T0287699

Mothers, Addiction, and Recovery

Copyright © 2018 Demeter Press

Individual copyright to their work is retained by the authors. All rights reserved. No part of this book may be reproduced or transmitted in any form by any means without permission in writing from the publisher.

Funded by the Government of Canada
Financé par la gouvernement du Canada

Demeter Press
140 Holland Street West
P. O. Box 13022
Bradford, ON L3Z 2Y5
Tel: (905) 775-9089
Email: info@demeterpress.org
Website: www.demeterpress.org

Demeter Press logo based on the sculpture "Demeter" by Maria-Luise Bodirsky, www.keramik-atelier.bodirsky.de

Printed and Bound in Canada

Cover artwork: Keriana Lily Hodson (age seven)

Library and Archives Canada Cataloguing in Publication
Mothers, addiction and recovery : finding meaning through
the journey / edited by Wendy E. Peterson, Laura Lynne Armstrong,
Michelle A. Foulkes.

Includes bibliographical references.
ISBN 978-1-77258-168-3 (softcover)

1. Pregnant women—Mental health. 2. Mothers—Mental health.
3. Motherhood—Psychological aspects. 4. Pregnancy—Psychological
aspects. 5. Substance abuse—Treatment. I. Peterson, Wendy E., 1962-, editor
II. Armstrong, Laura Lynne, 1981–, editor III. Foulkes, Michelle A.,
1967–, editor

HV4999.W65M68 2018   362.29082   C2018-903311-8

MIX
Paper from
responsible sources
FSC® C004071

Mothers, Addiction, and Recovery

Finding Meaning through the Journey

EDITED BY
Wendy E. Peterson, Laura Lynne Armstrong,
and Michelle Foulkes

DEMETER PRESS

To all mothers and their children living with addiction wherever they may be on the journey.

Table of Contents

Acknowledgements

We are so very grateful to have had the opportunity to engage with mothers living with addiction and researchers to create this book. The topic of mothers, addiction, and recovery originated with Demeter Press and came to our attention through a call for editors. In one of those precious moments, where inspiration prevails, each of us committed to this endeavour. Where would we be if there were no such moments! When a pursuit is one of importance that stirs passion within us, we cannot allow ourselves to be deterred by the amount of work or time that it may take to accomplish. With one email, we were committed. Not only were we committed, but we were welcomed and supported throughout by Andrea O'Reilly and the Demeter Press family. Accordingly, we begin with an enormous thank you to Andrea for providing this opportunity and helping us to succeed.

Thank you to all the contributors who have created this collection. Thank you for trusting us with your important work, for having patience as life occasionally interfered with our timelines, and, most of all, for having dedication to the important work you do. We extend a very special thank you to the contributors who have bravely shared their personal stories.

Thank you to Christina Cantin RN MScN, Rosann Edwards RN PhD(c), Karen Lawford, PhD, RM, Aboriginal midwife, and Danielle Macdonald RN PhD(c) for assisting with the review of manuscripts submitted for inclusion in this collection. Thank you to Ashley Desrosiers for helping all of us to conform to MLA formatting requirements, for your millennial understanding of technology, and for proofreading the entire manuscript multiple times. Thank you to the external reviewers who carefully examined the entire manuscript. Your thorough reviews and feedback absolutely enhanced the quality of this manuscript.

Thank you to Jesse O'Reilly-Conlin for your copy editing expertise and kindness. Your calm confidence was very reassuring when deadlines were looming. Thank you also to Angie Deveau, Casey O'Reilly-Conlin, and Tracey Carlyle—you have also provided wonderful support throughout this process. A big thank you to Keriana Lily Hodson (age seven) for your wonderful artwork featured on the cover of this book. And finally, many, many thanks to our families who have supported and encouraged us throughout. We are so fortunate to have you in our lives.

With sincere thanks to all of you,

Wendy E. Peterson
Laura Lynne Armstrong
Michelle Foulkes

Introduction

WENDY E. PETERSON, LAURA LYNNE ARMSTRONG,
AND MICHELLE FOULKES

ADDICTION OFTEN CONJURES UP ideas of desperate souls injecting themselves in deserted alleyways or illicit drug deals taking place in dark street corners. The popular media frequently portrays women as selling sex for money in order to pay for their substance of choice. Despite these narrow ideas around addiction, in this collection, we have not limited the topic of addiction to licit (tobacco, alcohol, prescription medication) or illicit (e.g. cocaine, heroin) substances. Writers also address addictions to food, idealized bodies, and technology.

Mothers with addictions, particularly related to substances, are often stigmatized and judged in our society and experience profound guilt and shame. When mothers are dichotomized into good and bad, those who admit to living with addiction are often categorized as bad mothers. This is evident through the way in which society treats mothers living with addiction—a lack of access to preventive and long-term services, judgmental care, child-focussed (rather than maternal-child focussed) care, incarceration, and perhaps the ultimate punishment, child apprehension by child-welfare authorities. The stigma experienced by mothers with addictions, or the fear of losing their children to the child welfare system, can inhibit treatment seeking. If they do access treatment, addiction treatment generally lags behind treatments for other mental health concerns, and relies upon approaches not supported with evidence. Furthermore, for all types of addiction, the concept of "recovery" is also unclear and may not fit the lived experience of those presenting with such concerns. Therefore, the aim of this book is to provide

1

a collection of personal stories, research, and policy commentary that gives priority to the voices of mothers living with addiction in order to better inform prevention, treatment, and a meaningful journey toward recovery.

In Part I of this collection, women describe their experiences of living with addiction and recovery while mothering their children (chapters one to four). Their insightful writing draws attention away from the addiction itself and promotes understanding of their experiences as a journey of meaning and hope. Through each of their stories, the authors describe how mothering has played a central role throughout their experience.

In chapter one, "Cholera Germs and Hummingbirds: A Spiritual Journey toward Recovery from Posttraumatic Stress Disorder and Addiction," Patricia Brethour shares the story of her suffering. She describes how she has journeyed from believing in her traumatic experiences as punishment to an understanding of this suffering as a gift that gives her life meaning. Her narrative touches on the trauma she endured, and the consequent feelings of guilt and shame that were effectively numbed with drugs. From there, she offers us a glimpse into the depths of her suffering and how being a mother to teenage sons led her back to developing trust in others, faith in God, and self-understanding.

The themes of traumatic childhood, loss of faith, use of substances to numb feelings of shame, and the long journey of recovery also emerge in chapter two, "From Winter to Summer." Author Renée Violette's use of time to frame her story underscores addiction and recovery as a lifelong experience. Through her description of a scene that could be from any day during a five-year period, the reader loses sight of the details of Renée Violette's life, as she did. However, her daughter is ever present, and while she hints at the intergenerational cycle of addiction, the reader leaves the story with a hopeful understanding of the resilient nature of mother-child relationships.

In chapter three, "Obesity and Recovering through Motherhood," Hadley Ajana introduces us to the destructive experiences of stigma faced by those living with obesity. Experiences that foster feelings of shame and guilt figure prominently again in this chapter. Hadley Ajana reflects on how relationships with her mother and son were key factors in her development and ongoing recovery from food addiction. The day that her mother died and her son was born marks both a literal and figurative point in time that empowered Hadley Ajana to change the way that she thought of herself. She describes how, over time, the part of her that mothers her son has helped to redefine her understanding of femininity and has provided her with a healing energy.

Chapter four, "Mothering through Addiction and Jail," is collaboratively written by six women: three mothers held in a county jail in the United States and three women who co-facilitate a writing workshop at the jail. Through their narrative, Chandera von Weller, Joni Joplin, Sam Pecchio, and colleagues draw our attention to the varied experiences and complex challenges encountered by mothers living through addiction and recovery while incarcerated. Using writing as a call for change, they appeal for alternative treatment methods that prevent rather than promote the incarceration of mothers with addictions.

To assist with the transition from these personal narratives in Part I, we have introduced some chapters in Parts II to IV of this book with fictional vignettes. Although these brief introductory stories are fictitious, they are composites that reflect the realities of women we are privileged to have encountered. Part II of this book is a collection of three chapters reporting the findings from studies that have prioritized the perspective of mothers living with addiction. Learning from mothers' lived experiences, the authors advocate for relational approaches to research and treatment.

Chapter five, "A Comparison of Justice-Involved and Nonjustice-Involved Mothers" begins with setting the context of women living with addictions in the United States by describing the factors that contribute to women's addiction, involvement in the justice system related to illicit drugs, and access to treatment. Then, author Erika Kates explores the similarities and differences between justice-involved and nonjustice-involved mothers in treatment in Massachusetts. Although further research is required, findings reflect the complexity of mothers' treatment needs, and the chapter concludes with recommendations for flexible, long-term services based on a public health approach rather than a criminal one.

In chapter six, "Mothering and Mentoring: The PCAP Women's

Quilt," Dorothy Badry and colleagues report the findings from a study using a qualitative approach to explore mothers' experiences participating in Alberta's Parent Child Assistance Program (PCAP). Mothers were invited to share the meaning of mentoring, a relationship-focused intervention, which is the main component of the PCAP program. This chapter offers insight into the use of quilting as a visual method to engage mothers in discussions of their experiences and the key role that a mentoring relationship played in their healing.

In chapter seven, "Mothering an Adolescent Who Misuses Substances: A Qualitative Evidence Synthesis," Masoumeh (Bita) Katouziyan and colleagues synthesize the research that has explored addiction during adolescence from the perspective of their mothers. Mothers describe their experiences of recognizing the problem and maintaining a good relationship with their teen, as they live with addiction. Particularly striking is the lack of accessible services encountered by mothers seeking support.

In Part III, we expand our view of addiction and turn to approaches for supporting mothers of daughters with eating disorders and for preventing smartphone addiction. Treatment and prevention strategies from meaning-centred second wave positive psychology approaches are provided in these chapters.

In chapter eight, "Confronting the Addictive Nature of Eating Disorder Behaviours: How Mothers Can Provide Meaningful Support to Daughters with Eating Disorders through a Meaning-Centred Framework," authors Caitlin Sigg and Laura Lynne Armstrong address eating disorders from an addiction framework. In the journey from addiction to recovery, existential issues as well as the central notions of secrecy, guilt, and shame for both mothers and daughters are discussed. Meaning therapy strategies are offered so that mothers may have tools to support their daughters experiencing eating disorders.

In chapter nine, "REAL Education to Prevent Smartphone Addiction—A Rational-Emotive, Attachment Logotherapy Approach for Expectant Mothers," Laura Lynne Armstrong describes addictive smartphone risk for new mothers. Smartphone addiction is framed within an attachment and meaning-centred lens as a surrogate for attachment or a response to boredom, loneliness, or a sense of meaninglessness. Prenatal educational tools from a second wave positive psychology approach called REAL are presented to promote resilience to smartphone addiction. Specifically, the tools presented in this chapter are aimed at enhancing positive mood and more balanced thinking, maintaining and building couple and parent-child attachment, and enhancing meaning and helpful coping.

In Part IV, the final two chapters of this collection provide a gendered analysis and critique of addiction programs and policy. The authors expand on harm reduction and restorative, healing approaches to the treatment of mothers' addictions, which have echoed throughout the chapters of this book.

In chapter ten, "Beyond Abstinence: Harm Reduction during Pregnancy and Early Parenting," Lenora Marcellus, Nancy Poole, and Natalie Hemsing provide a historical overview of the harm-reduction movement through a sex and gendered lens. They highlight the need to view harm reduction as an approach that expands well beyond the individual and requires us to situate substance use within a historical, political, and economic framework. Addictions arise from complex interactions between gender and socioeconomic issues of poverty and violence. This requires that we view substance abuse from an intersectional stance in which these cumulative factors acknowledge the role of stigma, shame, and disadvantage for many women.

In the final chapter, "Mothering and Illicit Substance Use: A Critical Analysis of the Implications for Healthcare and Social Policy Development from a Feminist Poststructuralist Perspective," Michelle Foulkes explores the social construct of motherhood. Motherhood is defined by patriarchal society within very narrow boundaries of what a good mother should be; all others who do not fit within the white, middle-class heterosexual confines are relegated to a less desirable notion of being a mother. There is no other collective of women who represent the lowest denominator of mothering than those with addictions issues. Society strips away any contextual understanding of how addictions arise; instead, it blames women who use substances during pregnancy or while mothering as an individual moral failing. The chapter reviews the complex interplay of variables that contribute to the development of addictions, and suggests the need to shift from a punitive stance against these mothers to one that is situated within a restorative justice framework. This provides the scaffolding for health and social policy to actively engage women in a healing process toward recovery that is both mother and child centred.

Our understanding of addiction has evolved over time. Addiction is not a personal failing; rather, it emerges from multiple intersecting factors. Biological, environmental, and social factors all contribute in varying degrees to whether an individual develops an addiction or not. Psychological aspects, such as trauma and mental health concerns, also play a role in the development of substance abuse issues. Similarly, spiritual factors, such as a sense of meaninglessness, are considered to be key precipitants to addiction, whereby people may turn to substances as a means to fill the emptiness. The complexity of circumstances that give rise to addiction in women requires treatment strategies that meet the unique needs of mothers with addiction. This requires that we remove individual blame from mothers with addiction and shift our focus to acknowledging that addictions arise from social and psychological structures of oppression. Furthermore, with respect to illicit substances, there has been a slow move away from criminal prosecution of women with addictions toward an understanding of the need to provide comprehensive health and social services. It is within a restorative justice framework that treatment programs grounded in trusting relationships between and among women must emerge so that mothers and their children can safely and meaningfully journey through the underlying factors that have contributed to their addiction.

I.
Lived Experience:
Mothers, Addiction, and Recovery

1.
Cholera Germs and Hummingbirds

A Spiritual Journey toward Recovery from Posttraumatic Stress Disorder and Addiction

PATRICIA P. BRETHOUR

IN 2011, I WAS DIAGNOSED with severe complex posttraumatic stress disorder (PTSD) comorbid with addiction. In the dark heart of my illness, there lay intense suffering. Suffering lay in dissociative flashbacks, nightmares, intrusive thoughts, an inability to trust, and the isolating hopelessness of addiction. Suffering also lay in self-pity and the age-old question "why me"? It lay in my family and friends from whom I had completely withdrawn. Worse yet, suffering lay in my children who had to watch their mother self-destruct. To heal from PTSD and positively adapt to living with the disease of addiction, I had to consider self-transcendence and the Divine. Today, I perceive my suffering as my gift. Without having experienced suffering, I would not have found my way out of the darkness by constructing a new way of spiritual being.

I grew up in a family subjected to the consequences of a multi-generational history of addiction and co-dependency. I was raised an Anglican and paraded to Sunday school most weekends. However, the God I learned about on Sundays did not seem to know about my house in which alcoholism, physical abuse, and chaos were the norm.

I was a child searching for love and approval. I found it in the arms of a forty-year-old pedophile. I believed he loved me and I loved him. In his arms, I tried drugs for the first time. He said that it would make it easier. It did.

After eight months, he abandoned me after my mother picked up the phone while we were arranging to meet. I never heard from him again. I was devastated. It was not long after that I had relationships with two other pedophiles. I remember celebrating my thirteenth birthday with one of them. The latter predators were more violent with me, but I accepted it because I thought it was what I deserved. For me, the God I learned about at Sunday school was punishing me for reasons I could not understand. The core principles of my self-preservation became simple: don't speak, don't trust, and don't feel.

Until 2011, I never considered what happened to me as sexual abuse. I willingly engaged in these relationships. I snuck out of the house to be with them. I lied to be with them. I lied to protect them despite what they did. Drugs were part of the ritual always taking me away to a safer place.

Until 2011, I never spoke about these relationships. I think the shame was the main reason I didn't talk about it. I knew at some level what had happened was wrong, but I believed it was my fault. As I got older, I didn't speak up because I tried to avoid thinking about those years. With time, when intrusive thoughts came up, I was so numbed by then that the flashes occurred as if watching a movie—as if happening to someone else. I also don't remember some of the more violent aspects of the abuse. I think when it was happening I would just go somewhere else in my brain. I remember my sisters calling me bubble brain and space cadet because sometimes I would be there physically, but mentally I was gone somewhere else, simply spaced out. Spacing out was a bit like taking drugs when I didn't have any drugs to take.

Until 2009, I continued to experience multiple traumatic events, including rape with a knife to my throat. Through these experiences, I came to believe my Sunday school God simply did not exist. My suffering from trauma manifested in intrusive thoughts and dissociative flashbacks:

I can feel his weight on top of me. I can smell his foul cigarette-booze breath. My heart is racing. I open my eyes. He is gone. "Get safe. Get safe."

I am sitting in class. The students around me disappear. I feel my nose start to bleed, and then my mouth fill with blood. I can taste it. It begins to spill out onto my chin. I wipe it with the back of my hand. I look at my hand. There is nothing there. "Get safe. Get safe."

I am driving home. A thunderstorm approaches. I am driving into a black void. The blackness surrounds me. It is inside of me. My very core is black. "Get safe. Get safe."

Taking drugs made the darkness fade and allowed me to "get safe."

The worst of the flashbacks were mostly associated with the first pedophile. It was the smell of his foul cigarette-alcohol breath. Even at present, I have an aversion to people with bad breath and yellow teeth. In the days when I was drinking in the bars when you could still smoke, I would from time to time smell that same foul breath. I would black out, dissociate, and find myself outside down the street. I was never quite sure what had happened other than I felt afraid. I used to blame these blackouts on my own drinking and drugging; I refused to acknowledge something was wrong with me.

I functioned fairly well for most of my life, unaware of the psychological impact of early childhood abuse and multiple traumas. I was functioning by self-medicating. Drugs made the inside hurt go away. Drugs let me focus, first, on my studies and, then, on my career. Drugs stifled the intrusive thoughts. I was unaware of how the abuse had affected everything and everyone I experienced. I had few emotions other than anger and its source—fear. My relationships with men were always dysfunctional and chaotic. I practised as a defense litigator for almost twenty years. What better career for someone who could not trust and could not feel?

The trauma and drug abuse came to a crisis when I defended a school board being sued as a result of a teacher sexually abusing multiple girls, aged eleven to thirteen. Their experiences were mine. Their suffering was mine. For the first time, the drugs failed to make me feel safe. The suffering I endured and experienced again through the eyes of the plaintiffs left me mute and numb. I was broken.

I was hospitalized in a dual diagnostic treatment centre offering intensive trauma therapy and a twelve-step-based addiction treatment program. The treatment centre used the *Seeking Safety* treatment manual, which is largely based on a cognitive behavioural therapeutic approach (Najavits 4). The treatment focusses on creating a safe environment, which helps participants trust enough to talk about their traumas as well as to understand how trauma interacts with addiction. I started the program as part of a group of twelve. We were down to six within the first two to three weeks. The six of us stuck through the eight-week program. Once I was off the drugs, I started to feel the pain, intensified by daily intensive therapy. I had nightmares almost every night and regular flashbacks. As a group of six, we shared our dirty secrets. The sharing, facilitated without judgment, allowed us to develop a bond of trust. The group became my safe place. I was with people who had gone through similar trauma and responded by self-medicating—we got each other. For the first time in my life, I felt safe enough to speak.

Through therapy, I understood what happened to me was not my fault. I learned pedophiles and other predators know how to pick their victims—those already abused in some way and vulnerable to manipulation. Learning it was not my fault eased my burden of shame. What occurred with the pedophiles did not represent love: they used and victimized me. I understood how early childhood abuse affected all of my relationships and many of my life choices.

On the addiction side, I learned my addiction was inextricably linked to trauma. I chose drugs because I did not have any other coping mechanism. I chose drugs to make the pain go away. The treatment centre encouraged a twelve-step recovery program. I had no trouble coming to terms with the first step: admitting I was powerless over my addiction and my life had become unmanageable. However, having abandoned God on the belief that He had abandoned me, I could not get past step two, which required coming to believe that a power greater than myself could restore me to sanity.

I left treatment raw from intensive trauma therapy, spiritually empty, and unable to work. At home without follow-up psychological support or a higher power to rely upon, the relapse came rapidly. I passively endured the suffering of a bleak, drug-infused existence for another eighteen months. During this period, I experienced the darkest nights of my soul, yet there was no light to guide me forward. I was killing myself with the drugs and glad about it.

As my addiction intensified, I needed more and more of the drugs to obtain the desired effect. I spent all of my savings trying to chase the high. I retreated from life—including caring for my teenaged boys—to the relative safety of my bedroom where I lived to use and used to live. Like a dog, I hung my head outside my bedroom window, blew smoke outside, and believed my kids could not smell it.

Documentaries about addiction always talk about hitting rock bottom. I hit rock bottom so many times, I discovered there was a whole elevator system there, but it only had a one way down button. I lost over forty pounds. I relegated cooking to my oldest son, and I gave up on housework altogether. Eventually, nothing mattered. I tried to get clean many times, but I could not stay clean for more than four days. My addiction was fully in control.

Each relapse just represented another failure. I endured this four-day cycle of slim hope followed by failure until I came to the belief that my life was over. I intentionally tried to overdose. Somewhere in my drug-addled brain, I believed it would be easier for the kids if I overdosed rather than if I died by suicide. While higher than high, I wrote my sons goodbye letters and then laid my head to rest for what I hoped was the last time. I woke up. When I read what I had written to my boys, I have never felt such shame. The letters were so self-engrossed, so pathetic; they totally disregarded my children's feelings. I despised this person I had become. I couldn't even overdose right.

While I burned the letters to my children, I found the strength to ask for help. I returned to the same treatment centre for three months. In asking for help, I knew change had to occur for there to be any possible future. I had to give a "voice to my suffering" in order to accept the past and make the necessary changes to learn to live with addiction (Soelle 69-70).

Through intensive trauma and addiction therapy, I reconstructed my life and gained a sense of control over what had happened to me and a sense of understanding for my behaviour. For me, one of the most important steps on the road to recovery was accepting the past and making a commitment to change. I had to accept that these events occurred in my life and I could do nothing to change them. However, I could choose not to allow these events to control my life. I could commit to change. This was the beginning of the transition from victim and addiction to survivor and recovery. I took art therapy, releasing my anger in forceful splatters of red and black paint. I took horticulture therapy, connecting both to earth and peaceful living. I took mindfulness training, learning to keep my mind focused in the present. I learned to identify my triggers and to apply coping mechanisms to (mostly) manage the flashbacks and anxiety attacks. I engaged in grief counselling and resolved my confusing feelings of love and anger toward my alcoholic father. I spent a huge amount of time learning to change the way I thought about myself and to challenge my core beliefs, which had previously centred on self-loathing and personal failure.

Hospitalization and intensive therapy enabled me to tackle the "first antidote for suffering": to gain control, to accept, and to commit to change. However, the "second antidote for suffering," hope and faith, remained elusive (Loscalzo 145).

Through daily attendance at Narcotics Anonymous, I understood there was no cure for addiction, but I could still obtain healing and recovery through the discovery of a higher power. I listened to, and talked with, other addicts about finding a higher power. Again, it was the "God thing" or step two that had me stumped. Although I learned how trauma had affected my life and interpersonal relationships, I still could not reconcile a loving God with what had happened to me.

I wanted to believe in a higher power that could support me in my battle with addiction, but I could not get my head around the question as to why God allows innocent children to suffer. I was in a place of "spiritual emergency" (Taylor 32). Something opened within me, perhaps planted with the spiritual seed of baptism:

It was 6:10 a.m. The sky was still dark; the stars and planet Venus clearly visible. In the quiet, I watched the snow softly falling. On the horizon, a dim line of grey began to appear in such a way that the spherical nature of planet Earth was apparent. As a pale line of pink began to emerge in the east, a shimmering rose-coloured light fell on one side of the snow draped trees. I watched a bird clean some of the fresh snow from its nest. Time ceased to have any meaning. I became aware of my connection to the earth, the birds, the trees, and the cycle of life. I became one with my surroundings. We were all unified in one cosmic harmony. I sensed a Creator behind what I saw. With sudden knowing, I became one with all of creation and, thereby, the Creator.

So began my undertaking of spiritual adaptation. How arrogant I had been to assume there was no power greater than me. I believe I experienced a suffering-induced transformational experience (SITE) (Taylor 49). I had discovered a higher power, the Creator, which enabled me to get past step two. I came to believe a higher power could restore me to sanity.

The next stumbling block was step three, which required that I make a decision to turn my will and my life over to the care of God as I understand him. The sudden relationship with a Creator was sufficient to meet the step-three concept of God as I understand him. However, my connection to the Creator did not lead to a sudden awareness of God. Before I could complete step three, I had to know whether the Creator could possibly be the loving God from Sunday school.

Despite having experienced a SITE, I could not reconcile my childhood suffering with the notion of a loving God. I researched spirituality and the concept of God with the same tenacity I had tackled law school, albeit without drugs. With cosmic unity and harmony as my starting point, I learned the principle of plenitude: "The principle of plenitude states that the richest and most desirable universe contains every possible kind of existence: lower and higher, imperfect and (relatively) perfect, ugly and beautiful, cholera germs and hummingbirds.... Even sin and its punishment belong to this harmony" (Nichols 69).

I could accept cholera germs and hummingbirds were necessary for cosmic balance. However, I continued to question whether my suffering was the result of sin and its punishment. I acknowledged having sinned in my adolescence and adulthood, but I could not find any action on my part to justify my childhood abuse. Further research led me to understand I was asking the wrong question. I understood God created us as finite beings with free will. Evil exists because we are imperfect beings. It is free will, not God, which enables dangerous and evil people to bring suffering to the innocent. Without evil, there would be no need for repentance, the very cornerstone of Christian faith. I considered the parable of the footsteps in the sand:

A woman walked along a beach with the Lord. The beach was her life. As she looked back, she saw that there were times when there were two steps of footprints and other times when there was only one set. The woman noticed that there was only one set of footprints in the sand during those times of her life that she had suffered most. She said to the Lord, "When I decided to follow you, you said you would be with me all the way." She questioned the Lord as to why he was not with her when she was truly suffering. The Lord responded that he was always with her, but during the worst of the suffering, the Lord was carrying her.

I returned home from hospital with a solid support system. I saw a trauma therapist on a weekly basis, attended a women's recovery house outpatient program, and went to Narcotics Anonymous meetings daily.

With a clearer understanding of why hummingbirds and cholera germs could exist simultaneously in a loving God's world, I began daily meditation and prayer. I did so not with a firm belief in God but with a desire to believe. It is often said that trust needs to be earned. In the course of my recovery, I saw that a spiritual journey requires trust be given. With continued prayer seeking strength and guidance, I found maintaining sobriety was becoming easier and my PTSD symptomology had lessened. I started to live the miracle of recovery. My dark soul found its light to follow. I had renewed strength and began to see the prospect of hope.

In completing step three, I surrendered my addiction and the wounds of my past to God. Paradoxically, surrendering and continued sobriety enhanced my spiritual wellbeing. As with millions of addicts before me, having surrendered to God, I became a living miracle and knew in my lightened heart recovery was possible. I began to experience hope.

However, before I could fully experience a new way of being, there remained a significant task. I had to make amends to my children for our lost years. Steps four to nine of Narcotics Anonymous do not require being forgiven for the hurt addicts have wrought. However, I could not move forward without seeking my children's forgiveness. When I received their unconditional and loving forgiveness, the heavy weight of guilt was lifted from my shoulders. My amends and their forgiveness confirmed my belief I was living in the forgiving, accepting, and loving presence of God.

As with the parable of the footsteps in the sand, today I recognize that a loving God has been carrying me all along. God kept me from dying at the hands of the violent pedophiles, from an overdose, and from suicide. God gave me the strength to ask for help after my relapse. God kept me alive for a reason. Today, as an addict in recovery, a work in progress, I am trying to fulfill that reason by finding purpose.

In completing the twelfth step, I carried the message to other addicts and trauma survivors. I regularly speak to and work with struggling addicts through Narcotics Anonymous. I am presently enrolled in a master's program in the healing professions. Through helping other suffering addicts, many of whom experienced trauma, the reason that God carried me through my suffering has become clear. I suffered so that I can fully appreciate the suffering of others and help them in their quest to find peace and recovery.

When I am speaking with addicts and I see that my words have touched someone in a fundamental way, I feel their hope within myself. Sensing their hope, I recognize I have reframed my own reality. I have turned my suffering into my strength.

Without having faced these challenges in my life, I would not have come to my present potential as a spiritual being; I can accept the reality of both cholera germs and hummingbirds. Without having suffered, I could not have become who I might be.

APPENDIX

The twelve steps of Narcotics Anonymous:

- We admitted we were powerless over our addiction, that our lives had become unmanageable.
- We came to believe that a Power greater than ourselves could restore us to sanity.
- We made a decision to turn our will and our lives over to the care of God as we understood Him.

•We made a searching and fearless moral inventory of ourselves.

•We admitted to God, to ourselves, and to another human being the exact nature of our wrongs.

•We were entirely ready to have God remove all these defects of character.

•We humbly asked Him to remove our shortcomings.

•We made a list of all persons we had harmed and became willing to make amends to them all.

•We made direct amends to such people wherever possible, except when to do so would injure them or others.

•We continued to take personal inventory and when we were wrong promptly admitted it.

•We sought through prayer and meditation to improve our conscious contact with God, as we understood Him, praying only for knowledge of His will for us and the power to carry that out.

•Having had a spiritual awakening as the result of these Steps, we tried to carry this message to addicts, and to practice these principles in all our affairs.

WORKS CITED

Loscalzo, Matthew. "Psychological Approaches to the Management of Pain in Patients with Advanced Cancer." *Pain and Palliative Care,* vol. 10, no. 1, 1996, pp. 139-155.

Najavits, Lisa. *Seeking Safety: A Treatment Manual for PTSD and Substance Abuse.* Guilford Press, 2002.

Narcotics Anonymous World Services. *Narcotics Anonymous.* Narcotics Anonymous World Services Inc., 2008.

Nichols, Aidan. *The Shape of Catholic Theology.* The Liturgical Press, 1991.

Soelle, Dorothee. *Suffering.* Fortress Press, 2008.

Taylor, Steve. "Transformation Through Suffering: A Study of Individual Who Have Experienced Positive Psychological Transformation Following Periods of Intense Turmoil." *Journal of Humanistic Psychology,* vol. 52, no. 1, 2012, pp. 30-52.

2.
From Winter to Summer

RENÉE VIOLETTE

1987

ICRACK OPEN THE BIG BLUE PLASTIC CASE of make-up my Godfather gave me for Christmas. It is the best gift of all the gifts—blue eyeliner, eight shades of blue eye shadow, blue mascara, and hot pink blush.

It is a bright Sunday morning. I move my face left and right, and search my reflection for zits in the bathroom mirror. My mother scurries around me picking up wet towels and yelling for my sisters and brother to eat their cereal. We are always late for church. I hate being late because then I don't get to choose my seat, and Alex, Pastor John's son, will already be seated. Every Sunday when we enter the small, white steepled church, I scan the congregation for his face. My heart flutters and pounds against my chest when my eyes find him. If he hasn't sat yet, I slip ahead of my mother, and nonchalantly lead her in his direction so I can accidentally sit by him.

I have covered my small blue bedroom with paper signs reading "I love Alex" in fluorescent marker calligraphy. But Alex is sixteen, two years ahead of me. Although there are whispers by the kids and adults when we mingle in the front hall after church that he likes me too, I am told he is not allowed to ask me out until I am officially in high school.

Those are the rules.

My parents met in their first year of high school. I can tell my mother is hopeful he may be "the one." I am hopeful too. I am finally fourteen, and in six more months, I start my first year. The wait is torturously exciting. I lie awake at night, stare into the darkness, and play all the possible scenarios of our first date over and over in my head. What I will wear. What he will say.

I need to look good, so he doesn't decide to like someone else before he asks me out.

I bend toward the bathroom mirror and paint my eyes. I line the inside of both bottom and top lids with bright blue eyeliner and then layer four shades of eyeshadow—white, light blue, sparkly blue, and bright blue—in a rainbow pattern up to my eyebrows. Pushing my stomach into the sink, I lean an inch from the mirror and blink my eyelashes over the thick clumpy blue mascara brush. I finish off my base-covered cheeks with thick brush strokes of hot pink blush, and I step back to examine the masterpiece.

Perfect.

I hear my father's deep voice in the distance.

Oh no, no, no.

One of my sisters has accidently woken him up by playing too loud in the living room. He is on his eleven-to-seven shift at the mill, which means we need to let him sleep.

I hear the pounding of his feet. My shoulders tense. The footsteps grow louder.

I feel his heat to my left in the doorway, but I pretend I don't know he is there.

He looms in and sneers, "Where do you think you are going looking like that?"

"Church," I reply as innocently as possible.

"You have too much make-up on. You look like a clown! Take it off now!"

Mom flutters nervously behind him. "It's time to go. We have to go," she sings out, attempting to pleasantly distract the interaction.

"You HAVE"—he steps forward—"too much make-up on!"

I see it. He is going to snap.

Okay, let's get it over with.

"Whatever." I flit, and my mother gasps in the hallway.

He lunges, grabs my wrist, and twists it behind my back, I lean away from the pain, and he kicks, kicks, and kicks at my leg with his white-socked foot. I helplessly crumble back toward the wall.

"Whatever?" He booms, "WHATEVER? I WILL SHOW YOU WHATEVER!"

Mom pleads meekly, "Roy, Roy, stop.... We need to get to church."

He doesn't listen.

He lets go of my arm and grabs me by the throat and slams me up against the wall.

Go completely limp Renee, I coach myself. *Maybe if you make it look like you have lost control of your body, he will think he has gone too far and stop.*

I close my eyes and force all of my muscles to relax. He feels my weight falling. He holds me up by the neck, grabs my left arm, and picks me up from the ground. I can't stay limp; my body defies my commands, and I flail grabbing at the wall, at anything. He turns and throws me into the shower, and my head bounces off the edge of the plastic tub with a hollow "THUD!"

"Wash your face!" he yells as he storms out.

"Jesus, Donna!" He snaps at my mom as she passes into the bathroom.

She should have known better than to let me look like that.

I am having a hard time catching my breath. Sobs come in unmanageable jerks, and I shake as she helps me out of the tub. I stand there vibrating, gasping in small breaths of air that make little yelps on the way in.

Mom is shaking her head "no" in small little sad swooshes as if trying to shake it all away.

She wets a facecloth and hands it to me, her lips pressed together. When I grab it with my shaking hand, she looks down from my eyes and walks out of the room.

"We are going to be late for church," she whispers. "Wash your face and get in the car."

The car ride is silent except for the sporadic uncontrollable gasps of air my body insists on retrieving to calm my nerves. I hold the white facecloth covered with blue blotches to my red puffy eyes and squint out the dirty passenger side window to see how bad I look in the side view mirror.

I look worse than I thought.

I lean my head against the window and close my eyes.

We bounce into the pothole-ridden dirt parking lot and park next to the other minivans. I am last to climb out, and I shuffle behind my mom and my siblings into the basement entrance where the Sunday school classes for the little kids are closing with a song. I cross the concrete floor and climb the stairs to the sanctuary. The vibrant children's voices echo off the newly dry-walled stairwell: "Obedience is the very best way to show that you believe. Doing exactly what the Lord commands and doing it happily! O-B-E-D-I-E-N-C-E! Obedience is the very best way to show that you believe!"

1993

Mom asks if I am pregnant after I vomit bile between my clamped fingers while she makes eggs in the kitchen.

I say no. And then I do it again.

When I decide I can't go through with the abortion, I tell her the truth. She rushes to me, as if she has rehearsed this moment a hundred times, hugs me too tight, and mumbles, "It's okay. It's okay. It's okay."

I just stand there, arms at my side, and glare over her shoulder at the decorative wicker baskets hanging off the flowery wallpapered wall. I am twenty, jobless, and living in my childhood bedroom. Adding "pregnant" to that equation is definitely not okay.

Later that day, she rushes out to the dirt driveway and accosts my father with the news as he is getting out of his small Toyota truck. I watch out the window as he briskly walks around the house, scowling and shaking his head.

"You told him?" I hiss at my mother when she walks back in the house.

I hear Dad bang open the basement bulkhead door, and he yells for me to come down.

Giving my mother the most evil look I can muster, I turn and storm down the hall toward the small wooden basement door. Silly high-pitched cartoon voices echo out from the television in the living room where my youngest sister and brother are playing.

I hesitate at the barrier, breathe in and out quick, turn the knob, take two steps down, and sit at the top of the stairs.

Dad paces at the bottom of the stairs on the grey concrete.

"The guy beats you up, and you still fuck around with him! What the fuck?"

He kicks a wooden box full of rags; it bounces past a clear garbage bag of empty beer bottles and off the cinderblock wall.

"I thought you were smarter than that! I didn't raise you like…"

I sit blank and stoic, a statue staring above his head.

"What is wrong with you?" His voice quivers.

I look down at him. *Is he … crying? Oh my God, Dad is crying.* I have never seen him cry.

A ripple of cold runs over my skin. I become hyperaware of my sex. I swing around, run up the two stairs, and fling open the door.

He hollers at my back, "No babies in this house!"

I sit across from Tammy—my bouncy, permed, adoption case-worker—at a chain restaurant and thumb through a three-inch dull black binder of family profiles encased in individual cheap clear pocket inserts.

Tammy is rambling. Her life is blessed. She has three children and a husband. She gave up her firstborn for adoption because she wasn't married when she got pregnant. The father is the same one she married. Adoption is the right Christian thing to do. Blah blah blah.

I hate her.

A waitress walks by with a plate of scrambled eggs and sausage, and the smell cuts through the musty reek of the carpet. I glance over at a brown bucket in the middle of the browner floor, which catches loud drips from the arched ceiling, and I think about how I have never been in one of these restaurants that didn't smell of musty carpet. *Huh. Must be a bad roof design.*

Tammy stops rambling and taps two manicured fingers on the open photo in the black binder and clears her throat. I look back down and flip one silky page to the next and the next: white man and wife in front of their home, white man and wife in front of a Christmas tree, white man and wife at the start of a hiking trail. They all embrace each other and beam joyfully. They all look stable.

Bullshit. I judge them all.

I keep my head down. At the bottom of each photo, there is a paragraph from the hopeful parents about gardening, hiking, travelling; all the wonderful things they will do with a child. Any child. My child.

I scan the pages for any who are not Christian.

At seven months along, I lie on the couch with my hands on my extended belly. Summer has the hiccups. She always gets the hiccups in the evening, and my stomach jerks up into my ribcage every few seconds. I pull up my shirt, watch my stomach for the lurch, and rub my stretched skin trying to soothe her. I've named her Summer, but no one knows that.

I'm due in two weeks, and I go in for my last ultrasound. I can now see all of the little contours of her face, her little fingers, and her knees on the monitor.

My doctor is on vacation, and there is a plump blond replacement bustling around me creating the small talk that attempts to take away the fact that my bare legs are spread wide in the stirrups. She asks me where we live.

I tell her I am living with my parents, but after I give birth, I am going out west. I tell her I am giving her up for adoption.

I wait for the usual response: "Wow, what a selfless thing to do" or "You are so brave." Or some other variation of praise I will swallow in hopes it will convince me I am somehow noble, but I know it won't.

But the blond woman stops, turns to me, tilts her head and says, "What do you think is the most important thing you can give a child?"

I'm quiet for a moment and then respond, "Love."

She says, "Can you give her that?"

I whisper, "Yes."

She smiles, snaps off her blue plastic gloves, pats me on my bare knee, and walks out of the room.

Two weeks later, Summer is born at 2:35 p.m. Twenty minutes later, the phone rings in the maternity room. I answer; it is Tammy.

She asks me if I am ready, if she can come get the baby. I tell her no, I am keeping her. She sighs, says "good luck," and abruptly hangs up.

ANY DAY BETWEEN 1994 AND 1999

Summer is spending the night at my mom's, or Uncle Joe's, or home with a teenage babysitter again.

"Renee!" voices yell out above the music from the dark smoky corner under the dartboard as I walk through the door.

I return the cheer with a smile and a broad sweep of my arm, and I turn toward the bar. I circle past Joe at his every-night place on the end stool. He cradles his draft, and methodically eats pretzels from the small bamboo bowl. The evening news silently playing on the television above the bar has mesmerized him.

John saw me come in and has already begun service. I read the back of his rock-n-roll tour shirt as he pours my draft beer. It streams rich gold out the silver spigot and into the pint glass, churns into the bottom, spins upward, and the foam rises to the top.

I rub my palms together and lean both elbows on the bar.

John turns, grins, and slides the pint of amber ale across the bar toward me, leaving a wet streak on the polished wood.

"Start a tab," I say and grin back.

He winks and turns to write my name on a long slip of paper.

I lift the glass to my mouth, and the bitter bubbles bite my tongue; the burn, that beautiful burn, envelops my throat. I love the burn. I close my eyes slowly and feel it. Savour it. Absorb it. It slides down my esophagus and lingers, pulses, in my middle right beneath my heart, before it spreads slightly outward. Another sip pushes the burn further down into my belly. The heat coats the inside of my stomach; it shoots warmness up my spine, into my shoulders, which caresses the back of my skull and finally crawls up over my brain in a loving embrace. My cheeks flush.

I close my eyes and breathe in the beauty.

"It is all okay," it whispers. "It is all going to be better now."

Today sucked. Or it was great. Or it rained. Or it was the first day of spring. Or I got a bad grade on a big test. Or it was Thursday. Or Summer was whiny. Or my Mom said something that pissed me off. Or I have too much work to do. Or I just got a raise. Or the winter has been too long.

None of it matters.

I glow.

My shoulders take their rightful position away from my ears. My cheeks and fingers tingle.

I light a cigarette and join the laughing voices in the smoky corner.

1999

I have a party, and I invite everyone I know. It is just what I need, a break from the monotony of a single mother work week.

After the invitations are given, I call my mother, my sister, and my uncle and ask them to babysit, but they are all busy, so Summer is here.

The open kitchen and living room of our small red home are bright and loud. After years of bouncing in and out of low-income housing units and finishing my bachelor's degree at the local college, I landed a job helping at-risk youth get into job training programs. I bought the house all by myself at age twenty-six when most of my friends were ski-bumming out west.

Most of the alcohol has been absorbed, and people shout stories at one another and laugh louder than they need to over the music.

Summer sits alone in a pair of pink shorts and a yellow tank top among the feet of my friends on the blue carpet. She quietly plays with the body crayons I bought her for her seventh birthday, and covers her arms and legs in bright yellow sunshine and blue and green flowers.

It is late, and I am wildly drunk. I didn't intend on getting this drunk, but then again, I never do. I've finished a six pack, and I sneak swigs off the bottle of bourbon I have hidden in my freezer.

I hear splashing and laughter in the back hot tub room and stumble down the hall stripping off my shirt and bra as I walk. I crash though the French doors and bend down to pull off my pants. I fall against the wall as I yank to free them from my calf.

Climbing naked into the hot tub I hear my brother yell "God!" and he covers his eyes with the hand not holding a beer as his friends look on in horror in their bathing suits. I fall, splash in, and my brother picks carefully past the submerged bodies to climb out.

The heads bobbing in the bubbles are no longer laughing.

"You're no fun!" I yell to no one in particular and slide back out of the tub.

I wrap myself in a small white towel and stumble back into the living room.

I plop next to my friend Kate on the couch and tell her I want to have another baby.

"I am tttwenty-ssseven," I slur, "don't you think that is a gooood age to have another baaaby?"

As a parent would speak to a child, she leans in and firmly states that it is an important decision to talk about when I am not drunk. That pisses me off. She is always so fucking judgmental.

I get up and go into the kitchen to find out what is so funny in there. Paul is swaying with a beer laughing and pointing at Caleb who is crouched on the peach kitchen tile. The backdoor opens into the kitchen, and Tristen, a friend from high school I haven't seen in years, and a woman, dressed conservatively in a button up blue sweater, slacks, and clogs greet everyone with a somewhat surprised hello. It's as though they thought they were walking into one thing but did not expect what they saw.

They look bright eyed and sober.

Tristen says hi to me and introduces me to his female friend. I yell "grab a beer!" He looks confused, and she looks at him and back at me, probably wondering why I am soaking wet and wrapped in a towel.

Summer runs through the wavering bodies and into her room covered in paint. Tristen refuses a beer and asks Paul how he has been. His female friend follows Summer into her bedroom. I stand in my towel drinking a beer in the kitchen, and watch the two of them through Summer's open door. The conservatively dressed stranger kneels down and asks Summer about the drawings on her legs. Summer points to each drawing, smiles, and explains her art. The woman asks Summer if she wants to hear a story. Summer nods, and the woman picks up a book from the floor and starts to read.

I feel the burning from the beer in my belly rush up to my face.

I bet she is judging me.

The next morning, I come-to in my pink comforter, naked and alone. I hear Summer playing with her dolls in the living room. I roll over, stare at the ceiling, and put my hand on my shreaking forehead. I feel the familiar horror burn right above my stomach and wait for the memories to make their way in. They show up in stabs and flashes: the horrified look on my brother's face, Kate talking to me as she would a child, the stranger helping Summer. The shame burn pulses stronger in my gut with each vision. I breathe deep and try to will the thoughts away.

I slowly push myself up, plop on my blue terrycloth robe, and feel my way into the living room. Bright sun streams through the windows. I squint at Summer who is sitting in a pool of light, playing with two plastic dolls and some blocks. Without looking up, she calls out "Hi, Mama. Look at what I made. Can I have some cereal?"

"One minute hun," I mumble and shuffle into the bathroom.

I glance in the mirror. My cheek is red and purple. *What the..?* I lean toward my image, poke at it lightly, and wince. I try to get my brain to make connections but it refuses to cooperate. I just stand and stare at myself. Slowly a cloudy image appears. I see myself naked, crashing off the toilet into the corner of the wall before crawling to bed.

I lean way in, two inches from the mirror, and focus on my bloodshot green eyes. I look deep and say, "I hate you. I fucking hate you."

2005

Ellen, the publisher and my supervisor at the *Maine Business Journal*, can tell something is wrong with me. I have stopped selling; my numbers are in the toilet. I show up late and never feel good: tired, sick … hungover.

My name rings out over the sales pit, a cluster of cubicles, from Ellen's glass office. My shoulders drop, and I look at the ceiling. *Fuck. This is never good.*

I saunter through her office doorway, and she says, "Take a seat." She opens a file on her desk with my name on it. I stare at her blankly as she pauses to flip a few pages. She looks up from the folder over her glasses and tells me she is worried I am not going to make my goals. I squint at her with my bloodshot baggy eyes. Three cups of coffee on a sour stomach after two hours of sleep—if you can call being passed out, sleep. I may vomit right here.

She says if we don't do something now, it is going to be a problem. She knows I can sell; she saw me blow everyone else out of the water last year.

"Let's try a life coach," she suggests.

"A life coach?" I perk up. "Like Margaret, the woman I am proposing a media package to next week?"

"Yes," she says. "See if she will accept trade. We will run her ads, and in trade, she can work with you."

I like this option. It's better than getting fired. And I really like Margaret. When we met in her small office, we chatted about more than just advertising. She was kind and bubbly and easy to talk to. And honestly, I want someone to help me get back on track. I keep telling myself that I am still young, I am just having fun, but at thirty-two, the excuse is starting to wear thin. My life feels like a bad carnival ride I can't get off.

Margaret happily agrees, and we start weekly calls. We identify my goals. My number one goal is health. I want to feel better. I tell her I want to eat better, exercise more, and drink less.

We break down the goals into small action steps. I will walk the hill by my house every day. I will always start the day with a protein breakfast. I will only drink on the weekends.

Every Thursday morning at 9:00 a.m., I sit under my fuzzy blue blanket on my Santa Fe patterned couch and report on my progress. Margaret is great. She is kind and gentle and cheers me on whenever I accomplish one of my small steps. But week after week, I dread talking about the "drink less" goal. I am failing. I know it. I don't know how not to. I can make it a day or two, like Monday, maybe into Tuesday evening, but then something in my head congratulates me for a whole thirty hours of not drinking and tells me it would be great to celebrate with a drink. *Why the hell not? It's not that bad. I deserve it. I am making this drinking thing into something it is not. All I have to do is be okay with it, and then I will be okay.*

29

But the next morning, I am never okay. I am angry at myself for giving in, and I vow not to do it again.

And then I do.

After about six weeks of coaching, I flop back on the couch in front of the bright living room windows and make my 9:00 a.m. morning call. It is 9:10 a.m. I overslept and had to rush Summer to school in my pajamas because she missed the bus. I forgot about the call. I feel like shit. I am shaking with my lips stained and crusted with red wine.

She asks me how I am, and I admit that I am hungover. I tell her I only wanted to have one glass, just one, but I drank the whole bottle and then chased it down with the bourbon I keep stashed in the freezer. I want to stop, but I can't seem to figure out how.

She suggests what I have been expecting her to say—a self-help meeting in town for people with alcoholism. She explains her husband got sober by going to a similar meeting.

I feel fire in my chest.

"I can't!" I respond, trying to control the irritation in my voice.

"I don't want to hear any of that God shit. I used to pray all the time when I was a teenager, when Dad was out of control, and nothing happened. God didn't listen or care or whatever; it didn't work. People who believe in God are weak, foolish, stupid, ignorant."

I hear my voice strain and pleading. "They are going to tell me I have to believe in God. And, then ... and then they will have won."

"Who has won?"

"My mom and the church."

The line is quiet for a minute.

"Well, you could try it. And if you don't like it or it seems like too much God for you, you don't have to go back," Margaret gently suggests.

That night I slink through the cracked white side door of the church and descend into the musty basement. The scent of coffee wafts up the stairs from a corner room brightly lit from big squares of florescent ceiling tiles. I hear laughter. My knees wobble on each step. I wish I had a big paper bag. I would put it over my head.

I follow the light into the room and slither into the back of the five short rows of metal chairs facing four wooden tables arranged in a square. People laugh and joust another while they get coffee.

I keep my head down but peer up.

Shit.

A woman I went to church with is at the front of the room.

I knew it.

I remember how once, when I was about seven, she reached over and placed her hand directly on a piece of paper I was reading while Pastor John prayed, trying to get me to pay attention. I was embarrassed, and I haven't liked her ever since.

A man with big coke-bottle glasses and thin shaggy hair smiles grandly at everyone at the table and starts the meeting. He reads a few guidelines and asks everyone to pray.

I cringe.

After the prayer, he reads from a book. He pauses occasionally and talks about his life and how what he has read applies to him. The others raise their hands intermittently and talk about their experiences too.

I listen. I listen for how I am not like them.

A large man with a mustache raises his hand and shares that before he started coming to meetings, he was lost. He would wake up in strange places, and he once pissed himself on a park bench. Strangely, a few of the other people in the room nod and chuckle.

I relax, as I realize I have a lot of drinking left before I piss myself on a park bench. I can still drink. I am okay.

When the chairperson asks everyone to stand and hold hands for the Lord's Prayer I swoop out the aisle, up the stairs and drive to the corner store to grab a six pack.

A month later, I come-to in my bed thirsty and shaking again. I roll onto my back and look out the open door into the kitchen. Brown beer bottles litter the counter. There is a half full bottle of beer on my nightstand... never a good sign.

I feel the panic under my sweaty skin and search my cluttered foggy head for memories. *Who did I call last night? What did I say?* The shame floods out from the center of my chest through my body. I can't remember anything. I exhale a breath of sharp fumes and struggle to sit up.

Summer is awake. I have no idea how long she has been up, but I hear a spoon clink on the side of the bowl as she hums to herself while munching on cereal and milk.

I fucking suck.

I get it. This is it for me. This is how I will be forever. All the things I wanted to be... it is over for me. I can't do it differently. I am going to have to feel like this, be like this, until I die. I wish I could end it now, but I can't because of Summer. Fuck. I will just struggle through and try to hide it until she graduates, and then I will disappear—to an island or somewhere where no one knows me.

I'm fucked.

A snapshot of the basement room and the laughter breaks through my thoughts. I lay my pounding head back on my pillow.

Maybe.

A surge of anger bolts me out of bed. I stumble into the kitchen and grab the slim yellow phone book from the top of the refrigerator. I don't care anymore. I need help. Anything. Anyone. I grab the phone and dial the only person I recognized at that meeting: the woman from church. She is way too fucking happy to hear from me, but something about that makes me feel better.

There is another meeting at the church tonight. This time I walk in and sit in the middle of the middle row. People shuffle in and around. They laugh and pat one another on the back and shake hands. I just sit quietly and watch. No one pays much attention to me. I exchange a few shy smiles.

As people sit and quiet down, I feel a hand on my shoulder. I turn to look directly in the eyes of the bartender from the bar I frequent the most. He smiles and chuckles at what I can only guess is the size of my eyes and the confused look on my face.

"Welcome" he says.

"Oh... Hi," I stammer.

He squeezes my shoulder, and I turn back toward the front.

I listen.

I hear a woman share she hated herself because she kept drinking even though she didn't want to. I hear a man talk about how hopeless he felt before he did the recovery work to get better. How many times he tried to quit and couldn't.

I identify. I hate myself and I feel hopeless. And I can't stop.

I realize I don't care anymore about who will see me, or what I have to do, or what I have to give up. I am scared, scared shitless, but I don't care. I don't want to feel like this anymore— horrified, disgusted at my own behaviour, and ashamed at the damage I am causing Summer. I swore I would be better than this, better than my dad. I keep trying and trying, but my drinking is hurting her, and I can't stop.

If this is what it takes, I am in.

I scan the room for someone who looks okay to talk to. I focus on a woman who seems happy. When she speaks, her words are deliberate yet calm. She is about my mother's age; she has glasses, short ash hair, and a soft smile.

The moment the meeting closes I jump up and walk directly to where she is sitting at the table. I say, "Hi, my name is Renée; this is all new to me." I tell her I need to stop drinking but don't know how.

She chuckles and says, "Yes, yes, that is why we are here."

I ask her if she will help me, and she says she would be happy to.

The next day, I walk by the tall shelves of books in the university library and climb down the cement basement stairs. Wendy, the woman from the meeting, is seated at one of the two mahogany university chairs in a glassed-in study space. A book and a note-pad lie on the round wooden table in front of her. She smiles her soft smile when I walk in the door, and says "hello" in a gentle, joyful voice.

I sit, and she explains all she has to offer is what she was given to recover. I nod and she opens a book and begins to read. She pauses after each paragraph to explain what the text has meant to her and how it relates to her recovery experience.

I listen.

A few paragraphs in, I bristle at the word God. She notices, and I explain I just can't go there. I tell her about the church. I tell her I prayed for years for something to change at home and God did nothing. I don't believe in it. I think Christianity is stupid and hurtful and responsible for pain and wars in the world. I refuse to be a part of that.

She listens, nods, and then says to do this recovery work, I don't need to believe in a specific God, I just need to be open to the possibility there is something bigger than me out there—I am not the only person running the show. She asks if I can be open to that, and I figure there are so many loopholes in that idea that I can. I know I have felt something, something beautiful, usually at a concert or hiking or when I was high. I guess I can be open to the possibility there is some kind of vibration or power that isn't of me or of this world. I ask her if we can call it "the spirit of the universe" instead of God, and she says yes.

When we are done I stand to go, and she stands with me and gives me a hug. She smells flowery. I am not a big fan of hugging flowery strangers, but it feels alright.

We make plans to meet again.

As I walk out the door she says, "Renée, you know that spirit of the universe you sometimes feel?"

"Yeah," I respond.

"Ask it for help."

I pull out of the university parking spot, and I begin to talk. I watch the people driving by to see if they are watching me. I must look crazy talking in an empty car, but sometimes I scream profanities in the empty car, so I guess I can't look any worse than that.

"Okay, here I am. I don't know how to do this. Please help." I beg with every ounce of me. "Please show me how. Please, please help me not drink today."

An overwhelming sense of rightness, calm, and relief fills me.

I drive past the store where I buy my daily beer and straight to the local dance studio to pick up Summer.

I don't drink that day.

Or the next.

Or the next.

2016

I sit in a plastic white camping chair on the balcony outside my room at Bolvin's Retreat Center in North Central Oregon. My coffee is just hot enough. I cup it with both hands and sip, letting it warm my fingers and throat. A large flap of moss hanging from one of the looming pine trees twitches as if in a hip hop dance; it jerks randomly from the force of the bulbous drops of rain that have fallen from the sky for days.

I should probably get ready. The seminar on empathy healing and changing reactivity patterns in the brain is starting in the resort conference room in ten minutes, but I need this time to sit and reflect.

It's been a long road to get here. Ten years.

Ten years. So short, so long. Ten years since I chose recovery.

It hasn't all been great. There are the ongoing relationship issues. I keep dating tragic addicts or alcoholics, although I am aware this is a symptom of my family abuse history. And I still struggle with reactionary parenting. Sometimes, I react to Summer's life choices with anger, even though she is twenty-two and living on her own in Philadelphia. And when she calls me crying, hurting because her depression is debilitating, or she has just been abandoned by another boyfriend, or she feels like she can't make it a day without smoking pot, I feel the panic—the nauseating plummet in my stomach, the depth of my despair, that her pain is my fault. I believe I am at least half responsible for her struggles to thrive because she grew up in my alcoholic home. The first twelve years of her life she lived with me while I was actively drinking and emotionally stunted. But even after sobriety, I had to learn to live without drowning my feelings, and she experienced my bouts of self-pity, which resulted in frequent overcompensation in the form of gifts and unreliable boundaries. The whole time I knew I wasn't doing it right. But I didn't know how else to do it.

Sometimes the guilt outweighs my gratitude.

Although sobriety has been bumpy and sometimes dramatic, it has provided clarity, hope, and healing, even if it wasn't fast enough to halt every bit of damage. We continue to work at it, and search for a way to connect, relate, and heal. I am learning how to set healthy boundaries from a place of love, understanding, and support. I strive to offer her a nonjudgmental, gentle, empathetic ear; to hear the deep needs under her works so that I may respond with love and kindness. I am noticing I can do this more and more every day. And when things go wrong in her life, when she is overwhelmed, I am the one she turns to. There is beauty in that.

My recovery is sacred. Sometimes it may be messy, but I am committed to the process. When I think about what my life looked like in 2005, I am blown away by the progress I have made one day at a time. I now have the capability to accept and appreciate my humanness—perfectly imperfect. I am grateful recovery has given me the opportunity to be present and feel the completeness of my feelings, the highs and lows, and the beauty and pain of motherhood and relationships.

3.
Obesity and Recovering through Motherhood

HADLEY AJANA

I was ten years old the first time my mother insisted I go on a diet with her. I don't remember ever feeling or thinking I was fat before then, but I quickly learned that to others, including my mother, I was "heavy." During the two weeks of the diet, I begged for food on a daily basis (the breakfast—a piece of dry toast and half a grapefruit—was particularly crummy) and was told repeatedly to stick to the regime. The end result was a loss of five pounds, something I couldn't have cared less about, but which I understood was supposed to make me very happy and which was celebrated with a hot fudge sundae, the eating of which I actually did take joy in.

That I had done something to warrant this kind of eating regimentation is the earliest feedback I remember about my developing body. The idea was brutally reinforced by both my parents, but especially my mother, who once told me her hero was a horse jockey—a man she had read about in a magazine who was so meticulous about his weight that he allotted himself one peanut to eat on a transcontinental flight. He ate half the peanut upon takeoff, set the other half on the tray table in front of him, stared at the half nut rocking back and forth as the plane crossed North America, and then ate it upon landing. I thought this was silly, but that kind of discipline was something my mother admired very deeply, and I believe I deeply disappointed her.

To be fair, the damage diets can cause was not well known in the 1970s, certainly not to my mother, who had been raised to believe weight management was her duty as a woman. For her, dieting was a sacred female obligation, which she dutifully passed on to me with the best of intentions. I would have a better life (husband) if I were beautiful, and to be beautiful meant being thin, and being thin meant not eating. This thin duty was a part of the female bond I unconsciously rejected and rebelled against at every opportunity: I dieted occasionally to please my parents and then ate. And ate. And ate some more.

My mother managed her weight by drinking coffee and diet soda, smoking heavily, and starving herself most days until she would break. I would find her huddled in some private space inhaling a bag of Cheetos and a hot dog. The next morning would always bring a return to severe rationing. Weight was her greatest enemy—an intimate adversary she fought to the death. Its closest ally was food, and she fought bitterly to turn them against each other, but even my mother finally admitted they could not be driven apart for long. I absorbed by osmosis this toxic relationship to eating at a very young age and never put a thing in my mouth that wasn't accompanied by a side of shame and a sauce of guilt. Where my mother found happiness in discipline, I found a sort of liberation in indulgence, yet it was always bittersweet as the results were so harmful.

My weight rose steadily as I matured into adulthood, and as my mother intensified her campaign to slim me down, the more the pounds accumulated. This continued into my mid-twenties. Her most valiant effort was a very expensive summer at fat camp the year I turned fourteen. She had been at war with my body for as long as I could remember, and this was her Waterloo. The summer left me thirty pounds thinner, but I wasted no time in packing it back on and was obese by my sixteenth birthday.

For a long time that was all you needed to know about me. Such is our culture that obesity is all defining. If you're a drug addict, you might be considered a recreational user. Alcoholics can be "high functioning." But fat people are defined by their addictions always. If you're fat, you're fat, and obesity affects every area of your life, including sex, and necessarily, conception, pregnancy, and motherhood.

My own pregnancy at forty-one was no exception. The circumstances were less than ideal, and although I was thrilled, I knew others would be concerned, to say the least. I wasn't quite prepared, however, for the response of my father, who rather than announcing the arrival of his first grandchild with great joy wrote a scathing indictment of my situation to family and friends—an indictment beginning with "She's already obese and about to gain more weight." He would by the time my son was two have had two weight-loss surgeries himself in an attempt to reduce his own mass from about 380 pounds to something more manageable. Both of these attempts failed miserably—after much pain and a lot of expense—and my father died shortly after my son's second birthday. Although he died of a cause unrelated to his weight, no one to whom I announced the news of his passing failed to say "Oh, I thought the weight surgery helped." He had been sure I was too fat to survive a pregnancy, and everyone else was sure he had been too fat to live.

I admit to being slightly jealous when it was announced around the end of my first trimester that Kate Middleton got to go to hospital for her severe morning sickness while carrying Prince George. My body's first response to pregnancy had been to pack on about twenty pounds, and after that, I began to throw up four or five times a day, just shy of the six times the doctor said would warrant a visit to the emergency room. Although I couldn't keep much down, I continued to gain weight at a steady rate of one to two pounds a week for the first three months, which the doctor said was due to some terrible behaviour of mine. Every visit to the scale brought an ever direr look of concern to the nurse's face, making each appointment a bit more awkward for me. I explained my eating patterns had not changed much, but being obese to begin with, no one believed me.

During my last trimester, I was diagnosed with gestational diabetes, which meant medication, restricted diet, and regular blood testing. Instead of making me feel even more anxious and ashamed, I found it one of the most liberating experiences of my life. Confronted with a medical need to care for my child ("If you do not control your blood sugar, your baby may become too big to deliver," it was explained to me), I easily and happily conformed to the prescribed diet and exercise program. I had the documentation to prove it, since the doctor demanded detailed records of what I ate, my blood sugar readings, and activity. With the confidence that my eating was healthy and controlled, I gave myself permission to not care how I looked or how much I weighed. In this loving way, my baby announced his revolution because his arrival dramatically changed all my relationships, not the least of which was the one I had with my own body.

I think it was this inner confidence that led me to say something to my mother I had wanted to say since she put me on that first diet at ten years old but for which I had never found the words. My feelings were so simple, yet they had been so hard to find. My mom had been sick for quite some time, and I knew she was dying. We had been peeling away the layers of our relationship for a couple of years as her health declined, and we had finally come to the tender heart of our connection. I flew across the country to see her one more time before I gave birth and made my confession: "I am so sorry that I'm fat. I am so sorry I disappointed you. I know you. I know how hard that must have been for you." I cried uncontrollably. How had the incredible amount of love between us become so tightly braided with my weight? It seemed so inconsequential now. Yet it had defined our relationship for my entire life. "You were never a disappointment," she said and stroked my hand. "You're my beautiful baby girl." I was not sure if she meant that or just wanted to mean it, but I knew she forgave me. I rubbed my pregnant belly and thought about how much I loved my own baby. I promised to come back with her grandchild as soon as I could and said goodbye to my mother for what would be the last time.

That was the seventh month of my pregnancy, and on the plane ride, I had to ask for a seatbelt extender on the flight. Normally, this would have caused me the deepest shame. (Before I take a trip, I usually research the length of seatbelts on the plane to see if I'm going to need one and then diet like crazy if I think it will be a problem.) This time, however, I felt being pregnant was a good cover and looked the flight attendant right in the eye with a big smile when I asked for the help. She still handed the gadget to me discretely, as if we were consummating a drug deal, but I was okay with it. For the time being, I had surrendered my body to this miraculous process, and as long as I was doing what the doctors said, I was not going to worry about what other people thought or what I weighed. I realized that it was a lot easier to make good eating choices when I gave myself permission to stop hating myself for what my eating had done to my appearance and health.

As the little body grew inside me, I never daydreamed about my baby's looks or great intellect. I never imagined being the mother of a president or being named in an Oscar acceptance speech. In my heart, I only held one deep hope for my child (beyond "a healthy baby"): I hope he isn't fat like his mother. I prayed he would be spared that stigma and I would find the strength to lead him away from the food addiction haunting my family.

By the time I went into the hospital to deliver, I weighed well over three hundred pounds and had gained what I estimated to be about sixty pounds total. My doctor wanted to schedule a delivery as soon as possible out of fear of complications, and I was not sure what to expect. After taking the medicine to induce labour, I had contractions and my water broke, but the baby did not want to come out. I laboured almost forty hours before delivering my son by caesarean section.

I felt vulnerable lying in the hospital bed alone those two days (the person who had promised to stay with me during labour was called away for many hours at a time), and the weight added to my concern. Knowing I would be difficult for the delivery nurses at the hospital to manage if anything happened to me added shame to my feelings of vulnerability, nervousness, and anxiety about delivering a baby for the first time and being alone to do it.

There were two or three nurses assigned to me during my labour, and one seemed particularly disgusted with my size. I asked if I could eat, which she agreed to look into. When I said I had to take a pill for acid reflux before the meal (this is something that developed during the pregnancy, as well), she gave me a look of contempt so scorching I thought my face might actually be charred. I wondered if she would have felt the same about another type of medication. I also wondered if this was abnormal behaviour of mine somehow. In my half-conscious state, waiting for my baby to arrive, with a million things to worry about, I lay there pondering sincerely whether this was this part of my food addiction (the wanting to eat in the middle of labour) or whether it was something a normal (thin) person would want, too. The neurosis around eating accompanying a food addiction is relentless and exhausting, but it did not prevent me from eating all the food brought to my bedside.

About thirty-six hours into the labour, I asked for the pain relief that comes from an epidural. The paralysis exacerbated the anxious feelings I had, as I was now dependent on the nurses completely. I worried when I asked for help adjusting my legs that I was asking for something that would cause injury to my caregivers. By that time, I felt almost as if I had no right to be there at all.

As they prepared to take me to the delivery room, I wondered if my weight would be an issue in transferring me. The delivery team used some sort of inflatable device to move me from my bed to the table, and this didn't seem to be much of a problem for them. I waited patiently for my baby to be brought into the world, as I listened to the doctors and nurses, whom I couldn't see, banter back and forth. In the back of my mind, I was also waiting for someone to make a comment about fat patients, but the only person who addressed me at all was the anaesthesiologist. He looked down and said, "You have beautiful eyes." The next voice I remember hearing was that of my son.

I found out by text message the day after giving birth that my mother had died while I was in labour. As anyone who has lost someone close to them knows, a death can actually mean a lot of work during a time of great sorrow. My case was no exception. The doctor kept me several days in the hospital because of concerns over high blood pressure. Once I was finally released I got down to business figuring out where my mother's remains were and how to proceed with her wishes for after life.

In addition to dealing with my mother's situation, I also had to quickly find a place. (As luck would have it, I suddenly had to leave the home where I had been living prior to giving birth.) It was a difficult time to say the least. During all of this, my biggest concern was breastfeeding, as I had been told this not only was good for the immediate health of my child but would be the best thing I could do to keep my child from becoming obese in the future. Unfortunately, my son did not latch well, and, as was explained to me by the lactation consultant, I had "the wrong kind of nipples for nursing." This meant a lot of people coming by the hospital room to check us out—my breast and his mouth. I couldn't help but wonder how much worse the weight issue was making all this. Are my breasts just too big? How come I can't make them do what everyone else's do?

Because the baby had jaundice, the doctor insisted I start adding formula right away to get him eliminating waste, and for weeks, we struggled on a diet of about 3/4 formula and 1/4 breastmilk. I did everything I was told. I spent a couple of days in bed drinking water and trying to nurse; I ingested weird teas, and ate oatmeal and large amounts of herbs. Nothing helped. Despite this, six weeks after giving birth, my baby was doing well, and I was, too. I actually weighed a few pounds less than when I had gotten pregnant. The diabetic diet and months of not being able to keep anything down had done some good.

It was a great relief not just to have the baby himself out of my belly, but to be a little smaller than I was. Breastfeeding helped keep some of this weight off, and I was so happy with my baby that I sometimes forgot to eat, but eventually I was back to where I started—now with a belly that was all stretched out and floppy! I felt worse about my body than ever before, despite it having just delivered the most perfect thing I had ever seen right into my arms. Plus, I was back to eating whatever and whenever I wanted, something that made me feel bad about myself.

At one of our first visits to the paediatrician, I mentioned to the doctor the history of obesity in my family and my concerns about my son's future. I was relieved that my son seemed to have his father's body shape, all lanky and slender, but I didn't want to take his good metabolism for granted. "Breastfeed and keep him away from juice and sugar as long as possible." That was the extent of her advice.

The words refocused my attention on the breastfeeding, and after one more failed attempt to get myself pumping more milk, I looked into alternatives. I found I could get donated breastmilk pretty easily. That began nine months of a lifestyle revolving around begging for donated milk, running around town to get it (although the donors were from incredibly different backgrounds, I noticed they were all young and impossibly thin—is that what it takes to produce so much milk?), and borrowing other people's freezers to store it. If this is what it would take to get my son the healthy gut bacteria he needs, to set his palette, to get him all squared away for a healthy (thin) future, I was eager to do it.

As a single mother, I worried not only about my son's nutrition and the other things parents worry about—(such as quality day-care, paying for preschool, surviving adolescence, and getting into a good college and the cost)—but also about how my obesity and relationship with food would affect the trajectory of my son's life in general. Although I know my son does not care about my size at this point, I noticed immediately differences between me and the thinner moms. There was the failed attempt to set my son on my lap and swing him, for instance. My belly was so round there was no place for him to sit, and we fell off. And I worried I wouldn't fit down the slide. I wondered if his future girlfriends and wife would be fat, or maybe extremely thin. I also noticed other mothers didn't seem to agonize over their children's eating the way I did. At swim classes, my son liked to have some fruit-flavoured snacks (really candy). These sat on a table by the pool and were provided by the instructor as a distraction. Was this okay? Would having these snacks set up a lifetime of weight problems for my kid? I worried. The thin mothers didn't seem to scruple about this, as they handed over anything from the snack tray without compunction. "She doesn't eat junk food at home, so I don't worry about it," said one mother to me. *I don't eat junk food at home, and I'm a mess*, I thought to myself. *That's no solution.* Every encounter with food was charged with shame and guilt before my kid was even two years old. Even if I gave my son healthy eating habits, which I doubted I could do, I worried my psychic toxicity would always be with him—the way my mother's weight obsession haunts me.

Other experiences fed my anxiety. One weekend I made the mistake of watching *What's Eating Gilbert Grape*, a film about a boy with many problems, not the least of which was a morbidly obese mother. It made me think of how beautiful my own mother had been. Like all teenagers, I found my mother completely ridic-ulous at times, but one thing I never had to worry about was being embarrassed by her appearance. She was clearly attractive to my friends' fathers and their adolescent sons. What would my son's life be like? "Oh, that's John's mom. The fat one," they would say and laugh. Or worse, would my addiction to food get so bad that I couldn't keep up with John anymore? Would I become a recluse, an immense burden to my child? I could not let this happen to my son.

It was not just for him I was worried, though. Being alone with a small child brings its own kind of social isolation. Without my family, or the baby's father, and with the priority of being home to care for my child, I had no distractions from myself for the first time in my life. I was alone with my body and didn't like her. There was no escape on the horizon. At the same time, the mother I had become wanted to nurture myself as diligently as I cared for my child. It was me and the baby now, and for both our sakes, I wanted to heal my relationship with food. Not just be thin but finally be free.

Medicine offered little or no help. I knew being overweight is a health hazard and that losing weight would likely add years to my life, years my son might need me, yet I also knew there was no cure for my condition. The extent of the medical advice given to me about my food addiction was this: "You need to lose weight. Have you tried the Mediterranean diet?" Other types of addicts may get offered rehab programs, cutting-edge therapies, or drugs, but for weight loss there really isn't much that's known to work outside of surgery, which is no guarantee, and appetite suppressants, which can have severe side effects and cease to work once you stop taking them.

Convinced I had to do something to relieve the self-hatred, which was both a fuel to and result of my obesity, and cognizant of the ineffective medical treatments available to help me manage my weight, I considered I might have to spend the rest of my life as a fat person and wondered how I could find a way to like myself as such. I wasn't sure if accepting this fate was life beating me down or the wisdom that comes with age, but I saw no other way forward. I had to learn to like myself, as I was at risk of poisoning my son and wasting the rest of my life wishing for a miracle.

The acceptance of my obesity brought a great deal of peace. It also created the space for change. When I stopped denying my situation, I could talk about my eating with others and open my mind to a new way of relating to myself. During a frank discussion about my weight with a friend, I first learned about the possibility of healing obesity and eating disorders through inner work, especially dream work.

This idea disrupted the uneasy truce I had recently forged with food and weight. The part of me that nurtured my son fought valiantly against the part of me that hated myself—the latter still asserted the only way out of my self-hatred was more discipline. It was only logical I had to be thin before I could like myself and I had to exert more control if I wanted to be thin. I was fat due to my laziness and poor character, I would say to myself: "It was so easy for your mother. What's your problem?" Eventually, however, the positive mothering instincts that my son had awakened developed a stronger voice, and I became willing to examine the inner dynamics that compelled me to eat unconsciously when consciously I wanted so badly to be thin. The part of me that mothered my child now stepped forward to mother myself.

The more time I spent with my son, the more I honoured my role as a mother, and the stronger my maternal instinct became, which gave me confidence, I could confront the dark energy within, driving me to compulsive eating. In trying to understand why I ate food I knew was not good for me or why I ate more food than I knew I needed, I drew on my intuition and feelings to interpret dreams and pictures and to heal through yoga and dance. The same feminine energy that I suspected had pushed me to overeat in the first place was now being used therapeutically.

Listening to my inner voice led me to realize the critical feminine regime I grew up with— the one that made my mother anorexic and said to be beautiful required being thin—had to be replaced. It is not easy to let go of one's value system and grab onto another. It was as if, at forty-four, I was leaving my mother's shadow for the first time, rejecting everything she had taught me about being a woman, and forging out on my own.

That is difficult inner work and tricky, too, because the ego itself is invested in the weight. That is why diets fail and only bring on more weight gain. The ego feels threatened by any loss and fights back ferociously; it defends its very existence by adding even more weight as a defence against future attacks. It is crucial, then, the inner work be done in a way that builds the person rather than destabilizes her. And I knew I couldn't do it for the goal of finally being thin because it was entirely possible I might heal to the point of having an ordered, healthy relationship with food and still not lose much weight—or enough to meet others' expectations of beauty anyway. I was too old and had been fat for too long.

As I became more aware of the psychological drives underlying my addiction to overeating, I realized denying the part of me that wanted to be a mother and homemaker had repressed potent feminine energy, which, angered at being denied, took revenge on my body through compulsive eating and destructive food choices. For years I had delayed having children because I didn't find the right person, was in school, or wanted to get my career going. No situation was ever perfect enough, just as I could never be thin enough.

On a typical day, I worked diligently at the office, practised my tennis strokes, communed with friends, ate a healthy breakfast and lunch, and then went home where, at night, the dark energy of the archetypal female (who had been repressed all day) surfaced. Enraged, she emerged from the depths of my psyche, ate a whole pizza or a few pieces of cake, and then disappeared once again into the unconscious realm to which I confined her. Sometimes, I wouldn't even remember she had made an appearance—forgetting I had eaten at all.

Through dream work, drawing, and therapy, I could bring much of this energy into consciousness. Once I honoured the female qualities I had been suppressing—the feminine qualities my mother's strict diets and severe judgments had driven underground—I found it natural to want to eat better and to be conscious of what I ate. There are still days when I find myself eating out of anger or frustration, but they are less and less as time goes by.

Many people who become addicted to drugs or alcohol find a change in situation or relationship goes a long way toward breaking their addition. I had always hoped that somehow, some way, a change outside of myself would bring about the inner change I needed to control my eating. Some women find the right mate gives them the peace to slim down. Others do it when they leave home and get away from judgmental parents. For me, the birth of a son and death of my mother coincided to force a new consciousness, which spurred me on a journey toward self-acceptance and better eating. Being a good mother to my son has also meant being a good mother to myself as well as an end to living as my mother's unconscious daughter.

4.
Mothering through Addiction and Jail

CHANDERA VON WELLER, JONI JOPLIN, SAM PECCHIO,
TOBI JACOBI, KATE MILLER, AND LARISSA WILLKOMM

*The single story creates stereotypes, and the problem with
stereotypes is not that they are untrue, but that they are
incomplete. They make one story become the only story.*
—Chimamanda Ngozi Adiche, "The Danger of the Single
Story"

*People don't look at me and see "felon" stamped across my
forehead. They should see me as a person. I'm a mother,
a sister, a wife.* —Sam

THE UNITED STATES CURRENTLY INCARCERATES over two
million people, and, as Adiche and Sam suggest above, their
rich and complex stories are often reduced to a single story that is
easily dismissed. Indeed, society assumes a great deal about incarcerated women: they are poor women of colour; they are neglectful,
single mothers of two or more children; they are uneducated and
immoral; they will move in and out of jail and prison throughout
their lives. Simply put, they are seen as incapable of change. This
is the trap of "single stories"; they dehumanize individuals, and
their stories become anonymous and easily dismissed (Watterson).
Our experience tells us that women inside prison are much more
complicated than these stereotypes suggest.

Here are some alternative ways to know us. We are six women
from different walks of life, different stages of motherhood. We
can motivate one another to think about how to move forward.
We are mothers before addicts. The past can define us, but we can't

49

let it control us. We have dreams. We have cherished memories of childhood and family. We are not monsters or terrible mothers. We are making the decision to change.

This collaborative chapter—co-authored by three women who co-facilitate writing workshops at a county jail and by three women who are held at the jail—argues that mothering, especially when complicated by the factors of addiction and incarceration, does not occur in a vacuum. We authored this chapter across three months, spending time together on Friday mornings at the jail. We began most meetings with a series of five-minute free-writing on collaboratively developed topics surrounding identity as related to mothering, addiction, and recovery in jail. As a group, we drafted several versions of the chapter and worked together to revision. We negotiated the content and structure of the writing to represent ourselves and our ideas in ways that felt comfortable to all of us. The chapter represents our collaborative attempt at an inclusive process and an effort to address the complexities of living apart from children while grappling with addiction in jail. By reflecting on the challenge and necessity of mothering from afar, our varied voices document the complexity of addiction and recovery. We also call for increased attention to alternative methods for treating addictive behaviours, which often end with incarceration and interrupted parenting rather that mental and physical care.

We began this project by grappling collectively with definitions of the key concepts that hold this connection together and by exploring them from behind bars.

The concept of "incarceration" often brings the usual social stereotypes as well as a sense of chaos for many women. Sam claimed that some people are terrified at the thought of being in jail, but she sometimes found comfort in it: "I find peace of mind knowing that I'm safe, sober, and healthy. After my first extended stay in jail, I realized I wasn't arrested—I was rescued." Although jail provides all necessary amenities for life and some protection from the self and others, it comes with a lot of baggage. As Chandera claimed, "A majority of people are put behind bars and guilty until proven innocent, which is unfortunate! Isn't it supposed to be the other way around?"

For us, "mothering" is an identity and an action. When motherhood is complicated by incarceration, a barrier is placed between mother and child, which is difficult to overcome as Chandera experienced firsthand. "I want badly to be there for my child right now, but I'm stuck here in jail, and the clock just keeps ticking as his childhood is passing. I feel robbed of these moments that I can't be there for him, but I did this to myself." She goes on to list many questions haunting the incarcerated mother: "Can this be a hurdle that we both can overcome? Will he feel loved by me? Does he feel abandoned?" We perform mothering behind bars. We feel that so many take mothering for granted until the opportunity to parent is gone.

"Addiction" seems to follow the same pattern: you think that you have control, we all do; it's not until you've lost everything and become what you swore you wouldn't that you realize your addiction has taken over. Addiction is complicated by incarceration because jail provides a sort of refuge from the addiction, as mentioned above. Jail becomes a catalyst to escape for some, such as Sam, who described her battle with substance addiction since her incarceration in the following way: "I carved my name in the stones at the bottom of the pit I found myself in, and I stood back up, determined to fight and claw my way back out. I don't want to be another statistic... I refuse to be any kind of stereotype." Addiction often takes the form of substance abuse (with its many complexities) for women in jail, which is how it is referenced in this chapter.

"Recovery" is a notion people often romanticize as a linear path, something done once with a permanent and happy ending. Recovery in jail is never this simple and is far more complicated, as Joni reflected:

> The act of actually quitting doing drugs was so absolutely terrifying to me. A morphine/heroin addict has to maintain to avoid getting violently ill. Withdrawals from opiates can be fatal. It is a hell all its own. This is where the fear comes in. You have to take more drugs to avoid being sick. This is how the cycle continues. The truth, however, is I know the person who takes drugs. This sober person, I do not

know any longer. I am beginning to understand who she is in my recovery process.

With these key concepts in mind, we unpacked the complexity of balancing addiction recovery and mothering from afar. In the following sections, we name the physical and material realities of women's incarceration in the United States and the challenges resulting when jail separates women from both their children and their physical addiction.

UNDERSTANDING THE CONTEXT OF
MOTHERING BEHIND BARS

Although the number of women behind bars is not equal to men, their numbers have been among the fastest growing prison population in recent decades as the chart below indicates.

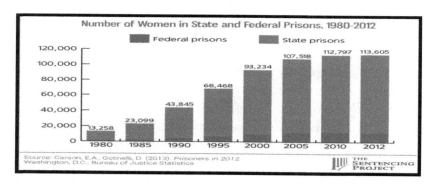

There are currently 2.1 million women involved in the United States justice system (Sentencing Project). Drug and alcohol use and abuse influence many of these arrests. About half of all women held in state prisons acknowledge the influence of drugs and/or alcohol at the time of their offense (Greenfeld and Snell). In 2014, 59 percent of all federal women prisoners committed drug offenses (Carson). For many women grappling with prison or jail, motherhood is a primary concern. According to the Bureau of Justice Statistics, seven out of ten women in the correctional system have children who are minors—a number translating to 1.3 million minors who often depend upon women as their primary caregivers. Two-thirds of all women in state prison and more than half of women in federal prisons leave behind at least one child while doing time (Greenfeld and Snell). Substance abuse complicates this separation: it often increases the likelihood of involvement with drug-related criminal activities and the likelihood of lost guardianship of their children (Harp et al. 687).

Once inside, mothers experience structural, economic, and institutional barriers. In *Mothering from the Inside: Parenting in a Women's Prison*, Sandra Enos names five issues emerging from her work with mothers in prison: arranging care, demonstrating fitness as mother to officials, managing mothering tasks and identity, negotiating ownership of children, and balancing crime and/ or drugs and motherhood (19). Based upon twenty-five interviews, Enos ultimately argues there are four trajectories women may take as they parent through prison time: motherhood accepted, motherhood terminated, mother on leave, or sporadic and shared mothering (132-34). These graphs represent "situational contingencies," which imprisoned mothers may experience and how they affect their connection to motherhood. Enos's conclusions point to four possibilities— ranging from termination of parental rights to full and positive return to motherhood.

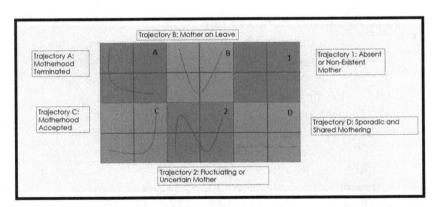

We felt at least two additional representations were possible (represented by one and two). The first (Trajectory 1) represents a roller coaster model of motherhood in which parental involvement rises and falls regularly as women engage and disengage with their children as other pressures (economic, addiction, systemic) intervene. Our second addition (Trajectory 2) represents an absence of identification with the role of mothering, although children may be present. In both additional trajectories, substance use influences how women can engage with children before, during, and after incarceration in ways that Enos's initial examples do not fully account for. We offer this extension to name the multiplicity of ways that addiction, recovery, and incarceration intersect for mothers.

LETTERS TO INCARCERATED MOTHERS

We also recognize the deep trauma many women experience as they arrive in jail or prison. Many times they are in grave need of support to understand the often overwhelming emotions that come with separation from their children. Although some institutional resources are available, this support usually comes from other confined women in the form of talk therapy and empathetic listening. To demonstrate the issues bound up in initial separation, we spent time imagining letters to newly incarcerated women to counsel them through the initial trauma of incarceration and separation from children:

> Dear Newly Incarcerated Mom,
> My dear, this is but a bump on the road of life. It may steer you off course for a while. You will soon see it is a necessary part of your future. You will have an experience that few moms get—what not to do, and the consequences from that action. Your children will be fine. You are their mother, and they know this and they love you. They will still love you no matter what you do or where you go. In a child's eyes, a mother is someone who loves them no matter what they do or say. Often, we do not realize it, but our children take on some of the blame for our mistakes. Reassure them that it is not their fault and this is your mistake to take care of. Lead by example. Be strong and supportive on the phone and in letters, and let them know you love them. That's all it takes.
>
> —JJ

Hey Rookie :-)

Do yourself a favour and breathe. It's all gonna be alright, I promise. They won't keep you here forever. I know, trust me. I know that you're probably, definitely, freaking out. I'm here to help you through this. Jail happens to the best of us. It's not the end. Your little one at home won't forget you. You can't forget "mommy." If they're still really young, there's a real good chance they won't even realize that you've been gone as long as you will be. You know how most young kids have no real sense of time. If your child is old enough to understand, then do your best to explain your situations to them. You're not gonna walk outta here with "criminal," "convict," or "felon" stamped across your forehead, my dear. The world there will continue to see you however you choose to present yourself. You made a mistake and got caught up. That is all. You being here right now doesn't mean that you're a bad mom, and don't you dare let anyone make you feel like you've abandoned your kids. They don't know you or your story. When you look back at this brief time about ten years from now, it's gonna seem like nothing. I promise you with all that I am that in retrospect to the many, many years you have spent and will spend with your kids on the other side, this is just a little blip on the radar. Keep your chin up. You'll be just fine.

—Sam

Dear Incarcerated Mother in Shambles,

Breathe. It's going to be okay. I want to help you know that you can still be a parent from behind bars. It may seem hopeless right now, but hang on.

If allowed, contact your child regularly through letters and/or phone calls. Let them know the current situation is temporary. Ease their young minds of the uncertainties they have. Humble yourself and let them know that you have made mistakes that landed you in jail, but you are picking up the pieces and moving forward.

Comfort them by giving them a timeline once you

have an out date. Encourage them to make a calendar or make them one, so that days may be marked off, and the end is in sight. The day of freedom can be a day of new beginnings. A day of hope.

Chandera

As these letters demonstrate, there are common fears and emotions sparked by the initiation of incarceration, especially when children and the Department of Human Services are involved. Creating community through these moments of trauma is essential. The more we connect the more shared difficulties we find. The challenges facing mothers are complex, daunting, and irreducible to mere physical separation. In the following section, we unpack four of the challenges that have emerged repeatedly through the drafting of this chapter, our ongoing writing workshop program inside a county jail, and our additional research on how incarceration affects mothers' work toward recovery.

THE CHALLENGES OF MOTHERING
THROUGH ADDICTION AND RECOVERY

How did drugs affect me? My personality changed into a person who could speak up, a person people wanted to be around.... I had confidence I had never before felt. Soon I could not handle any type of stress without the help of drugs. I felt like I belonged in this world—I deserved to be here. (Joni)

The intersection of mothering, addiction, and recovery is often interrupted by incarceration, which creates new difficulties beyond what nonimprisoned mothers face. The systemic and cultural structures surrounding mothers become interwoven with their life experiences, values, and social and familial identities. The problems facing mothers when it comes to substance abuse and jail are numerous and variable. Therefore, we focus on four that seem particularly relevant to contemporary women and families based upon our collective experience and research on parenting while incarcerated (Enos; Harden and Hill; Lawston and Lucas;

Talvi): lack of support during and after incarceration, mothering through damaged relationships, lack of institutional and community trust, and the difficulty of recovery.

Lack of Support During and After Incarceration

> Mothers are often forced to manage their own drug use-related problems while simultaneously trying to adequately care for their children in order to avoid criminal justice system or family intervention. This likely causes significant stress, and some have reported increasing their substance use to cope with the stress of parenting. (Harp et al. 687)

In our research as well as our experience, we echo the assertion made by Harp et al.: support provided for mothers and women in jail is absent. This lack of support is marked not just in terms of legal recourse, but also in physical and mental healthcare, parenting instruction, and postincarceration support. The current legal, economic, and social systems in place often prove to be more challenging than helpful. Many women are placed in jail because they cannot afford the kind and quality of mental healthcare they need, which results in jails becoming a holding area rather than an opportunity for change (Nowotny et al. 782-83; Whitehead et al). The cycle of incarceration does not just happen to individuals; it can create cycles of addiction and imprisonment within families. As family members are exposed to the environment inside jails and the disruptions of addictions, other family members can be drawn into the system and illegal habits. Having an incarcerated parent increases children's chances of ending up inside themselves by 300 to 400 percent (Gladwell 245). This cycle—which often starts with "alienation from mainstream health services ... [and] mothers feeling judged by the staff and other mothers (Fowler et al. 2835)"—could be interrupted by well-designed parenting outreach programs.

Postincarceration support beyond parenting instruction is vital. Leaving jail is often abrupt and can often lead to reincarceration if individuals are not prepared to re-enter the responsibilities of life all at once. As Malcolm Gladwell argues, the consequences of the three-strike rule include psychological damage, loss of employment prospects, loss of noncriminal friends and financial stability (245-46). Employment is particularly important. Women need to get a job to support themselves, their children, and to avoid illegal means of gaining income. Yet many jobs—including entry-level jobs, which are most easily applied to after a long period of being out of work due to imprisonment—insist on background checks and exclude people based on their criminal record, even if it does not affect their ability to perform the job. Moreover, the strong social stigma associated with addiction is difficult to escape. Thus, the people expected to take responsibility for their actions cannot move on with their lives after incarceration. In many cases of imprisonment, then, "the collateral damage starts to outweigh the benefit" (Gladwell 246).

Mothering through Damaged Relationships

Mothers battling addiction often experience "feelings of inadequacy, anger, and self-blame" (Fowler et al. 2836), which are often exacerbated by the geographic separation of jail, as Joni's reflection demonstrates:

> I have been an addict for fifteen years, and I have been a mother for twenty-four and a half. I have two absolutely wonderful girls. They are kind, loving, intelligent, and thoughtful. Even though my oldest daughter is angry and not communicating with me, I do know she loves and deeply respects me. The only reason she is glad I am locked up is because she believed it would save my life, and she's absolutely right—it did. In the span of three minutes, I made a decision that would change the course of my life forever. I went from being a preschool teacher to an inmate waiting for, what feels like, an execution. What have I done to hurt my children? They both have emotional turmoil—My youngest with a severe anxiety disorder, attempting suicide at age eleven, and almost being successful at it. It breaks my heart to know I may be to blame for it. Actually it kills me!

Most of us understand parenting comes in many shapes and sizes.

Yet for many women working through addiction and incarceration, it seems like an "all or nothing" ultimatum. We want to be there for everything with our children, but part-time parenting becomes imposed during incarceration by institutions looking out for "children's best interests"—a painful concept for both parents and kids to live with. Sam often mentioned how jail became a rescue and a means of removing temptation to help her reset her life. For those who are reoffenders, time spent in jail can become an opportunity to "go on leave" from the challenging work of parenting. For some, this "break" can become an attraction, not because of the separation from children but because of the separation from responsibility. Choosing to stay away after incarceration sometimes results in an easier slide back into substance use and abuse. Yet Sam, Joni, and Chandera all mentioned that staying with their children and spending time with them helps to keep them on the path to recovery. Rekindling relationships becomes more important to them than the fear of dragging their children with them through the process of recovering from addiction and its impacts. Chandera's fear of being "robbed of these moments" is made more real as she tries to deal with her troubles away from her son while still being a part of his life. These mothers also felt the need to prove their ability to parent to themselves, to society, and to their children. Cultural expectations and social norms regarding parenting in the United States reveal a gendered double standard for women: mothers are expected to parent instinctively, with or without a spouse, and to handle the stresses of life without complaint or failings. This ideal is difficult to achieve.

Institutional and Community Lack of Trust

> I think many behind bars are tormented souls. They are misunderstood and then mistreated, rather than being helped or treated for their shortcomings. (Chandera)

Another complicated barrier to recovery from both addiction and incarceration stems from the suspicion and distrust women experience from medical professionals, community members, and even family. Although being a mother with a substance dependency significantly increases the risk of harm for children, it does not automatically mean harm is occurring. As noted earlier, issues such as poverty, mental illness, isolation, and lack of support potentially increase the risk of harm to children, but these are also many nondrug using families (Fowler et al. 2836).

"There are assumptions that people make about the allure of drug use. 'You're high. You're high!'" reflected Sam as she recalled accusations made by her mother shortly after she was released from jail. "It's a difficult thought process to overcome. If everyone assumes you're this type of person, why prove them wrong? It's a self-fulfilling prophecy." The lack of trust runs deep. Catherine Fowler et al. affirm that "the women's feelings of guilt and fear, and being judged by others may have been unfounded in many instances. Nevertheless, all the women provided examples of negatively judging themselves" (2839). Social norms and responses often reinforce these feelings for women and the culture at large.

Institutionally sponsored recovery can underscore these perceptions of failure and make trust difficult to rebuild. In many halfway houses and community programs, curfews are strictly maintained. Work placement is restricted and monitored. Getting a ride from the perceived wrong people can result in write ups. Cell phones are strictly regulated and cameras aren't allowed. As Joni reflected, "We are so often set up for failure. Small mistakes land women back in jail." Parole often means daily urine analyses, weekly therapy sessions at certified treatment centres and other community sessions (e.g., Alcoholics Anonymous or Narcotics Anonymous), and monthly meetings with probation officer on top of requirements to find employment, housing, and childcare.

Difficulty of Recovery

The pressures of motherhood sometimes push the work of recovery to the side as women try to meet the needs of their children and lives. Sam knows this dilemma well, as she's struggled with how to think about her recovery process. The following mantra has emerged for her: "You're selfish when you're using because you are focusing on yourself. You're selfless during recovery because you are focusing on your family and pushing yourself toward change." Yet jail complicates the difficulties of recovery. Sometimes imprisonment can force sobriety, something that many women may not want or be ready for at that time. Recovery and sobriety are things that must be worked toward and desired. People who are not ready to be sober are at risk for being incarcerated again and again, which makes it harder and less appealing to change. On the other hand, the forced sobriety incarceration creates can act as an opportunity to refocus if the necessary supports are in place:

> To recover is to save oneself—to regain control, to bring back to a normal condition. Quite literally, recovery is the act, fact, process, possibility, or power of recovering or state of having recovered. To recover takes close observation and care of oneself during the process. The power to recover. I have the ability to recover, and I will. (Chandera)

> How do you keep fighting something that isn't tangible? It's all in your head, in your chemical makeup now, and you can't just rid yourself of it like the common cold. I don't want to be another statistic.... I refuse to be any kind of stereotype. I have accepted that my addiction and I will live together forever, unhappily ever after … but I sure as hell am not gonna let it continue to control me. I'm taking back the crown … taking back my life, on my own terms. (Sam)

This determination and hope exemplify the attitude toward recovery pervasive among some incarcerated women. They are determined to reclaim their lives and are fighting to claim a motherhood role for themselves that feels right (even when this means saying goodbye to their children). The individual and systemic challenges highlighted here are pervasive, and without adequate and intentional support, many women will not have the opportunity to realize their aspirations of successful parenting and/or recovery. We call for increased attention to the diverse and multiple needs of mothers struggling through addiction within the criminal justice system.

RECOGNIZING THE PUSH AND PULL OF ADDICTION, MOTHERING, AND RECOVERY FROM BEHIND BARS

> When an incarcerated woman begins a story with "I," she is, for one thing, explicitly inviting the listener/reader to "know" her, to imagine her humanity. When she says "I" and the next incarcerated storyteller starts her story with "I," too, and then the next, we begin to imagine a community of incarcerated women, speaking to us and also to each other ... building community in the midst and against the insanity of imprisonment. (Solinger et al. 7)

We have penned this multivoiced chapter with a few goals in mind. We want to offer alternative stories about our mothering selves as a way to represent the complexity of managing our identities rather than having them only managed for us. We also want to call for change. We see opportunities for better systems of support for women before, during, and after incarceration, especially when it comes to defining how parenting happens. We believe alternative programs can better support mothers' efforts to reclaim their lives and repair the harms of addiction with their families and communities.

Community-based programs, such as weekend community service, offer women opportunities to give back to the community through project-based work (e.g. building houses for Habitat for Humanity or cleaning at a senior centre) while maintaining the rest of life (i.e., working, and caring for their children and homes). This approach allows mothers to use time productively and to feel invested in both their own recovery and their community by building meaningful relationships. As Sam said, "You don't feel like such a criminal. You don't feel stuck in the system."

Restorative justice approaches also make more space for intervening in the cyclical nature addiction and incarceration that mothers face as they juggle the consequences of active or even past addictions in remaking their financial, physical, and emotional lives. Working toward repairing harm that has happened both individually and in the community could help offset the punitive approach adopted by most facilities. Such approaches begin by treating people as people; they are not seen only as their sentences or addictions. Through the more humanizing lens of restorative justice, mothers with addiction issues can better navigate their lives and better connect with their families during the healing process. They can demonstrate to the community they are not bad people, but people caught up in difficult situations, in cycles, and in different ways of life.

As we move toward understanding the power of narrative to create change, we turn again to Adiche: "stories have been used to dispossess and to malign, but stories can also be used to empower and to humanize. Stories can break the dignity of a people, but stories can also repair that broken dignity." We want our stories to challenge readers' understanding of how and why women choose to mother their way through incarceration. As we try to understand and address the harms of addiction and incarceration, we have written a collaborative letter to speak and demonstrate our complicated relationships to the children in our lives:

To our kids,

We miss you every single day that we wake up without you, but we find solace in knowing that we are one day closer to being with you again. We are writing to let you know we have made some mistakes and are in time out for a while. None of this is your fault. We were sick when we left you, and we want you to know that we are getting better. We humbly ask you to give us a chance to show you we can change and provide a better life for us and hope you can find it in yourselves to forgive us someday. It is going to take some time and love for us to gain your trust back.

We hope that you are taking good care of yourselves and each other and that you are continuing to talk through your feelings of sadness or frustration instead of keeping them locked inside. We know that this isn't easy on any of us right now. Keep looking toward the future and the years that we will have to spend together on the other side of all this, and we'll get through it together. It's a stepping stone to a promising future to create new and better memories.

You are our drive, the fire that burns within us to keep fighting.

We love you more than jellybeans. We love you more than the sun, moon and stars. Know that we will be together again soon.

♥ forever,
All the moms

In their collection about using narratives to change the world, Solinger and colleagues argue that narratives are powerful agents of change: "The story can have a different ending from the one we already know. You can 'hear' the story differently from me. We can compare. We can rewrite/re-enact/redraw and retell it again. The story becomes a way of remaking the world; being a storyteller in these contexts means being an activist" (6). We believe the telling of stories of addiction, recovery, mothering, and jail can help to complicate what we think we know about social order and social responsibilities. We believe we are capable of, and are indeed, moving toward the changes that will restore our abilities to have strong and positive relationships with our families. We end with an excerpt from "I Am More Than the Storm" by T-Town that was published in the *SpeakOut! Journal*—a biannual publication of a creative writing program inside the jail (67-8). We, like T-Town, are telling our stories and hope readers wide and far will hear them anew.

> Through all storms come recovery
> And without my storm
> I couldn't have made it to the "brighter days"
> Without the mistakes and lessons
> There would be no value to a
> Seemingly "sunny blue skied day"
> * * *
>
> I am not the storm I created years ago
> I am rewriting my story
> And this chapter in my life
> Remembers the storms
> But reached in the direction of

Beautiful
>Sun filled
>>Days
I am the rainbow after the storm

WORKS CITED

Adiche, Chimamanda Ngozi. "The Danger of the Single Story." Ted Talk Global July 2009. www.ted.com/talks/chimamanda_adichie_the_danger_of_a_single_story. Accessed 8 May 2018.

Carson, E. Ann. "Prisoners in 2014." *Bureau of Justice Statistics*, September 2015. www.bjs.gov/content/pub/pdf/p14.pdf. Accessed 30 Apr. 2018.

Enos, Sandra. *Mothering from the Inside: Parenting In a Women's Prison*. State University of New York Press, 2001.

Fowler, Catherine, et al. "Experiences of Mothers with Substance Dependence: Informing the Development of Parenting Support." *Journal of Clinical Nursing,* vol. 23, 2014, pp. 2835-843.

Gladwell, Malcolm. *David and Goliath: Underdogs, Misfits, and the Art of Battling Giants*. Back Bay Books, 2015.

Greenfeld, Lawrence, and Tracy Snell. "Women Offenders: A Special Report of the Bureau of Justice Statistics." *Bureau of Justice Statistics*, December 1999, www.bjs.gov/content/pub/pdf/wo.pdf. Accessed 30 Apr. 2018.

Harden, Judy, and Marcia Hill, Eds. *Breaking the Rules: Women in Prison and Feminist Therapy*. The Harrington Park Press, 1998.

Harp, Kathi, et al. "Social Support and Crack/Cocaine Use Among Incarcerated Mothers and Nonmothers." *Substance Use and Misuse,* vol. 47, 2012, pp. 686-694.

Lawston, Jodie Michelle, and Ashley E. Lucas, Eds. *Razor Wire Women: Prisoners, Activists, Scholars, and Artists*. SUNY Press, 2011.

Nowotny, Kathryn, et al. "Risk Profile and Treatment Needs of Women in Jail with Co-Occurring Serious Mental Illness and Substance Use Disorders." *Women & Health,* vol. 54, no. 8, 2014, pp. 781-95.

Sentencing Project. "Incarcerated Women and Girls." *Sentencing Project*, 30 Nov. 2015. www.sentencingproject.org/publications/

incarcerated-women-and-girls. Accessed 30 Apr. 2018.

Solinger, Rickie, et al. *Telling Stories to Change the World: Global Voices on the Power of Narrative to Build Community and Make Social Justice Claims*. Routledge 2008.

Talvi, Silja. *Women Behind Bars: The Crisis of Women in the U.S. Prison System*. Seal Press, 2007.

T-Town. "I Am More Than the Storm." *We Make Our Future*. Ed. Mary Hill. *SpeakOut! Journal,* Fall 2014, pp. 67-8.

Watterson, Kathryn. *Women in Prison: Inside the Concrete Womb*. Northeastern University Press, 1996.

Whitehead, Chaundra, et al. "Forgotten Women: Incarceration and Health Concerns of Minority Women." South Florida Education Research Conference, 2014, http://digitalcommons.fiu.edu/sferc/2014/2014/6/. Accessed 30 Apr. 2018.

II.
Research with Mothers

I wanted a better life for my little girl. Being a department store cashier meant that I had enough to pay for food and rent in our one-bedroom apartment, but little else. I was thankful that our neighbour would watch her when I was at work and didn't want to be paid. I don't know how I could have gone to work if I'd had to pay for a babysitter. Our neighbour never had children of her own and was lonely in her older years, so she simply enjoyed the company, becoming Grandmama to my child. Now that I think about this life we lived, it doesn't sound so bad. There was no money for dance lessons or birthday parties, but I had my little girl and my neighbour and we were happy.

One day, while walking to the bus after work, I met a man who seemed to like me. He never spoke about his job, but I didn't ask too many questions. I thought that this was my daughter's chance for all the opportunities that her friends at school had. At first, everything seemed okay. He was romantic, paid for nice dinners, and even paid for dance lessons for my child. But he didn't respect my boundaries and didn't accept "no." I welcomed dates with the future in mind, but I also became scared every time I saw him.

Most dates were at my place, with my daughter next door at the neighbour's. He gave me drugs to dull the pain of his leisure, and I gladly accepted. I began to welcome the drugs and crave them. He had a steady supply, as I eventually learned that he was a drug dealer. I even let him hide his stash at my house, as he said his place might be under surveillance. That was when the police came and I was arrested.

I don't belong here in jail. I just wanted a better life for my child. She's in foster care now, away from the mother and Grandmama who love her. I just want to go home, back to my old life."

—Aliyah, age thirty-two

5.
A Comparison of Justice-Involved and Nonjustice-Involved Mothers

ERIKA KATES

THE INCREASING USE OF HEROIN and other opiates has been described as a national and global epidemic (United Nations 5; Centers for Disease Control 1; Massachusetts Governor's Opioid Working Group 1). This chapter highlights women and their experiences in this epidemic because women, though heavily involved in substance abuse, are often marginalized in policy debates. Although white, affluent, and suburban women have become the fastest growing group of opiate users (Centers for Disease Control 1; Cicero et al. 822), this chapter focuses on low-income women—disproportionately women of colour—who, as the following sections show, are less likely to find their way to private treatment centres and are more likely to become enmeshed in the criminal justice system.

The chapter's first section provides information on the factors contributing to women's substance abuse and pathways to addiction. It discusses how women's imprisonment, like that of men, expanded enormously as a result of drug sentencing laws enacted in the 1980s and 1990s, and how this has affected their children. Finally, this section outlines recent advances in treatment for mothers with addictions as well as the dilemmas some face in seeking treatment.

The second section describes new research by the author that takes a unique look at mothers who have entered substance abuse treatment in Massachusetts; it compares the characteristics of those who are justice involved with those who are not. Justice involvement is defined as a wide range of interventions, including arrest, probation, bail, and incarceration. The research is a case study combining quantitative analysis of statewide caseload data of women seeking treatment together with qualitative data obtained from focus group interviews with addicted mothers. This approach provides valuable insights into these women and the breadth of their treatment and justice-involvement experiences. Most importantly, it adds women's voices and opinions to the analysis. Finally, the chapter concludes with recommendations incorporating these women's suggestions, centred on the premise that future policies should stop criminalizing addicts and focus instead on family-centred treatment.

ADDICTION, JUSTICE INVOLVEMENT, AND ACCESS TO TREATMENT

Pathways to Addiction

In 2015, almost eleven million (or 8 percent of) females in the United States aged twelve or older used illicit drugs, not including marijuana (SAMSHA 205). Alcohol, while not illicit, is the most commonly used drug among addicted women. One particularly troubling trend is that the rate of heroin use for women doubled between 2002 and 2013 (Centers for Disease Control 2). Moreover, women's overdose deaths increased 400 percent between 1999 and 2010. Addiction in women can be attributed to many factors: physiological, psychological, experiential, and medical. For example, women's physiology (i.e., hormones and reproductive cycles) can make them more sensitive than men to the effects of drugs. As a result, they can become addicted using smaller amounts, find it more difficult to stop using them, and relapse for different reasons (National Institute for Drug Abuse, "Sex and Gender Differences" 2). Women with histories of physical and sexual abuse are particularly vulnerable to addiction, as those who fail to secure early psychological and medical care may turn to alcohol and/or drugs as self-medication. Mental illness is frequently associated with addiction and is diagnosed as a co-occurring disorder (National Institute for Drug Abuse, "Other Sex and Gender Issues" 1). More recently, physicians have also come under scrutiny for their poor management of prescription drugs, especially for women.

Alarmingly, one recent study estimates that between 14 and 22 percent of pregnant women have received an opioid prescription (National Institute for Drug Abuse, "NIDA Editorial" 1). The fact that heroin is now cheaper than prescription drugs has contributed to the escalation of opioid use.

Women in poverty who need drugs have few options, and they may turn to stealing or trading sex for drugs and/or money. Their lack of resources and the inability or unwillingness of family members to help them can lead to homelessness, and to losing custody of their children (Raphael 104). The following section addresses the extent to which women's justice involvement results from drug-related offenses.

Substance Abuse and Justice Involvement

The United States has become known as the "incarceration nation"; over two million people are in prison on any single day. Often overlooked, however, is the fact that in 2012, this population included over 212,000 women, more than anywhere in the world (Walmsley 5). Moreover, the rate of growth has doubled since the 1980s, resulting in an 800 percent increase.

The prison population expansion is due more to the harsh and inflexible federal sentencing policies enacted in the 1980s than to an increase in crime. The Criminal Sentencing Reform Act, of 1981, and the Anti-Drug Abuse Acts of 1986 and 1988, imposed mandatory and lengthy sentences for drug offenses (The Sentencing Project 2). Importantly, these laws adopted a blanket approach—meaning the punishments were equally harsh regardless of the role a person played in committing an offense. Thus, a woman whose boyfriend stashed money in her apartment without her knowledge could serve as long a sentence as he would for trafficking in drugs. Much has been written about the impact of these laws on African American men (Alexander), but African American women have also borne the brunt of these draconian sentences. Between 1986 and 1991, black women's incarceration in state prisons increased 78 percent (Mauer and Huling 5). Following changes to the drug laws in 2005 and 2007, there was a decline of 24 percent (Mauer 26) among African American women. Still, many people remain incarcerated as a result of the earlier laws.

The population in prison with substance abuse problems remains high, and on some measures, the problem is worse for women. Although in the general population, women's drug use is half that of men (6 percent compared to 12 percent), Jennifer Karberg and Doris James's 2002 survey shows the percentage of women in prison with a substance abuse problem exceeded that of men (61 percent compared to 54 percent) and more women in prison were dependent on drugs compared to men (51 percent compared to 44 percent). Another study shows prison treatment resources are variable and poorly integrated, and monitoring outcomes is problematic (McCarty and Chandler S92).

Research has shown consistently that 60 to 80 percent of women in prison are mothers, with an average of two children under the age of eighteen years. In 2009, over three-quarters of mothers in federal and state prisons had lived with their children prior to their incarceration (Glaze and Maruschak 5). Thus, from the moment mothers are arrested, their children are displaced.

Research shows that adults' substance abuse has powerful psychological, behavioural, and biological effects on their children—stemming from initial fetal exposure to alcohol and other drugs to witnessing substance abuse. Children develop a vulnerability to becoming substance abusers (Johnson and Leff 1085). In addition, there are long lasting social and economic costs (Allard and Green i-iii). Typically, over 80 percent of women's offenses are nonviolent, so many women serve short sentences initially: for prostitution, disturbing the peace, and larceny. However, each time women are removed from their homes, the chances increase that they will lose custody of their children (Johnston 18). Thus, worry over their children and remorse becomes a constant factor in women's lives.

Recent Advances in Substance Abuse Prevention and Early Treatment

Early access to substance abuse treatment for women is essential to prevent the intergenerational effects—genetic and learned—from being passed on to children (Worley et al. 105). Such access has been a key objective since the late 1980s when federal funding first became available for treating pregnant and parenting women (National Institute for Drug Abuse, "Sex and Gender Differences" 3).

Currently, the trauma-informed approach is considered to be the preeminent model for successfully treating women. First identified in the late 1990s (Cottler 111), it gained recognition for justice-involved women in the early 2000s (Covington 379; Markoff and Finkelstein 7). The approach works on the premise that women with posttraumatic stress disorder (PTSD) develop high levels of anxiety, become hypervigilant, and exhibit "fight and flight" responses (i.e., fear and anger). They require environments where people know how to recognize, defuse, and prevent conditions likely to trigger such responses.

Another key factor in women-centred treatment care is peer support. Women feel less isolated and hopeless when they share their feelings with women in similar situations. This approach acknowledges women's responses as authentic and rational within the context of their lives, and strives to be voluntary, nonjudgmental, empathetic, and respectful. A central tenet of the peer-support approach is that women's strengths are emphasized rather than their deficiencies. Finally, women-centred treatment models respond to women's roles as mothers and address concrete needs, such as childcare, housing, education, and job training (Blanch et al 13).

Yet many women still cannot afford or access the resources they need (Wechsberg et al. 1278). Although women may be well aware that using drugs while pregnant or breastfeeding will have direct and negative effects on themselves and their children, they are scared that if they admit to drug use, child welfare agencies will take custody of their children and increase their chances of becoming justice involved. Another obstacle to entering treatment is the lack of reliable and affordable childcare (Grella and Greenwell 246). Thus, although considerable advances in treatment responsiveness to women's circumstances have been made, these obstacles likely extend their addictions and increase their chances of becoming justice involved.

COMPARING JUSTICE-INVOLVED AND
NONJUSTICE-INVOLVED MOTHERS IN TREATMENT

It is important to understand that not all women with substance abuse problems become involved with justice agencies. The author learned about available treatment options especially designed for women in Massachusetts in a prior study when visits to residential programs for women revealed that women who were justice involved were being treated in a nonstigmatizing manner side by side with women who were not (Kates 25). The purpose of conducting the study discussed here was to explore further to what extent justice-involved (JI) and nonjustice-involved mothers (NJI) are different or similar to one another and to what extent their treatment needs overlap.

Caseload Analysis

The research to address this question was facilitated by the cooperation of the Massachusetts Department of Public Health's Bureau of Substance Abuse Services (BSAS). All cases referred to BSAS in 2013 were used to create a "tailor-made" database. The key selection variable was mothers of dependent children. This group was then divided by whether women were JI or NJI. The data came from intake forms with justice involvement being defined by referral source, previous night's residence, current justice status (including an involuntary civil treatment petition), and the number of arrests within the previous thirty days.

There is an important caveat regarding the data: the analysis is based on the number of admissions, 33,000, not the number of individual women clients, which is likely closer to 17,000. This difference is explained by clients seeking assistance more than once a year (multiple entries of clients within a year). Analysts at BSAS estimate that the average number of relapses per person seeking assistance is eleven to thirteen over a lifetime. In 2013, there were 100,000 admissions to substance-abuse treatment services in Massachusetts. Women made up 33,000 of these admissions, and about 15,000 of these were mothers. Almost three-quarters of the mothers (11,000) were nonjustice involved (NJI) compared to just over a quarter (4,000) who were justice involved (JI).

Table 1 shows that the two groups of mothers were virtually identical on many characteristics: namely, the percentage with children under eighteen years, the percentage of those who were pregnant, and the percentage of those who had lived with their children. Similarly, there were almost no differences in the type of treatment they entered (residential, detoxification, or outpatient); the number of overdoses experienced within the past twelve months; the mental health status; or the average age. No data, however, were available on trauma and violence.

The racial/ethnic percentages appeared similar for the two groups, but it should be noted, underrepresented women of colour, since in Massachusetts, white people are 83 percent of the state population, Latinos are 10 percent, and African Americans are 8 percent.

Education levels show areas with slight differences between JI and NJI women. A larger percentage of JI women had higher education credentials (some college and higher) and a lower percentage with high school or less (Table 2).

Almost one third of JI had employment experience compared to 15 percent of NJI women; and almost three times the percentage of fulltime employment. Over 40 percent of NJI women were not looking for work, compared to one-third of JI women.

Table 2 shows noticeable differences between the JI and NJI women, including their employment status, the primary substances used, referral sources, type of treatment, and outcomes. For example, twice the percentage of JI women as NJI used alcohol as their primary substance, and almost 60 percent of NJI women used heroin compared to 40 percent for JI women. Twice the percentage of NJI women used opiates compared to JI women. As might be expected, almost 60 percent of JI women were referred to treatment by the courts, compared to 3 percent of the NJI women; and over 60 percent of the NJI population was self-referred, compared to 11 percent of the JI women. The percentage of women referred to more intensive treatment by an initial substance abuse treatment program was similar for the two groups. However, twice the percentage of NJI women were referred to detox/stabilization as JI women; twice the percentage of JI women were referred to residential treatment as NJI women (13 percent compared to 7 percent); and medically assisted treatment (MAT) was provided to a much smaller percent of JI than NJI women (3 percent to 15 percent). A higher percentage of the JI women had positive outcomes with over three quarters of the JI women being discharged or having completed treatment compared to 64 percent of NJI women. The dropout/relapse rate was higher for the NJI group.

Table 1.
Selected Characteristics of JI and NJI Women

Demographics	JI %	NJI %
Children		
Children under eighteen	46	46
Lived with children	39	35
Pregnancy		
Pregnant, with another child	2.4	3.3
First pregnancy	1.4	1.7
Race/Ethnicity		
White	83	83
Black	5	7
Hispanic (nonblack)	7	8
Multi/Other	4	4
Average Age	33 years	32 years
Education		
Less than high school	19	23
High School/GED	38	42
Some college	23	22
Associate degree	6	4
Bachelor degree or higher	14	8
Employment		
Fulltime work	22	8
Part-time work	12	7
Unemployed	23	28
Not looking	33	44
Disabled	10	13

Table 2.
Mental Health and Substance Abuse History

	JI	NJI
Overdoses within previous 12 months		
None	87	87
1-2	10	11
3-4	2	2
5+	1	1
Mental Health		
No prior treatment	34	37
2+ hospitalizations	15	15
Primary Substance		
Alcohol	40	20
Heroin	41	59
Marijuana	3	3
Crack cocaine	8	5
Other Opiates/Other	8	16
Referral Source		
Self-referred	11	62
Substance Abuse program	28	32
Court	58	3
Other State Agency	3	4
Treatment (Type)		
Detox/stabilization	26	52
Out patient/case-mgt.	26	22
Residential	13	7
MAT (medically assisted)	3	15
Outcomes		
Completed/Discharged	78	64
Assessment only	4	7
Dropout/Relapse	18	29

These data provide a unique opportunity to compare women in addiction treatment who are involved with the justice system with those who are not. Their status as mothers is very similar, as are their histories with mental illness and overdoses. Interestingly, while they are very similar in race/ethnicity, women of colour are underrepresented in both groups. The greater use of alcohol by the JI women rather than heroin and other opiates may be related to their higher education and employment levels; perhaps, they are not as debilitated by their addictions. Also, it may be related to histories of abuse. Although there were no data in this analysis on the abuse and trauma they had experienced, one study has found that alcohol abuse was more likely to be related to trauma in women's lives (Pirard et al 57).

Although these data provide indicators of women's experiences with both justice involvement and treatment, they do not address the scope and range of these experiences or whether justice involvement helped in directing women to treatment. To enrich the research analysis with women's personal narratives, focus group interviews were added with addicted women living in residential treatment centres.

THE EXPERIENCES OF MOTHERS WITH ADDICTION DISORDERS IN RESIDENTIAL TREATMENT

Method

Women with substance abuse and justice involvement are considered a vulnerable research group. Therefore, the research methodology and all protocols were reviewed by the Institutional Review Board at the Wellesley Centers for Women. The women were not promised a reward for their participation, but were given twenty-dollar gift certificates at the conclusion of their interviews. The principal investigator, who had considerable experience in interviewing vulnerable populations, was assisted by a research assistant responsible for the audio recordings and transcriptions.

The residential houses were selected with the assistance of staff at a nonprofit agency under contract with BSAS to screen mothers with substance abuse and find them appropriate treatment settings. Agency staff assisted the researchers in identifying houses that would provide racial/ethnic diversity to the analysis. House One was located in a rural area in central Massachusetts. Children did not live with their mothers but were allowed to visit, and some women earned weekend passes allowing them to visit their children. House Two was located in a very low-income neighbourhood in Boston; House Three also was located in a low-income Boston neighbourhood and was purposely selected because it had a bilingual, Spanish-speaking staff. Houses Two and Three permitted children to live with their mothers in the houses through an arrangement with the Department of Children and Family Services. There were no limits to the number of children a woman could have with her, or on their ages. Children were reunified with their mothers within thirty days of the mothers moving into a residence.

During the summer of 2014, twenty-five women participated in three focus groups held at the residential treatment houses in Massachusetts. Twenty-two of the women were mothers, and one woman was pregnant. All the women who volunteered to participate completed a brief questionnaire prior to the focus group and chose names by which they could be identified for the tape recording and transcripts. This step provided anonymity to the women while allowing their comments to be matched to their demographic data using the NVIVO qualitative analysis program.

Findings

Because residential treatment houses are required to accept women from throughout the state, they were expected to be representative of the population of women with substance abuse histories. However, each house had a distinctive population. In House One, all the women except one were white; in House Two, all the women except one were either African American or of mixed race/ethnicity, and in House Three, seven out of eight women in the focus group were Spanish speaking.

Also, there were noticeable differences among the three houses in women's age, education level, and employment experience. The mean age of women in House One was twenty-seven years, compared to thirty years in Houses Two and Three. The education level of women in House One was higher, with 57 percent having some college, compared to House 2 with 40 percent, and House

3 with 25 percent. All the women in House One had employment experience, whereas 30 percent of women in House Two and 50 percent in House Three had none (See Table 3). The kinds of work done included the clerical, retail, and food service sectors.

Table 3.
Age, Education, and Employment by House

	Mean Age	Some College	Employment Experience
House One	27 yrs.	57%	100%
House Two	30 yrs.	40%	30%
House Three	30 yrs.	25%	50%

These differences continued into their justice involvement and treatment encounters. In House One, only one woman had no treatment history, and only one had no justice-involvement history. In House Three, there were two women without prior treatment and two women without justice-involvement histories. When women were asked why they did not have justice involvement, they revealed it was luck, as they had engaged in similar risky behaviours as their counterparts who had justice involvement. The staff referred to them as the "not yet [justice-involved] women."

Most noticeably, there were distinctive ethnic/racial differences in the extent and scope of justice involvement and treatment among the three houses. As Table 4 shows, in House Two, the population of African American and mixed-race women consistently had the highest treatment and justice involvement, as well as the highest average count per woman. In House Three, the Spanish-speaking women had the lowest number of treatment and justice involvement encounters, whereas in House One, the experiences of the white women were closer to House Two than to House Three.

Table 5 shows the types of treatment women had experienced. In Houses One and Three, about half of the residents had experi-

Table 4. Mothers' Treatment and Justice Involvement Encounters by House

	Number of Treatments Encounters		Number of Justice Involvement Encounters	
	Range	Mean	Range	Mean
House One	0-21	7	2-33	7
House Two	2-23	8	2-34	17
House Three	0-8	3	0-13	4

Table 5. Type of Treatment Experience by House

	Percent Detox	Percent Treatment	Percent Recovery House
House One	57	71	48
House Two	90	90	60
House Three	50	38	50

enced detox, compared to 90 percent in House Two; and around half had had prior residential treatment in Houses One and Three compared with 90 percent in House Two. The Latina women had the lowest prior treatment history, whereas the African-American/mixed race group had the highest.

Table 6 shows a similar trend with the type of justice involvement. House Two had consistently high percentages on all types of justice involvement: 100 percent had experienced arrest and probation. The Latinas in House Three had the lowest percentages for all four categories. In House One, over 70 percent of the mostly white women had been arrested, but less than a third had been sentenced and imprisoned.

Table 6. Type of Justice Involvement by House

	Percent with Arrest	Percent with Sentence	Percent with Probation	Percent with Prison
House One	71	29	57	29
House Two	100	70	100	60
House Three	63	13	14	38

The data show that most of the women had both treatment and JI experiences, and some had been hospitalized for mental illness. As Beverley, a mixed-race woman living with her two children in House Two stated, "This is my first long-term [substance abuse] program ... [but] I have been to the [state prison] quite a few times; I've been in mental institutions, and detoxes, and holdings [jails]."

In summary, the three houses appear to have distinct populations as defined by ethnic and racial grouping. Women of African American and mixed-race backgrounds had the most treatment and justice-involvement experiences, whereas Latina women had the least. Clearly, no conclusions can be drawn from such a small-scale sample, but this finding raises many questions about the difference between the BSAS caseload data, which underrepresents women of colour, and these findings. They suggest more research should be conducted to explore the racial differences.

Women's Responses to Key Questions

Women were asked about how they had negotiated the complex treatment and justice-involvement terrain; what factors had helped and hindered their treatment; and what effects these experiences had on their children.

Did Justice-Involvement Help You to Get Treatment?

It is not uncommon to hear judges, probation officers, and correction personnel argue that justice involvement for women with substance abuse problems often provides an essential safety net for women. By locking women up "for their own safety," they are removed from dangerous living situations, and they are provided with food, shelter, and basic medical care. In short, they help to save lives. Some women agreed being locked up had saved their lives by affording an immediate break from their destructive ways of life. One woman who entered treatment as a condition of probation stated the following:

> I'm in recovery because of them…. Everyone says I have to really want to be here, but I have to be honest, no one wants to change their life. "Oh yeah, I'm doing drugs, I'm doing alcohol, let me turn myself in." This [idea] is ridiculous … things have to happen. Now time is passing by, and I'm realizing the process of learning. You get the knowledge of it, [and] then you change. I have changed my views.

> After [my] overdosing, the judge came to my ER room and sentenced me to eleven days in the [state prison], no bail. That was for violating pretrial probation for charges they knew I didn't do. I just don't think I should have gotten thrown in jail…. [But] It saved my life.

All the women were clear about the lack of treatment in the state prison:

> As awful as it may sound, it is easier to cop [drugs] in jail than it is on the street. Drugs are right there amongst everybody…. Even in the awaiting trial unit. [In addition] you have to be there [prison] for thirty days before you can go to NA or AA [Narcotics Anonymous or Alcoholics Anonymous] groups. I was sentenced to twenty-three days [for violation of probation], so it's like pointless.

Several women talked about justice personnel who humiliated them, or were unwilling to accommodate pregnant women:

> The last time I was there the judge said to me, "It's women like you who ruin children's lives. You should be ashamed

... your child isn't even borne yet, and it doesn't stand a chance."

My probation [officer] isn't very understanding. I went up there to clear my warrant and do what's right. I was homeless. I didn't have an income, and I was seven months pregnant with the twins. And he wanted to throw me in jail for a month and a half.

In the latter case, the judge intervened on her behalf, and she entered treatment in lieu of prison. However, other women who had been seven-, eight-, and nine-months pregnant when they went before the courts had been refused access to outside treatment and were sent to prison. Several women who had been to prison and other types of treatment programs spoke about their reluctance to enter a long-term residential program because they feared it would be like prison. None of the women said anything positive about the prison experience and treatment, but some mentioned probation officers had treated them with respect in drug and prostitution courts.

What Kind of Treatment Helps You?

Women spoke about the importance of understanding the nature of addiction, and how recovery involves more than simply not using drugs: "There is real recovery and [then] there is abstinence." Most women expressed positive opinions about their current treatment. The houses offered a trauma-informed support base for women, in which the staff encouraged women to make decisions governing house management. House One was a social model program that encouraged women to run the house with the assistance of case managers who were in long-term recovery themselves. As one woman said, "The staff understands; many have been there themselves.... they let us make decisions and we run the house ... we help each other."

As the literature suggests, peer support was an essential component of treatment in all the houses. After overcoming their initial mistrust of the other women, many talked about the importance of peer support in their recovery: "The expectation here is learning how to be a sober woman with honor and dignity and also [to] be a mother.... If other women here can do it, it gives me a lot of hope that sobriety and motherhood, I can do both of them." Others discussed gaining a feeling of independence and agency, within the confines of the house and its treatment structure. They felt accountable to themselves, their children, and one another. Thus, the factors helping women were those related to definitions of resiliency: gaining knowledge about the nature of addiction; claiming independence; being responsible for their actions; acknowledging their struggles; requesting assistance; feeling grateful; and supporting others.

Does it Help or Would it Help You to Have Your Children with You in Treatment?

Women worried constantly about their children, even when they were not in their custody, so a key question concerned whether women thought it was a good idea to have their children with them while they were in treatment.

All of the women in Houses Two and Three where children could live with their mothers agreed that it was. Some thought it created a positive atmosphere: "It puts you in a better mood when you see a kid laughing and being with their parents." Others thought that learning to balance their needs with their children was a crucial factor: "I believe this program is really teaching me how to balance being a mother and being in recovery, and how to put those two things together." For others still, it reminded them how important it was to succeed so they did not repeatedly put their children through the experience. One woman stated, "It doesn't make it any easier to have my daughter. She's ten and she's been here twice with me." Another woman, however, found it a great strain having her children with her because they were unwell. As a result, she had not slept in days and had to miss many activities and group sessions. It should be noted that a caregiver was available for mothers who needed to go to outside appointments or take a rest in House Three, but not in House Two. Women in House One who did not have their children in residence missed their children, but they appreciated the time to themselves. One woman explained, "I look at it like this is my time. Six months, nine months, is a very short time in all of it. If I can get my mind right, get myself right, then I will be able to take care of my kids;" and, "I need to figure out who I am before I get back home with them."

Finally, women were asked about their ideas on opportunities and resources essential to their long-term recovery.

RECOMMENDATIONS

Access to Treatment

Some women had stopped using drugs on their own; however, most understood they needed a more structured treatment setting. Yet, when they had applied to some programs, they were told they needed to be under the influence of drugs to be accepted. They suggested these rules should be changed and access to treatment be expanded. Although some judges and probation officers, as well as personnel at mental hospitals and trauma centres, had referred women to the houses, information about such resources is inconsistent. Several women had been unaware of the existence of family recovery houses.

Reinforce Women's Strengths and Motivation

Women carry so much remorse, shame, and self-anger at how their addictions have affected their children that they do not need to be constantly reminded about their failings. Courts and other agencies should respond to women's need to be treated with respect despite their histories.

Flexible Family Policies and Childcare

Some women refuse to enter treatment early because of the fear they would lose their children by admitting to a drug problem; and some refuse to enter outpatient care because of a lack of childcare. Women should be encouraged to admit to a problem without threat of imprisonment as early as possible to avoid the risk of developing a long-term addiction that becomes harder to quit as they age.

Informed Response to Relapse

Relapse is a normal occurrence on the journey to recovery. The common response of probation officers to women who violate the conditions of probation by using drugs is to punish them with a prison sentence (even when the original offense had not warranted incarceration). This disrupts their lives and removes their children, but it does not help them with treatment. In fact, it creates a spiral of increasing justice involvement. This practice is in contrast to the policy in recovery houses, where the staff uses a client's relapse as a tool to help her understand how to anticipate, avoid, or overcome similar situations in the future. This self-knowledge is regarded as one of the more crucial components of recovery. By helping women to understand how and why they have relapsed and avoid situations where they are vulnerable, the staff enable women to make different and healthier choices.

Enable Trauma-Informed and Peer Support Approaches

A trauma-informed approach is essential for women to feel safe enough to benefit from treatment, and peer support is often the key to an understanding that recovery is possible. Since these approaches can rarely be offered effectively in coercive settings, women should have access to early trauma screening and community-based treatment wherever possible.

Ensure Housing Is Available Posttreatment

Almost every woman expressed a concern about where she would go after the recovery house. Transitional or group housing, as well as permanent affordable housing, are important factors in promoting recovery and reunification with children.

CONCLUSION

The purpose of this research was to explore women's experiences with addiction and to identify how they fared in JI and NJI settings. Certainly, a case study in Massachusetts cannot be generalized to other states and countries, but it can raise awareness and point the way to future research. Policymakers in the U.S. and elsewhere (Pugh 15; Malinowska-Sempruch and Rychkova 19) acknowledge that instead of defining addiction in terms of moral weakness and criminal behaviours, it would be more productive to define it as a serious medical condition requiring therapeutic involvement and concrete resources (i.e., a move to a public health paradigm). Such a shift would be particularly important for women, and it should accommodate their circumstances and family responsibilities. A more promising policy approach would be to ensure and facilitate women of childbearing age and mothers to voluntarily enter treatment early without the threat of having their children permanently removed, and to provide childcare for outpatient treatment. The best remedy would be early intervention, in which the justice system would be used as a screening mechanism instead of a punitive one.

If, in reality, diverting women with substance abuse problems from justice involvement requires justice intervention, it should be the least harsh available measure. The research limitations of snapshot analyses and small case studies should be overcome through the use of longitudinal analysis to learn more about women's pathways into and out of addiction, the costs of treatment, and the consequences for women and family members. Finally, the inclusion of women's voices is a crucial element of efforts formulating policy change.

WORKS CITED

Alexander, Michelle. *The New Jim Crow: Mass Incarceration in the Era of Colorblindness*. The New Press, 2010.

Allard, Patricia, and Judith Greene. *Children on the Outside: Voicing the Pain and Human Costs of Parental Incarceration*: Justice Strategies Report, 2011.

Blanch, Andrea, et al. *Engaging Women in Trauma-Informed Peer Support*: National Center for Trauma-Informed Care, Center for Mental Health Services, 2012.

Centers for Disease Control. "Today's Heroin Epidemic." *CDC*, July 2015. www.cdc.gov/vitalsigns/heroin. Accessed 30 Apr. 2018.

Cicero, T.J., et al. "The Changing Face of Heroin Use in the United States a Retrospective Analysis of the Past 50 Years." *Jama Psychiatry*, vol. 71, no. 7, 2014, pp. 821-26.

Cottler, L.B., et al. "Gender Differences in Risk Factors for Trauma Exposure and Post-Traumatic Stress Disorder among Inner-City

Drug Abusers in and out of Treatment." *Comprehensive Psychiatry*, vol. 42, no. 2, 2001, pp. 111-17.

Covington, S.S. "Women and Addiction: A Trauma-Informed Approach." *Journal of Psychoactive Drugs*, 2008, pp. 377-385.

Glaze, L., and L. Maruscak. *Parents in Prison and Their Minor Children*. Bureau of Justice Statistics, 2009.

Grella, Christine E., and Lisa Greenwell. "Treatment Needs and Completion of Community-Based Aftercare among Substance-Abusing Women Offenders." *Women's Health Issues*, vol. 17, no. 4, 2007, pp. 244-55.

Johnson, J.L., and M. Leff. "Children of Substance Abusers: Overview of Research Findings." *Pediatrics*, vol. 103, no. 5, 1999, pp. 1085-99.

Johnston, Denise. "Effects of Parental Incarceration." *Children of Incarcerated Parents*, edited by Katherine Gabel and Denise Johnston. Lexington Press, 1995, pp. 68-76.

Karberg, Jennifer C., and Doris J. James. *Substance Dependence, Abuse, and Treatment of Jail Inmates, 2002*. U.S. Department of Justice, 2005.

Kates, Erika. *Promising Gender-Responsive, Community-Based Programs for Women Offenders in Massachusetts: A Resource for Policymakers*. Wellesley Centers for Women, Wellesley College, 2010.

Malinowska-Sempruch, Kasia and Olga Rychkova. *The Impact of Drug Policy on Women*. Open Society Foundations, 2012.

Markoff, Laurie and Norma Finkelstein. "Integrating an Understanding of Trauma into Treatment for Women with Substance Use Disorders and/or HIV." *The Source*, vol. 10, no. 1, 2007, pp. 7-11.

Massachusetts, Commonwealth of. *Recommendations of the Governor's Opioid Working Group*. June 2015. www.mass.gov/files/2017-08/recommendations. Accessed 8 May 2018.

Mauer, Marc. "The Changing Racial Dynamics of Women's Incarceration." The Sentencing Project, 2013,

Mauer, Marc, and Tracy Huling. *Young Black Americans and the Criminal Justice System: Five Years Later*. The Sentencing Project, 1995.

McCarty, Dennis, and Redonna Chandler. "Understanding the

Importance of Organizational and System Variables on Addiction Services within Criminal Justice Settings." *Drug and Alcohol Dependence*, vol. 103S, 2009, pp. S91-S93.

National Institute on Drug Abuse. "Sex and Gender Differences in Substance Use." *Drug Facts: Substance Abuse in Women.* National Institutes of Health, Sept. 2015, www.drugabuse.gov/publications/research-reports/substance-use-in-women. Accessed 30 Apr. 2018.

National Institute on Drug Abuse. "Other Sex and Gender Issues for Women Related to Substance Use." *Drug Facts: Substance Abuse in Women*, National Institutes for Health, July 2015, www.drugabuse.gov/publications/research-reports/substance-use-in-women. Accessed 30 Apr. 2018.

National Institute on Drug Abuse. "NIDA Editorial urges Safer Opioid Prescribing Practices for Pregnant Women." *Drug Facts: Substance Abuse in Women*, National Institutes for Health, Jan. 2016, www.drugabuse.gov/news-releases/2016nida. Accessed 30 Apr. 2018.

National Institute on Drug Abuse. "Sex and Gender Differences in Substance Abuse Disorder Treatment." *Drug Facts: Substance Abuse in Women*, National Institute on Drug Abuse, July 2015, www.drugabuse.gov/?ppublications/drugfacts/substance-use in women. Accessed 30 Apr. 2018.

Pirard, Sandrine, et al. "Prevalence of Physical and Sexual Abuse among Substance Abuse Patients and Impact on Treatment Outcomes." *Drug and Alcohol Dependence*, vol. 78, no. 1, 2005, pp. 57-64.

Pugh, Tracy, et al. "Blueprint for a Public Health and Safety Approach to Drug Policy." *New York Academy of Medicine*, 2013, pp.1-81.

Raphael, Jody. *Freeing Tammy: Women, Drugs, and Incarceration.* Northeastern University Press, 2007.

SAMHSA. *Tip 51 Substance Abuse Treatment Addressing the Specific Needs of Women.* U.S. Department of Health and Human Services, 2009.

United Nations. Office on Drugs and Crime. *Substance Abuse and Care for Women: Case Studies and Lessons Learned.* United Nations, 2004.

Walmsley, Roy. *World Prison Population List.* Institute for Criminal Policy Research, Birkbeck College. University of London, 2015.

Wechsberg, W.M., et al. "Reaching Women Substance Abusers in Diverse Settings: Stigma and Access to Treatment 30 Years Later." *Substance Use & Misuse*, vol. 43, no. 8-9, 2008, pp. 1277-279.

Worley, L.L.M., et al. "Building a Residential Treatment Program for Dually Diagnosed Women with Their Children." *Archives of Women's Mental Health*, vol. 8, no. 2, 2005, pp. 105-111.

6.
Mothering and Mentoring

The PCAP Women's Quilt

DOROTHY BADRY, KRISTIN BONOT, AND RHONDA NELSON

"The Meaning of Mentorship," Quilt square designed by a participant in the
Parent Child Assistance Program (PCAP) Women's Quilt Project.
Image Credit: Dorothy Badry, Kristin Bonot, and Jamie Hickey.

THIS CHAPTER INTRODUCES and describes the Parent Child
Assistance Program (PCAP) Women's Quilt Project completed in Alberta, Canada, in 2015. The PCAP program works with
vulnerable women who struggle with addictions and have given
birth, or are at risk of giving birth, to a child born with alcohol

exposure in utero, which can often lead to a diagnosis of fetal alcohol spectrum disorder (FASD)—a lifelong disability. In 2012, program mentors created quilt squares to express their experience of being a mentor. They named the quilt "Pick-Up-Sticks," as mentors worked closely with women and described this work as gathering things back together (Job et al. 73-77). The PCAP women's quilt was developed as a qualitative research project inspired by the PCAP mentor's quilt. A small grant was provided to the PCAP Council to develop a women's quilt after mentors indicated that creating a quilt was such an inspiring project; they felt the women they work with would gain from this experience. Women participating in PCAP were invited to share their experiences as participants in the mentoring program through the creation of a quilt square in locally hosted workshops. A master quilter completed both quilts through an interpretive and creative process. The PCAP women's quilt was named "Woven Together," wherein women were invited to identify the meaning of this program in their lives through the use of visual imagery—namely, creating a quilt square through workshops offered in Alberta in 2014 and 2015. The quilt depicts women's experience in PCAP and highlights the influence of mentoring relationships as well as women's experience as mothers. It is their voices and experience of mothering that truly ground this work. The use of visual research offers an opportunity to look at women's lives and culture, particularly for women who struggle with addiction and have often been marginalized from their children's lives.

The use of visual methods to reflect women's lives is gaining ground, as it offers a means to explore the meaning of relationships through nontraditional research approaches. Laura Ellingson has indicated that qualitative research should consider using differing approaches and even transcend methodological approaches to reflect human experience; she suggests a place exists for research that is distinct to diverse groups (413). Dorothy Badry and Aileen Felske suggest that a visual methodology such as Photovoice offers a way to conduct research on complex health and social topics with women in rural and remote Indigenous communities (169). Through a quilting activity, the participants in our research created images that were reflective expressions of a place and time in a woman's life. Jon Prosser highlights how visual research offers a role for researchers to look at the world differently (2). Although lived-experience research has not historically held the same status as quantitative research, new models show that understanding lived experiences means programs and services will be better designed to fit client needs. Visual methodologies, from a social science and feminist inquiry perspective, offer compelling ways to explore women's lives and understand their lived experience in PCAP. With this in mind, we embarked on a project inviting women to reflect on their lived experience and to visually share this through contributing to the creation of a quilt.

THE PCAP WOMEN'S QUILT RESEARCH QUESTION

PCAP has been influential in developing approaches to effectively support women to parent their children while they deal with addictions, historical trauma, and other social problems requiring ongoing support and caring interventions. Qualitative research offers a means to explore the human experience in innovative and creative ways. The focus of this research was on developing an in-depth understanding of the ways in which women through visual imagery, quilting, reflect their experience of and meaning attributed to mentorship. The experience of being involved in the PCAP program and working with a mentor can be, and often is, a major influence in whether women can keep their children when involved with the child-welfare system. The PCAP intervention work is based on relationships; it often disrupts discourses that assume all women with addictions cannot parent their children. The primary research question focused on asking women to represent through creating a quilt square the meaning of their experience of having a mentor in their lives. The question stated: what does having a PCAP mentor in your life mean to you? We recognized the use of a visual approach would elicit unique responses from each woman. We knew some women were parenting, and others were not. We anticipated distinct reflections of these experiences. This project was undertaken to understand the impact of mentoring work in women's lives. Furthermore, we believed creating the quilt was a supportive activity in women's healing and recovery work through the PCAP program. This chapter focuses on the PCAP women's quilt and describes themes and discourses emerging from the project.

A BRIEF DESCRIPTION OF FASD—
THE CANADIAN SOCIAL CONTEXT FOR PCAP

A brief history about FASD will help to contextualize the emergence of this phenomenon. In 1973, Kenneth Jones and David Smith published the first article in North America on fetal alcohol syndrome (FAS), and this signalled the beginning of public discourse on the topic. As with all scientific research, it takes years and even decades for the information to filter out to the medical community. The University of Washington in Seattle was the primary hub for research into FASD. In the 1990s, there was increased concern for parents living with alcohol addiction and their children and in response, the FASD Community of Practice (2003 ongoing) was developed within children's services in Alberta. The research produced at the University of Washington was gaining attention in Alberta. To this end, Dr. Sterling Clarren and Dr. Therese Grant offered training in southern Alberta beginning in 1992. The focus of training was twofold: to develop a basic understanding of the effects of alcohol in utero and to consider the needs of women, children, and families engaged with the child welfare system while identifying ways to support intervention and prevention. To this end, the Parent Child Assistance Program (PCAP) was adopted in Alberta in 1999 and initially began with three programs located in Calgary, Lethbridge, and Edmonton. Today, there are over thirty programs in Alberta. Alberta has been recognized for its leadership in responding to children and families within the child-protection system (Badry 55).

THE ALBERTA PCAP PROGRAM

A primary goal of the Alberta PCAP is to prevent future births of alcohol and/or drug exposed children by focussing on women's health and wellbeing. Researchers have shown that the PCAP model is designed to provide services and interventions, and has had a positive impact on the lives of women, children, and families (Ernst et al. 20; Grant et al. 212). The theoretical framework and approaches guiding PCAP intervention include relational, stages of change, and harm reduction (Grant et al. 2011). PCAP's harm reduction approach recognizes the need to support women in their environments and to promote resiliency. Guided by these approaches, PCAP mentors make a positive difference. The support they provide often leads to a decrease in substance use and more access to resources. Their work also supports networks, which reduces isolation stress. The primary work of the PCAP program is to support women by establishing long-term mentoring relationships focussing on health and wellbeing.

The Alberta PCAP Council meets twice a month to review practice and policy in relation to program delivery and resources. The council exists in Alberta under the umbrella of the FASD Cross Ministry Committee (FASD-CMC)—a body that provides a linkage between all human service ministries and the community. A central role of the FASD-CMC is to carry out the work of the Alberta Ten Year Strategic Plan on FASD (2007-2017) through providing leadership, identifying best practice, reviewing and revising policy, engaging in knowledge exchange, and sharing information. The FASD-CMC has also endeavoured to hear the voices of those living with and supporting individuals with FASD, as identified in the ten-year plan.

PCAP works to prevent alcohol-exposed pregnancies while focussing on supporting women from a harm-reduction lens. Women also remain in the program if the pregnancy is terminated, miscarried, or stillborn. Mothering is a large part of mentoring work but not necessarily the main focus of the work, which is dependent on a woman's need at the time of intervention. Other key aspects of the work include crisis management and supporting stability in relation to housing, income, and supporting women involved with the child-welfare system. A harm-reduction focus in PCAP offers intensive support aimed at creating a safe space where women know they are cared for, particularly in the mothering of their children.

Responding to FASD from a feminist lens involves focussing on harm reduction while engaging in health promotion—a primary goal of PCAP. Social science research has not kept pace with biomedical research in FASD, but a determined focus on women's health as a critical issue in prevention is a priority within the Canada FASD Research Network Action Team on Prevention led by Nancy Poole of the Centre for Excellence in Women's Health. To suggest women simply refrain from alcohol use during pregnancy is far too simplistic. Nancy Poole and Lorraine Greaves have examined this topic from a women's health lens. They stress the importance of trauma-informed care and argue the root causes of alcohol misuse are grounded in women's health, relationships, historical trauma, and adverse experiences contributing to addiction (xii). Prevention is multifaceted, and PCAP embraces a harm-reduction and relational approach, which has a positive impact on the lives of many women, children, and families.

The challenges of addiction, recovery, and parenting are daunting when a woman comes into contact with the child-welfare system. The Alberta PCAP program offers specialized and holistic support to pregnant women with alcohol and other health or social problems. In PCAP, relational support and intervention take into consideration the broad experience of women's lives, their social context, how addiction develops, and the role it plays in a woman's life.

A Qualitative Research Approach

The PCAP women's quilt was a qualitative participatory action research (PAR) project involving thirty women; it took place in the province of Alberta, Canada, from 2014 to 2015. This project was initiated and supported by the Alberta PCAP Council in collaboration with the Faculty of Social Work, University of Calgary, which granted ethics approval for the project. Women involved in the project shared the meaning of the mentoring relationship through contributing to the women's quilt. The Alberta PCAP Council provided some funds to cover the cost of the master quilter and supplies. Otherwise, the PCAP women's quilt was an unfunded project. Small quilting workshops were held in two urban centres and a number of rural communities from 2014 to 2015. Using felt pens and fabric quilt squares, women were invited to visually create the meaning of the program and to represent the change in their lives. Furthermore, women were asked to briefly share the meaning of their visual creation and to reflect on how the image was representative of changes in their lived experience. Most workshops were standalone activities, although a few workshops were attached to another activity or event within the host program. The researchers maintained a relaxed atmosphere for the workshop by allowing staff and participants to come and go from the room. Women could also bring their children during the workshop, as finding childcare arrangements might have been a potential obstacle to attending. The presence of women, children, and mentors at the workshops contributed to the creation of an engaged, connected, and lively space for working on the quilt.

Qualitative research methods intend to evoke experience, and Luc Pauwels identifies this work as both participatory and collaborative (96). Norman Denzin and Yvonna Lincoln suggest a qualitative researcher is akin to a quilter who brings together pieces of material to create a montage of differing views and perspectives (7). Qualitative research creates a space for differing voices to be added to the discourse—in this project the voice of women involved in supportive mentoring relationships. Furthermore, once the researcher has gathered together all the pieces of the work—in this case, a visually stunning quilt—a portrait emerges that reflects the experience of individuals and contributes to a perspective on collective experience.

The methodological approach included the creation of the quilt square, brief interviews, and conversations with women. Small focus groups were held with women participants, and these were recorded, transcribed, and checked for accuracy. Furthermore, the quilting activity and the quilt squares were photographed as well as the work of the master quilter, who also submitted an interpretive analysis after working so intensively in the quilting process. Through reviewing and reflecting on individual contributions and the collective work as a whole, this chapter gives voice to themes and experience.

Visual Methods

John Grady has identified visual research as a benefit to the social sciences through its contribution to understanding and appreciating emotional aspects of life (11). Jon Prosser and Catherine Burke suggest that participatory research, visual approaches in particular, has an emancipatory function for marginalized groups, such as children, and supports empowerment on the part of participants (270). They further identify the value of visual research in promoting change and offering a vehicle to address complexities in the lives of children and youth. Visual approaches are also appealing in working with women. In this project, the opportunity to engage in creating a quilt square with felt pens and vibrant colours was appealing to women. Women who brought their children to the workshop often worked side by side with them, as children could draw on fabric. This was clearly a joy for women participants. Visual approaches hold unique opportunities to communicate findings of social phenomenon

Gustavo Fischman suggests image-based research requires a focus on inquiry and reflection going beyond the notion of a picture being worth a thousand words (31). Looking at an image offers an opportunity to explore human concerns more deeply to engage in meaning making from a less traditional research stance. Research literature on visual methodologies remains thin, particularly in relation to quilting, but a growing body of work is emerging. Elena Bendien has used the metaphor "the last stitch in the quilt" as a means of reflecting women's narratives over a lifetime and referred to these as the following:

> The intricate quilts they have stitched together in the course of their lives. They have fitted together layer after layer with almost unbelievably diverse pieces of life events, managing to keep a hold on patterns that were in accordance with their characters and beliefs...they tied the layers together in order to comfort and protect those whom they loved. (718)

Lori Koelsch has used the metaphor of qualitative research as a patchwork quilt, which resonates with feminist approaches (823). In many ways, the PCAP Women's quilt was a patchwork quilt—stitched together to beautifully reflect the lives of thirty women who have faced many challenges throughout their lives. In alignment with the research conducted by Koelsh, each patch or square constructed held a woman's story. In a recent project, known as the Truth and Reconciliation Commission Virtual Quilt, an online quilt was created by Inuit women in Canada through Pauktuutit (Nipiqaqtugut Sanaugatigut). Through traditional activities such as sewing, storytelling, voice and community engagement, the experience and the ripple effect of the residential schools of Canada in northern Canada were represented. This project showed that for healing to occur voices must be heard, and the virtual quilt is

The PCAP Women's Quilt—Woven Together. Complete quilt photograph for women participants. Image Credit: Dorothy Badry, Kristin Bonot, and Jamie Hickey.

a remarkable example of the power of visual methodology.
Social Context for Women Involved in PCAP

In Alberta, the development and delivery of PCAP was closely modelled on the work of Dr. Therese Grant and colleagues at the University of Washington, many of whom have provided training and support to grow and develop mentoring work in Alberta. Given FASD has primarily been framed as a public health issue, PCAP's primary goal is to reduce both incidence and prevalence through focussing on women's health, which is a foundation for prevention. The issue of alcohol addiction and pregnancy is a hot-button topic. One does not need to look far in social media to find condemnation and criticism of women who drink alcohol while pregnant. It is important, however, to have an appreciation of the challenges associated with addiction. According to Gabor Maté, addiction is "any repeated behaviour, substance-related or not, in which a person feels compelled to persist, regardless of its negative impact on [her] life and the lives of others" (214), including shopping, Internet use, sex, and work. For the purpose of this discussion, we will focus on substance-related addiction, specifically alcohol. Although many reasons exist for alcohol misuse, Poole and Greaves indicate that self-medicating is not uncommon for women with histories of abuse and trauma (xii).

Maté argues it is important to understand the science of addiction and the complex factors contributing to maintaining the state achieved through the use of alcohol (213). We recognize women involved in PCAP often have complex trauma histories and these need to be understood as important factors influencing a woman's life trajectory. When a child receives a FASD diagnosis, there is often a long, complex trauma history that has contributed to these circumstances. The supportive relationships offered by mentors and allied health professionals can influence change in intergenerational cycles of alcohol addiction and the myriad of associated health and social concerns.

Based on intake assessments within the PCAP client population as indicated in the 2010 Alberta PCAP Council User Manual, approximately 50 to 60 percent of women report co-occurring mental health and substance abuse disorders at enrollment—the most frequent being mood disorders (depression, bipolar disorder), and stress, panic, and anxiety disorders, including posttraumatic stress disorder (PTSD) (36). Since women involved in the PCAP program have substantial mental health and substance abuse issues and since PCAP is concerned with preventing FASD, an understanding of the relationship between adverse childhood experiences (Robert Anda) and a woman's use of alcohol is essential for PCAP mentors if the program is to meet her mental, physical, and emotional needs.

In their mother-child study, *Breaking the Cycle* (BTC), Debra Pepler and colleagues show that women using substances often have strong connections to others doing the same and that unresolved historical trauma is often triggered in relationships as adults (29). Their findings indicate that women involved in "relationship-focused intervention at BTC had greater improvements in their ability to resist substance use" (38). Furthermore, they state that women involved in supportive, relationship-based intervention have a greater likelihood of remaining in the program and making improvements in their lives (41). The relationship between the mother and child is a critical factor in motivation for change. Supporting mothers through relational interventions focused on substance use reduction as well as parenting can positively influence motivation. The PCAP program understands that the mother and child are a dyad, and this position contributes to and supports engagement. The BTC study identifies the need to promote relationship-based interventions as early as possible for women, which is also important for mediating the challenges of children who may have FASD and developmental challenges. On the importance of relational approaches, Pepler and colleagues state the following:

> An authentic relationship-focused intervention hold mothers and their children together at the heart of program and service provision. All services and programs are directed towards building relationship capacity between women and children, and between women and others in their lives. This includes the organization that is delivering the services, so that women can build strong relationships with service providers and can see appropriate relation-

ships modeled by providers, both within and without the
organization. (41)

This review of the literature was important to clarify research,
theory, and practice as it relates to the PCAP program.

Creating the Quilt Square

The creation of a quilt square is a tactile, kinesthetic, and visual
experience; it involves reflection, choice, design, and applying
drawing and colouring to render an image. The quilting workshops
were open to any woman who wanted to attend, and the table
looked like a buffet of colour with fabric squares, markers, and,
of course, the essentials of coffee, muffins, and doughnuts. Women
were immediately drawn to the activity, which had two steps after
the completion of informed consent. First, instruction, demonstration, and practice in drawing on fabric with the markers took place
prior to the creation of the quilt square. Once the demonstration
was complete, researchers invited the participants to begin their
creation with the statement: "Represent your experience with [the
PCAP program name] in word, design, or drawing." It was also
explained that the relationship between the mentor and woman is
a central feature of the PCAP program. Once participants finished
illustrating their square, they filled out a piece of paper that asked
the participant's name, description of the square, and number of
years in the program. The piece of paper was pinned to the back
of the square to keep track of participant comments, which were
later documented.

In the second half of the workshop, participants were asked for
their permission to be recorded and then were asked the following two questions. How has the creation of the PCAP quilt been
meaningful or supportive to you? How has your participation
in this project contributed to your health and healing work in
the PCAP program? Women spoke deeply about the meaning of
the program. Many commented on how much they enjoyed the
activity of creating the quilt square. They also said it was exciting to be contributing to a quilt that would include others from
around the province. Once the workshop ended, photographs
were taken of the individual squares and the recorded questions

were transcribed. Squares were provided to the master quilters, Lin Taylor and Bev Ewan, for interpretation, design, and quilt creation.

The quilt itself is an amazing piece of art that when threaded together reflects the lived experience of thirty women, but its reach is extended to children, family, mentors and the community. The collective impact of the quilt images is powerful. However, each square reflects the life of one woman and identifies the aspects of her life representative of her experience with PCAP. This work is reflective of transformation on many levels, and some interpretation based on the workshops and women's voices is included with the imagery. It reflects the process and transformation of women's lived experience identified through participating in PCAP.

INFLUENCE OF THE PCAP MENTOR'S QUILT—"PICK-UP STICKS"

The PCAP Mentor's Quilt was inspired by an initial project undertaken in Alberta in 2012 involving forty-seven individuals, primarily mentors as well as a few supervisors, administrative support staff and program managers, working on the frontlines of FASD prevention work. Jenelle Job and colleagues identified PCAP mentors as FASD prevention specialists and undertook an analysis of the mentor's quilt through focus groups and thematic analysis of the quilt squares (73). The PCAP mentor's quilt was created in a one-day quilting workshop (to create squares) held in Edmonton, Alberta, at the annual meeting of the PCAP program in 2012. The quilt squares were then delivered to the master quilter to design and sew the mentor's quilt. After the squares were transformed through the work of the master quilter and returned to the PCAP program, the impact of this visual work was positively received. The PCAP mentor's quilt was presented and displayed at the Alberta PCAP Council Annual General Meeting and the Alberta FASD Conference, both in 2013. An image of this quilt was also used as a cover on the Alberta FASD Cross Ministry Report for 2011 and 2012.

The master quilters also provided an interpretation of the mentor's quilt from their perspective: the quilt was reflective of change and transformation in the lives of mentors through the relationships they have with women in the program. The work done by mentors is intensive, demanding, and challenging; it requires skills in supportive counselling, advocacy, and systems navigation, including child welfare, social assistance, housing, justice, and other allied programs. From focus groups held with mentors in 2012 and 2013, the idea emerged to create a women's quilt. Mentors indicated that creating the quilt was a meaningful experience, which highlighted the heart of their work with women, children, and families. The Alberta PCAP Council decided to move forward with creating a second quilt as women in the program were inspired by seeing the mentors' creation.

EMERGING THEMES

Thematic analysis of visual imagery took place through a review of the quilt squares individually as they were developed and as a whole once the quilt was woven together. Participants wrote a brief description of their quilt square, and these were moved into a table for the purposes of coding and looking for emerging themes. The primary themes emerging regarding the involvement of a supportive mentor in the women's lives included mothering and healing, love, support, relationships, family, nature, spirituality, connections, community, and resilience. Further thematic analysis is ongoing.

Mothering

For women who brought their children to the workshop, many started their square with tracing their child's hand. At one workshop, a participant started to trace her daughter's hand when the participant next to her went to help by holding the marker and tracing while the first participant held her daughter's hand. Images of mothering are prominent in the quilt: names of children, drawings of child, and symbols representing their child. Additionally, the informal conversations amongst women show their dedication and devotion to their children, and challenges the belief that mothers are always putting their addiction before their children. Their devotion to their children compels them to seek the help they need, and a relationship with their children motivates them to continue the program.

The presence of children in the lives of women participants was largely attributed to the mentoring relationship, which suggests that this intensive support is helping women retain and, in some instances, regain custody of their children. For example, one mother described her quilt square as "Being with my daughter in a happy home," and used the words "inspiring," "family," "love," "mom," and "daughter" to describe her image, which included a house, child, mother, and hearts. Another mother in the program used the words "love," "secure and safe connections," "trust," "female bonding," "mommy," and "child" in the description of her image. Another mother simply wrote "Being happy" and used the words "live," "love," and "laugh." In describing her quilt square, another mother simply wrote, "Being a woman, motherhood/ birthstones of children in a circle." Women in the workshop were enthusiastic about this creative activity and put a lot of care and thought into the work.

Healing through Mentoring Relationships

Regarding the quilting workshop, one participant said, "It lets me know where I am right now and where I need to go from here. And just putting the stuff down on the quilt allowed me to see where I am and how healed I am so far." This participant mentioned that she did not have trusting relationships with other women in her life prior to joining PCAP. Her relationship with her mentor helped her build a bond with another woman in the program. Other participants also reflected on how important the mentors were in their lives. One participant mentioned her mentor was like "a sister" to her. Another woman said it was because of her mentor supporting her through her struggle with addictions that she got to keep her son. Another woman said, "What am I going to do? I don't have anybody. No one is going to pay anybody to be a friend to me ... it starts out as like, something that you're doing for yourself and it ends up being an actual friendship ... it makes people that are down and out feel like they have somewhere to go." Another participant's visual representations included people linking hands, and her mentor. She included the mentor's name in the square and used the square to describe her mentor as "bubbly," which is clearly evident in this highly detailed creation. Brightness and positive outlooks are often present in the quilt squares. Women also noted benefits they experienced just by having someone care about them.

DISCUSSION

A visual approach to research can illuminate the experiences of women and their voices, such as the work undertaken in this quilt, aptly named Woven Together. When we offered the workshops and watched the quilt squares being developed, we heard women's voices and stories begin to emerge—both about struggle and resilience. Women for the most part highlighted the importance of having their children in their lives and how being involved with a mentor was helpful in their lives.

As researchers, we were interested in understanding and appreciating the ways a visual methodology approach can act as a supportive activity in women's healing and recovery work in PCAP program. The PCAP program mentors provide support for women to acquire basic needs for survival, such as food, funding, and housing. While mentors work with women, they gain over time an understanding of the pain and vulnerability in a woman's life; thus, their reflections on the women's quilt are interesting to hear. One comment made to the research team by mentors upon seeing the quilt was about how bright it looked.

A key aspect of the work mentors do in helping women is based upon a relational approach, which nurtures the development of trust and confidence, and helps women face challenging issues and move forward in their lives. For some women, this work can be focussed on issues such as alcohol and other substance addictions, getting visitation with children who are in foster care, regaining custody of children, or reducing the harms associated with alcohol addiction, including alcohol abstention or reduction during pregnancy. The overarching goal of the mentoring relationship is to support women in health and wellbeing.

Deeply powerful images reflective of children, relationship and support combined to construct a rich tapestry of lived experience. The symbols represent love (hearts), happiness (flowers) mothering (children, mothers), wholeness (circles), healing (medicine wheels), and growth (sun, trees, flowers). The words used in the squares emphasize the support, trust, and acceptance they feel from their mentors. They express the joy and gratefulness of motherhood. Whereas mentors see the hard work it takes, and the relapses and setbacks involved in the program, the PCAP women see the program as an opportunity, a second chance. The women's quilt shows the PCAP's foundation in relational theory: the relationship built between the mentor and participant can often be more meaningful than the concrete services received. In the words of Lin Taylor, a master quilter, "In summary, what is the mentorship program offering? The community of women suggest that the program offers safety, security, significance and hope so that the participants can do what every mother wants to do for her children, provide safety, security, significance and hope for a good life in the future."

In the PCAP Mentor's Quilt of 2012, Job et al. identified visual themes in the quilt squares showing a progression of recovery, connectedness, love, healing, growth, and a sense of hope and vision for the future (76). Relationship connects women and mentors, and it is this relationship that both quilts express. Knowing the hardships that the women in this program have faced in their life and understanding their trauma, grief, and loss, the researchers expected to see a similar emotional range in the quilt squares of the participants to that of the original quilt. Although PCAP mentors are often very involved in their clients' lives, they are also witnesses and onlookers in relation to the experiences of pain and sorrow that women express. For the mentors, then, the women's quilt reflects resilience. We do have plans in a current research project to conduct a focus group and elicit the viewpoint of mentors on the work completed by the women participants, including a review and thematic analysis of both quilts.

The project was disseminated to women participants through photographs of the individual quilt square as well as an image of the full quilt. Women knew that the quilt square was going to form part of a quilt, and we found this approach gave women a view of how they contributed to the whole project. Mentorship work is emotionally taxing work, and staff are at risk of burnout, compassion fatigue, and vicarious trauma. Disseminating the findings of this project may help remind mentors and frontline staff of the important work they do and the contributions they make in the lives of women.

A visual research product tells us about relationships to space and time. In relation to the PCAP women's quilt, temporality was an important concept. Women in mentoring relationships through the PCAP programs are on a lengthy journey. Women who participated in this project were in long-term relationships with mentors and wanted to be involved in this project at this particular time in their lives. When women are in recovery, there is space in their life to think beyond immediate needs. When women are in the throes of addictions, they do not necessarily have the capacity to reflect on the meaning of their experiences. We know not all the women participants stayed on the path they were on at the time the quilting project was undertaken. We also know many women continue to grow and heal with the supportive relationships they have with mentors. In the past five years, two quilts have been created. The first quilt involved the PCAP program mentors and staff and was called "Pick-Up-Sticks," which they felt reflected a theme of their work in helping women pick things back up again in their lives and carry on. We also know through the experience of women involved with mentors that these relationships have contributed deeply to the women's experience of feeling "woven together," as the theme of families staying together was evident. The work of PCAP is focused on women's health and healing, whether women have their children with them or not. With a focus on women's health, there are bound to be better outcomes for the future. When this focus is combined with the significant presence of a mentor in a woman's life, the results continue to demonstrate that this program makes a profound difference. In the voice of one mother: "Because I am part of this program, I get to keep my son. I get to be the mother to my son."

ACKNOWLEDGMENT

We express our gratitude and appreciation for the women's willingness to share their time and engage in the PCAP women's quilt. Your courage on this journey and your willingness to work with mentors are remarkable to observe. We thank the mentors and

PCAP supervisors and staff who supported this work, including the Alberta PCAP Council. Finally, we acknowledge the children who through their presence have encouraged mothers on the path. We also acknowledge women engaged in the work of FASD prevention and who may not have their children in their care. We acknowledge their struggle and heartache. This quilt reflects the voices of a community of caring, and we thank everyone who contributed to this work. We also hope this work inspires a discourse recognizing that many women who were part of creating the Woven Together quilt have faced many hardships and challenges, yet they show resilience in the face of adversity.

WORKS CITED

Alberta FASD. "Cross Ministry Annual Report 2012." *Alberta FASD*, fasd.alberta.ca/documents/4-AB_FASD_CMC_Final_2011-12_Annual_Report.pdf. Accessed 5 May 2018.

Alberta FASD. "Ten Year Strategic Plan (2007-2017)." *Alberta FASD*, fasd.alberta.ca/documents/FASD-10-year-plan.pdf. Accessed 1 May. 2018.

Alberta PCAP Council. "Alberta PCAP Council User Manual." *Alberta PCAP Council,* 2010, www.alberta-pcap.ca/ Accessed 1 May 2018.

Anda, Robert F., et al. "The enduring effects of abuse and related adverse experiences in childhood." *European archives of psychiatry and clinical neuroscience* 256.3 (2006): 174-186.

Badry, Dorothy. "Fetal Alcohol Spectrum Disorder Standards: Supporting Children in the Care of Children's Services." *First Peoples Child & Family Review,* vol. 4, no. 1, 2009, pp. 47-56.

Badry, Dorothy, and Aileen Felske. "Exploring the Prevention of Fetal Alcohol Spectrum Disorder in the Northwest Territories of Canada: Brightening our Home Fires." *The International Journal of Alcohol and Drug Research,* vol. 2, no. 3, 2013, pp. 7-15.

Bendien, Elena. "The Last Stitch in the Quilt." *Gender, Work & Organization,* vol. 20, no. 6, 2013, pp. 709-19.

Denzin, Norman K., and Yvonna S. Lincoln. *Collecting and Interpreting Qualitative Materials.* Sage, 2008.

Ellingson, Laura L. "Analysis and Representation across the Continuum." *Collecting and Interpreting Qualitative Materials,* edited by Norman Denzin and Yvonna Lincoln, Sage, 2013, pp. 413-45.

Ernst, Cara C., et al. "Intervention with High-Risk Alcohol and Drug-Abusing Mothers: II. Three-Year Findings from the Seattle Model of Paraprofessional Advocacy." *Journal of Community Psychology,* vol. 27, no. 1, 1999, pp. 19-38.

Fischman, Gustavo E. "Reflections about Images, Visual Culture, and Educational Research."*Educational Researcher,* vol. 30, no. 8, 2001, pp. 28-33.

Grady, John. "Visual Research at the Crossroads." *Forum Qualitative Sozialforschung/Forum: Qualitative Social Research,* vol. 9, no. 3, 2008. www.qualitative-research.net/index.php/fqs/article/view/1173/2618. Accessed 5 May 2018.

Grant, Therese, et al. "Maternal Substance Abuse and Disrupted Parenting: Distinguishing Mothers Who Keep their Children from Those Who Do Not." *Children and Youth Services Review,* vol. 33, no. 11, 2011, 2176-185.

Grant, Therese, et al. "Postprogram Follow-Up Effects of Paraprofessional Intervention with High-Risk Women Who Abused Alcohol and Drugs during Pregnancy." *Journal of Community Psychology,* vol. 31, no. 3, 2003, pp. 211-22.

Job, Jenelle M., et al. "Combining Visual Methods with Focus Groups: An Innovative Approach for Capturing the Multifaceted and Complex Work Experiences of Fetal Alcohol Spectrum Disorder Prevention Specialists." *The International Journal of Alcohol and Drug Research,* vol. 3, no. 1, 2014, pp. 71-80.

Jones, Kenneth L., and David W. Smith. "The Fetal Alcohol Syndrome." *Teratology,* vol. 12, no. 1, 1975, pp. 1-10.

Koelsch, Lori E. "The Virtual Patchwork Quilt: A Qualitative Feminist Research Method." *Qualitative Inquiry,* vol. 18, no. 10, 2012, pp. 823-29.

Maté, Gabor. *In the Realm of Hungry Ghosts: Close Encounters with Addiction.* North Atlantic Books, 2010.

Pauwels, Luc. "'Participatory' visual research revisited: A critical-constructive assessment of epistemological, methodological and social activist tenets." *Ethnography,* vol. 16, no. 1, 2015, pp. 95-117

Pepler, D.J., et al. *The Mother–Child Study: Evaluating Treat-*

ments for Substance-Using Women. A Focus on Relationships. Mothercraft, 2014.

Poole, Nancy, and Lorraine Greaves, eds. *Becoming Trauma Informed.* Centre for Addiction and Mental Health, 2012.

Prosser, Jon. *Image-Based Research: A Sourcebook for Qualitative Researchers.* Psychology Press, 1998.

Prosser, Jon, and Catherine Burke. "Image-Based Educational Research: Childlike Perspectives." *Inquiry: Perspectives, Processes and Possibilities*, edited by L. Butler-Kisbar, Learning Landscapes Journal. 2011, pp. 257-73.

Shankar, Irene. "The Making of a Medical Disorder: Tracing the Emergence of Fetal Alcohol Spectrum Disorder in Alberta." *Social Work in Public Health*, vol. 30, no. 1, 2015, pp.38-50.

TRC—Virtual Quilt Book Nipiqaqtugut Sanaugaqtigut. *Pauktuutit Inuit Women of Canada*, 2013, www.pauktuutit.ca/virtualquilt/. Accessed 1 May 2018.

Well it was a shock when my husband and I first found out, when we found the drugs in our son's room. We panicked and didn't know what to do. We thought we'd scare him, you know tell him about how damaging drugs are and how it leads to criminal behaviour. He promised that he would stop, and for a while, I think he did but then it started up again. And it wasn't just the drugs. He'd get into trouble at school and with the police. I worried about that—if he had a criminal record that really limits his chances of getting a job. I kept asking myself how did this happen. What did I do wrong? To make it worse, my husband would kick him out of the house as punishment, and I really disagreed with that. I'd worry the whole time about where he was sleeping, what he was doing. It was terrible. I didn't have anyone to talk to about it. Well maybe I did, but I didn't want to talk to anyone. I was ashamed. Eventually I did start opening up to other people. I didn't have much choice; it got to the point where people knew anyway. Looking back, that was good because that was when I found out about this program for parents and they've been really helpful for me. Mostly, it was good to realize that I'm not the only one facing these issues. It was terrible. It's not over yet. Things are better for now, but it doesn't just go away. We live with it; it's the way he is. And I'm learning the importance of taking care of myself so that helps too.

—Ellen, age forty-three

7.
Mothering an Adolescent Who Misuses Substances

A Qualitative Evidence Synthesis

MASOUMEH (BITA) KATOUZIYAN, AMANDA VANDYK,
AND J. CRAIG PHILLIPS

ADOLESCENCE IS THE TIME when substance misuse most commonly begins (Leyton and Stewart 2). It is the life stage between ten and nineteen years of age, and a transition period between childhood and adulthood that is characterized by major physical and psychological changes (Buitelaar 357; World Health Organization). Adolescents are more likely than people in other age groups to use drugs and alcohol, engage in risky patterns of use, and experience harms from use because of the physiological and psychological impact of substances on their developing brains (Winters et al. 417). Substance misuse is the harmful use of substances, such as alcohol, illicit drugs, prescription medications, nicotine, and solvents, including glue and paint thinners (Lifeline).

Mothers have been characterized as the main figures, as well as the source of emotional support, that assists in keeping a family together in Western industrial capitalist societies (May 473). In Western countries, mothers are frequently held responsible for their children's behaviour and development (Gillies 94). Therefore, when a family encounters a problem, such as adolescent drug misuse, the actions and abilities of the adolescent's mother are often called into question by the society (May 473). The societal blaming may cause negative effects on maternal wellbeing and mental health, including social and somatic stress—potentially leading to serious psychological illnesses, including depression, anxiety, fear of danger, or guilt, as well as grief associated with failure in the parental role (Barnard 14).

Although qualitative research on the effects of adolescent substance misuse on the family unit exists, the specific experiences of mothers are rarely captured. Furthermore, a systematic review and synthesis of these experiences have not previously been done. An accurate synthesis will provide an evidence-based foundation from which future healthcare interventions can better improve individual, family, and social supports for mothers of adolescents who misuse substances.

PURPOSE AND RESEARCH QUESTION

The purpose of this study was to synthesize existing evidence on the experience of mothering an adolescent with substance use issues. The research question was the following: based on existing evidence, what are the experiences of mothers of adolescents who misuse substances?

STUDY DESIGN

This was a systematic qualitative evidence synthesis (Grant and Booth 94) modelled on the Joanna Briggs methodology (The Joanna Briggs Institute 35) for systematic reviews. We chose to model our review on this methodology because it allows for the synthesis of qualitative evidence and one team member is trained in it. This review was designed to synthesize publically available literature on the experiences of parents, particularly mothers, of adolescents who misuse substances. The review team had expertise in the care of individuals who misuse substances, and the study was designed with input from an expert in maternal childcare. The search strategy was developed with the assistance of a library scientist.

Eligibility Criteria

Studies were included if they were primary studies using a qualitative design about the experiences of parents and/or mothers of adolescents who misuse substances, available in full text, and published in English from 1995 to February 2016. We excluded all nonresearch and reports not subject to peer review (i.e., abstracts, and unpublished theses, books, and conference summaries) as well as quantitative studies. The grey literature was excluded in this synthesis because the research team was interested in peer-reviewed studies.

Search Strategy

Three online databases were searched: OVID MEDLINE (1995 to February 2016), Psych INFO (1995 to 2 February 2016), and CINAHL (1995 to February 2016) using predetermined keywords and MeSH headings (e.g., "adolescent," "substance misuse," "mothers and experience"). A twenty-year timeframe was selected for this review. Given the exploratory nature of this study and the paucity of literature on the topic, we felt a twenty-year timeframe was more appropriate than the ten-year search period typically used. This timeframe was agreed upon by all reviewers in consultation with a library scientist. We tailored each search to ensure the most appropriate terms were used, and complete search strategies are reported. We also conducted a targeted search of all articles published in the *Journal of Child and Adolescent Substance Abuse*. This journal was chosen because of its relevance to our topic. Finally, in the preparation phase of this review, we conducted a hand-search literature review, and all additional pertinent articles were included.

Study Selection

After removing duplicates, we transferred the retrieved citations to Covidence, an online program useful for creating and managing systematic reviews (Covidence sec.1). Using this platform, we completed a two-level screening process for selecting studies to include. First-level screening was done by titles and abstracts. In this level, citations were a) excluded, b) kept due to their relevance to the inclusion criteria, or c) marked as unsure. Citations marked as unsure were retained for further screening. The primary reviewer screened all citations, and exclusion was confirmed by a second reviewer. Second-level screening involved screening the full texts of all retained citations, and this was done by all reviewers. Every full text was reviewed by at least two team members. Consensus among all reviewers was reached on the final set of included studies.

Data Extraction

The primary reviewer extracted data from the selected studies using summary tables created in Microsoft Word. Extracted data included the following: a) study characteristics (i.e., title, year, country of origin, study design, data collection approach and methods, data analysis strategy, and theoretical and conceptual framework); b) parent/mother characteristics (i.e., number of parents in the study, number of mothers, age range, type of family, marital status, and ethnicity, education, and employment); c) adolescent characteristics (i.e., sex, age range, misused substance, employment, living situation, education, adolescent's parenthood, and history of mental illness); d) study findings (including identified categories, themes, and their conceptual definitions); and e) quotes provided by the study participants. The above-mentioned characteristics and criteria were agreed upon by all reviewers and were selected to provide sufficient information and detail of the included studies to allow for transferability of the findings. The parent/mother and adolescents' characteristics were chosen to obtain information regarding the selected studies' participants. Ultimately the studies' findings and quotes were extracted in order to obtain information from selected studies in relation to the research question.

Data Synthesis

Study characteristics, parent/mother characteristics, and adolescent characteristics were summarized and described using frequencies and percentages. We aggregated the extracted categories and themes (subcategories and subthemes) and compared their conceptual definitions using a constant comparison approach (Lincoln and Guba 339-44). Similar definitions were grouped together to create new categories, which we named. New conceptual definitions for each new category were crafted to reflect the aggregated data captured within. Finally, quotes from the original studies were embedded within each new category to ensure confirmability of our findings and to give voice to the original participants. Data analysis was undertaken primarily by two team members; however, all steps of the data analysis were reviewed at multiple occasions by the full team, and we reached

100 percent agreement on them to ensure credibility (Lincoln and Guba 301-27).

RESULTS

The search strategies retrieved a total of 1461 citations, from which we removed 711 duplicate citations. First-level screening was carried out on 750 potential citations, and of these, 678 were considered irrelevant. Primary reasons for exclusion at this stage were a) they were not full-text articles or research studies and b) they were off topic (i.e., not about parents or parenting). A total of seventy-two citations were included in second-level screening, during which we excluded an additional sixty citations. The main reasons for exclusion were the following: a) inappropriate study design (i.e., quantitative methods or intervention evaluation); b) inappropriate population (i.e., adolescents who were interviewed about substance misuse or parents who were interviewed about adolescent's substance misuse, but it was not indicated that they were parents of adolescents who misuse substances themselves); 3) off topic (i.e., not adolescent substance misuse); and 4) inappropriate outcome (i.e., experiences of parents regarding their adolescents' treatment for their substance misuse). Two studies that met all eligibility criteria were excluded at the data extraction phase because they did not include data about parents' or mothers' experiences that could be extracted. In total, we included eleven articles in this qualitative evidence synthesis. Ten articles were retained from the database searches, and one article was found through hand searching (see Figure 1).

Study Characteristics

The eleven qualitative studies included in this review were conducted in the following countries: four in Australia; two in the United States; and one each in Brazil, Denmark, Ireland, the Netherlands, and the United Kingdom. Sample sizes ranged from one to 32 participants. Data were collected using conversational-style interviews in five studies, semistructured interviews in four studies, and focus groups in two studies. In all eleven studies, data were analyzed using a version of thematic analysis (see Table 1).

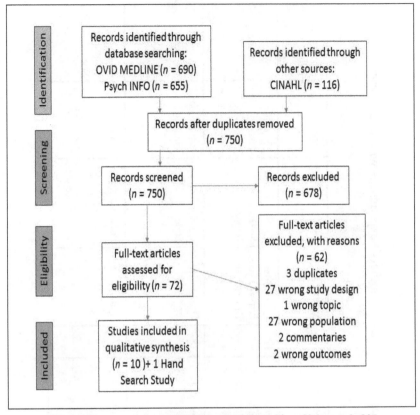

Figure 1. Literature review process flowchart adapted from Moher et al., 267

Parents' Characteristics

Participant characteristics were reported in all eleven studies; however, not all authors collected the same sociodemographic information. For example, marital status was reported in six studies; ethnicity of parents was reported in five studies; age of parents and parental education were reported in three studies; and employment status was reported in two studies. Given the information provided, participants in the included studies had the following demographic characteristics: marital status (44 percent married and 38 percent divorced); ethnicity (100 percent Danish, Dutch, or Anglo Australian); between thirty and sixty-five years old; high school educated (70 percent); and unemployed (6 percent). Interestingly, parental role (i.e., mother or father) was reported in

Table 1. Qualitative studies that describe parents', particularly mothers', experiences with adolescents' substance misuse

ID #	Title	Author (Year)	Country	N	Study Design	Data Collection	Data Analysis Strategy	Theoretical/ Conceptual Framework
1	"Then Suddenly He Went Off the Rails": Mothers' Stories of Adolescent Cannabis Use	Jackson and Mannix (2003)	Australia	12	Qualitative; Explorative-Descriptive	Conversation Style Interviews	Thematic Analysis	Feminist Research
2	Fractured Families: A Parental Perspectives of the Effects of Adolescent Drug Abuse on Family Life	Jackson et al. (2007)	Australia	18	Qualitative	Conversation Style Interviews	Van Manen-Thematic Analysis	NR
3	Communicating Trust Between Parents and Their Children: A Case Study of Adolescents' Alcohol Use in Denmark	Demant and Ravn (2013)	Denmark	37	Qualitative	Focus Groups	Thematic Analysis	Niklas Luhmann's Sociological

4	The Context of Alcohol Consumption among Adolescents and Their Families	Ribeiro Gomes et al. (2014)	Brazil	22	Qualitative	In-depth Interviews	Inductive Thematic Analysis	Symbolic Interactions; Family Systems; Calgary Family Assessment and Intervention Model
5	Parent Attitudes, Family Dynamics and Adolescent Drinking: Qualitative Study of the Australian Parenting Guidelines for Adolescent Alcohol Use	Gilligan and Kypri (2012)	Australia	32	Qualitative	Semistructured Interviews	Thematic Analysis	NR
6	Determinants of Binge Drinking in a Permissive Environment: Focus Group Interviews with Dutch Adolescents and Parents	Jander et al. (2013)	Nether-lands	26	Qualitative	Focus Groups, Interviews,	Thematic Analysis	NR

7	"That's What I Mean by a Hundred Little, a Thousand Little Deaths": A Case Study of the Grief Experienced by the Mother of a Substance Abusing Child	Dion (2014)	United States	1	Case Study	Conversation Style Interviews	Thematic Analysis Using Miles and Huberman's Approach	NR
8	From Every Direction: Guilt, Shame, and Blame among Parents of Adolescents with Co-occurring Challenges	Cohen-Filipic and Bentley (2015)	United States	23*	Qualitative: Phenomenology	Semistructured, Individual Interviews	Thematic Analysis	NR
9	Shattered Dreams: Parental Experiences of Adolescent Substance Abuse	Usher et al. (2007)	Australia	18	Qualitative, Hermeneutic Phenomenology	In-depth Conversation Style Interviews	Phenomenological Thematic Analysis	NR
10	Mothers' Experiences of Their Children's Detoxification in the Home: Results from a Pilot Study	Van Hout and Bingham (2012)	Ireland	9	Qualitative	Conversation Style Interviews	Thematic Analysis	NR
11	The Parents' Experience: Coping with Drug Use in the Family	Butler and Bauld (2005)	United Kingdom	10	Qualitative	Semistructured Interviews	Thematic Analysis	NR

Note. ID = study identification number assigned by research team. * Nine parents and fourteen clinicians participated.

all eleven studies. The percentage of participants represented by mothers in the studies ranged from 55 to 100 percent.

Adolescents' Characteristics

Adolescents' characteristics were not reported consistently in all studies. The most reported characteristic was the type of substance adolescents' misused, which was mentioned in ten studies. Other characteristics were not consistently reported. Ethnicity was only mentioned in two studies; adolescents' living situation, adolescents' mental health history, and adolescents' parenthood were each mentioned in only one study. Adolescents' employment was not reported in any of the studies reviewed. Adolescents' sex (male or female) was reported in four studies. The adolescents' age ranged from thirteen to nineteen years as reported in seven studies. Two studies included adolescents as study participants.

CATEGORIES AND THEMES REPORTED IN THE STUDIES

The authors in all eleven studies reported their findings in themes in nine studies and categories in two studies. In total, we extracted forty-three themes (supported by thirty-three subthemes) and five categories (supported by eight subcategories) on the experiences of mothers of adolescents who misuse substances from the studies. By comparing the conceptual definitions of these themes and categories, we regrouped them into ten distinct themes and categories. From this aggregated data, we created five new categories, supported by three subcategories. These new categories included a) "I love you, and we can talk no matter what"; b) "So this is really happening … My kid's on drugs"; c) "What have I done?"; d) "My family is shattered"; and e) "It's not my addiction." The category "My family is shattered" has three subcategories: "I can't believe what you're doing"; "I can't face this"; and" I've lost my baby" (see Figure 2). Each of these new categories is described below, and supporting quotes extracted from the original studies are embedded throughout. All supporting quotes are from mothers, and although some of the included data was based on father and mother perspectives, the following synthesis is largely reflective of the experience of mothers of adolescents who misuse substances.

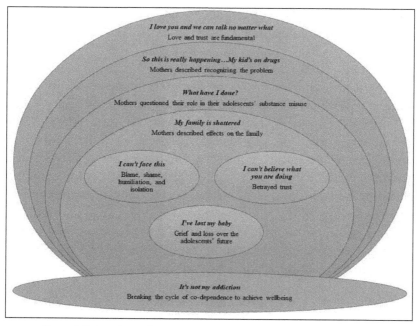

Figure 2. Categories and subcategories to characterize mothers' experiences with adolescents' substance misuse

I love you, and we can talk no matter what

This category was represented in five studies (1, 3, 4, 5, and 6). Parents, mainly mothers, described how love and trust were fundamental in their relationships with their children who misuse substances, and despite their adolescents' substance misuse, their love did not subside: "The door was always open and every time he came home I always told him I loved him even though I didn't like his lifestyle and I didn't like a lot of the people he was associating with. But I always told him I loved him and that home was always here if he wanted it" (qtd. in study one, Jackson and Mannix 176). Mothers also took steps to maintain their relationship with their adolescent despite active substance misuse, and they hoped that their good relationship would reduce or control their adolescent's substance use behaviours: "It's important to keep the communication lines open. The bottom line is that you have to trust them. It happens anyway so I would rather they tell me" (qtd. in study five, Gilligan and Kypri 3).

So this is really happening ... My kid's on drugs

This category was represented in three studies (1, 9, and 11) and is underpinned by the mothers' realization that their adolescents had problems with substance use. The mothers described their rousing suspicion and hypervigilance in watching their adolescents' behaviours, which changed markedly from their substance misuse. One mother said, "I had strong suspicions he was using drugs because he just changed as a person. His grades at school had started to drop; he became very aggressive and unpleasant to be around ... he broke things, he kicked in walls ... his father denied it, and it wasn't until I found a bong and I showed it to his father that he [father] took any notice, but by then it was too late" (qtd. in study one, Jackson and Mannix 172). Furthermore, another mother said the following:

> You know in the back in your mind, you know something isn't right, but instead of ... you just keep sort of going it "will clear up, it looks okay." But then she kept, she just started to lose a lot of weight; she never had money even though she was working a lot. Well sort of like I guess the real crunch for me that I knew something was wrong, she came home really late one night, and she sort of seemed to just fall apart, but at the same time be yelling and screaming, and it was all about a moth that was in her room, and it was a big giant monster and so I sort of started thinking "hang on you know there is something going on here" and then I would sort of sit down and just have a chat with her and she started saying "her friend had this drug problem," and I went "oh okay." (qtd. in study nine, Usher et al. 424)

What have I done?

This category was represented in four studies (7, 8, 9, and 11) and was described as the guilt and regret experienced by mothers regarding their adolescents' substance misuse. As one mother said, "I had to come to terms with my own drinking ... and I used to drink so much I was guaranteed drunk and throwing up ... I just realized ... as a parent your behaviour ... contributed to your child's behaviour, and there is not anything you can do about it now" (qtd. in study seven, Dion 399). Mothers recognized that their interpersonal life issues contributed to their adolescents' substance misuse:

> I had a relationship before that was mentally abusive to me and to my kids, and I was with him for seven years. So [my daughter] had to deal with that, too. So that's where a lot of her anger issues come from. And, yeah, of course, I blame myself for that. That I do blame myself for, because I knew better. But I didn't know how to get out. But [my daughter] doesn't understand that, so it was just making her more angry. She was always writing letters and saying, "I don't know why my mom is still with him." (qtd. in study eight, Cohen-Filipic and Bentley 448)

Mothers reported feelings of failing as a parent: "I failed as a mum. Why did I not see this, why could I not protect my son from this? Why couldn't I make him better? ... But until then it was where have I gone wrong?" (qtd. in study nine, Usher et al. 428). Regardless of whether the mother had her own history of substance use, her guilt was perpetuated by a sense that if she had recognized the problem earlier, it could have been prevented: "You do look back and you think to yourself 'well, where did we go wrong?' Or why didn't you see it—all these things go through your mind. You feel guilty. I do even now. You just wonder what you missed" (qtd. in study eleven, Butler and Bauld 39).

My family is shattered

This category was described by mothers in seven studies (1, 2, 7, 8, 9, 10, and 11). Because of the adolescent's substance misuse, the family unit was fractured. The family was faced with challenges and stressors caused by the adolescent's ill behaviour, which often included threatening, frightening and violent behaviour. As a result, the mothers described their families as dysfunctional and falling apart:

> When your child gets a drug problem, suddenly in your

> family you have someone who is intimidating, menacing, violent, abusive, can't be trusted, off the planet, you can't rationalize with them, they'll steal from you, you've got the other children fearful of them, and you're meant to just deal with it. That's your lot. Get on with it. There's nowhere you can really go for help... there's no ... daycare or anywhere you can get relief. Drug rehab couldn't help because he didn't want to be helped. (qtd. in study one, Jackson and Mannix 173)

Three subcategories were needed to adequately represent the variation in this category across the studies: a) "I can't believe what you're doing"; b) "I can't face this"; and c) "I've lost my baby."

I can't believe what you're doing

This subcategory portrays the mothers' shock and dismay at the actions taken by their adolescents in order to obtain and use drugs and alcohol. As one mother said, "When he was sixteen, he was stealing things; he stole things in conjunction with another young man that lived in our area, and it was stuff like lawnmowers out of peoples garages, that is how it started, and I found them in my car, and I was horrified, horrified" (qtd. in study nine, Usher et al. 425). Since the family had been fractured due to substance misuse,

> the verbal abuse is absolutely disgraceful ... It is a terrible thing for you to sit there and listen to what your daughter is saying to you. You know personal stuff, "you fat whore, whatever, I don't know all these words, you're nothing, good for nothing, blah, blah, blah, I hope you ...," what did she say, "I hope you die" and at one stage she was going to get bikies to come around and fix me up. (qtd. in study nine, Usher et al. 425)

Finally, some mother's went so far as to describe their child's behaviour as evil: "You know you still love him, he ain't evil. You know, I thought he was turning into the devil, that's what I felt" (qtd. in study eleven, Butler and Bauld 40).

I can't face this

This subcategory pertains to the mothers' feelings of blame, shame, humiliation, and isolation resulting from their adolescents' substance misuse. The mothers described how their parenting capabilities were questioned and how others (friends, family members, and society generally) blamed them for their adolescent's substance misuse. One mother said the following:

> I had to call the police in my house sometimes, and they'd be like, "Well, why don't you just take his cell phone and his car away?" Well, that's what I did, and that's why he's acting this way. Now what? I tried to do all these things, but it's like "Well, you know, you just need to have control over your son." Well, how? I mean, do you think I want to be in this situation? I mean, it was crazy, absolutely crazy.... How can I protect myself and my child? And they were like, "Well, you know, he's your responsibility and if he does anything, you're held accountable." I mean it was awful. I mean, I felt like I was losing my mind at times because ... there weren't the resources out there ... this is a crisis. I mean, where do I go? (qtd. in study eight, Cohen-Filipic and Bentley 450)

The mothers also described how they experienced blame in almost all situations, including while trying to obtain help for their child. They described how this attack on their character directly affected their family units: "It is a problem society needs to deal with, but because they don't want to look at it, you just get blamed with the whole lot. I would not go to the police or the ambulance ever again. There's too much blame that goes on ... Meanwhile the family just becomes more and more dysfunctional" (qtd. in study nine, Jackson et al. 426).

Mothers described feeling isolated from their friends and communities because of their adolescents' substance misuse: "I hadn't got a friend in the world left, and I mean that. I mean, I used to have quite a lot of friends, and not one of my friends or the family were there for me" (qtd. in study eleven, Butler and Bauld 40). This isolation was described as both a consequence of the substance misuse and a personal choice made to avoid feelings of shame and humiliation:

> You're on your own with it. The family ends up very isolated because people don't understand about it ... his brothers, they wouldn't have anybody come over to the house because there is too much stuff going on. The younger children ... I wouldn't let any of their friends come over, and I didn't make any friends. (qtd. in study two; Jackson et al. 328)

I've lost my baby

The final subcategory describes the grief and loss felt by the mothers because of their adolescents' substance misuse. The mothers described how they believed that drugs and alcohol would rob their children of their aspirations and happiness: "I still grieve for the person that he used to be" (qtd. in study nine, Usher et al. 427). These feelings of sorrow and grief were so powerful for some mothers that although their child was still alive, the mothers were so full of doom that it was as if their child had no future at all. One mother said the following:

Well I did go through a bit of a grief process like I said, denial first, and then definitely a lot of that bargaining went on, and just for the depression and the grief of it, you know and I do feel that I have lost my son, who my son could have been because he will never have a loan, he'll never own a house, or he'll never own land or anything like that because it is impossible for him to get a bank loan ... I don't know if he will ever have a full time job again because once you have these big spaces on your resume ... there is nothing to put down, it just becomes increasingly difficult to get work, so a lot of his things are already set in concrete now and a lot of his potential has disappeared down the drain now. (qtd. in study nine, Usher et al. 427)

It's not my addiction

This category represents the mothers' self-preservation, resilience and breaking of the co-dependence cycle. The mothers described how despite their adolescents' substance misuse, they needed to take back their lives and focus on their own health and wellbeing, which involved separating themselves from their child and the addiction. Participants indicated that this was necessary for their own survival:

> Well I am a fairly strong person but eventually I said, "this is too much for me." I told Paul that he was old enough and big enough to make his own decisions and we had carried him for long enough and he had to stand on his own two feet ... that was it ... I didn't have any more back pain, I didn't have any more migraines, I didn't have any more stomach aches. (qtd. in study nine, Usher et al. 428)

In all eleven studies, the mothers realized that the only healthy way forward for them and their adolescent was to come to terms with the fact that they needed to focus on their own health and wellbeing so they could support their adolescent through the healing process.

DISCUSSION

To date, few studies have explicitly studied the effects of adolescents' substance misuse on their parents (Choate 1359) or the experiences of parents related to adolescents' substance misuse. Our search strategy identified only eleven qualitative studies on this topic published in the past twenty years. Authors suggest that this is the first synthesis study of any kind on this topic and the first study to focus specifically on the mother's perspective.

Previous literature, much of it quantitative, links adolescent substance misuse with family risk factors—including low parental monitoring and lack of knowledge of the adolescents' activities (Borawski et al. 68; Martins et al. 920); permissive parenting styles; lack of closeness between parents and their adolescents; conflict among family members; parental substance abuse (Hawkins et al. 83); lack of parental-adolescent communication (Luk et al. 426); lack of parental support (Parker and Benson 520); and adolescents being raised in a single-parent household (Barrett and Turner 111).

Our first category, "I love you, and we can talk no matter what," can be influenced positively or negatively by these factors. For example, the importance of building a foundation of love and trust in the home is the essence of what is described in this category. Authors suggest that a parent-child relationship built on a foundation of love and trust may have a protective effect against problem behaviours in youth, (Ribeiro Gomes et al. 397); however, parents today may be misinterpreting these findings. As a growing trend, parents are giving their adolescents alcohol (and in some cases illicit drugs) at young ages to demonstrate their love and trust, and to facilitate adult decision making. Parents are choosing this strategy because of a commonly held belief that exposing one's child to alcohol in a supervised environment prevents adolescent substance misuse (Jander et al. 8). Unfortunately, studies consistently demonstrate that this practice leads to more adverse alcohol-related outcomes, including binge drinking and adult substance misuse (Irons et al. 276; Kaynak et al. 600-1). These research findings must be widely disseminated so parents can make sound and evidence-informed decisions regarding their parenting approaches to alcohol and drug use.

In the literature on adolescent substance misuse, single mothers are particularly criticized (Barrett and Turner 111; Daire et al. 60; Fauber et al. 1112). By teasing out the mothers' perspectives (from a sample comprised primarily of single mothers), our synthesis lends a more nuanced understanding of single mothers' experiences with adolescents who misuse substances; it provides information that may counter interpretations reported in previous quantitative research. Notable differences include the single mothers who offer affection and serve as protectors and counsellors for their adolescents, and who positively influence them against misusing substances. Also the adolescents value these mothers as women who sacrifice themselves and give everything they have to benefit their children (Ribeiro Gomes et al. 397). Our findings also highlight the complexities of navigating the social and contextual challenges that influence access to social supports. To ensure adequate access to services for these marginalized mothers because of their low socioeconomic status, it is imperative that the discourses surrounding them be consistent with their reality and nonbiased in their delivery of care.

Among parents specifically mothers who participated in the studies reviewed, the realization and acknowledgment that their adolescent was misusing substances was a critical turning point for them as parents. It was at this point that they recognized their parenting styles and relationships with their adolescents needed to change. This realization was the essence of the category "So this is really happening ... My kid's on drugs" and may be a pivotal transition point in the trajectory of the adolescent's substance misuse. With any transition point, there is an opportunity for change (Chick and Meleis 238-39), and with appropriate guidance, it may be possible for mothers to use this realization as a catalyst for positive change for their adolescent. Information useful for helping mothers navigate this critical time should be widely accessible. Although there is a plethora of self-help based interventions available through such organizations as Alcoholics Anonymous and Narcotics Anonymous—which offer advice on "what to do when you find out your child is misusing substances"—we could not find any evidence-informed interventions useful for parents that have demonstrated efficacy for promoting adolescent recovery. This highlights a very important gap in the literature. More research is needed to identify what is most effective for helping parents, especially mothers, and their adolescents once substance using behaviour is known.

After the initial shock of learning that their adolescent was using substances, mothers began to question their own actions and their implications. This emerged in the category "What have I done?" Hallmarks of this category included maternal guilt attributed to their own personal substance misuse, maternal interpersonal life issues, and perceived failure as a mother. Healthcare providers working with these mothers should encourage both mothers and adolescents to engage in care by facilitating access to family-centred programs. These programs aim to foster positive coping skills in all family members, and are shown to be protective against continued adolescent substance misuse (Brody et al. 113-14). Building capacity for all family members may promote healthier lifestyles and behaviours in subsequent generations. More research is needed to support the development and testing of such programs.

Among the mothers who participated in the studies reviewed, the effects of adolescent substance misuse on the family was evident and is characterized in our category "My family is shattered" and its three subcategories: "I can't believe what you're doing"; "I can't face this"; and "I've lost my baby." In the studies, mothers described how parenting adolescents who misused substances was stressful and challenging. Keeping the family intact was almost impossible because of the adolescents' menacing behaviour and criminal acts. Anger, violence, and stealing are examples of risk-taking behaviours. Adolescence is, by definition, a transitional developmental stage when risk taking is common because of the heightened reward responsiveness of the adolescent mind (Geier 338-39). When substances are used regularly or in a binge pattern (typical of adolescent use), individuals may experience a compulsion to continue their use, which can also lead to increased risk taking to acquire and consume the substance (Leyton and Stewart 29). Examples of these behaviours may be stealing to pay for substances or exchanging sexual acts when money is not available. The combined effect of risk taking related to age and risk taking related to substance use and addiction cannot be ignored.

Harm reduction is a philosophy of care directed at reducing harms associated with certain behaviours (Leslie 53). A harm-reduction approach is appropriate with the risk-taking behaviours and experimentation occurring in adolescence (Leslie 53). Two harm-reduction programs for adolescents' alcohol misuse have been successfully implemented and evaluated. These programs are the Alcohol Misuse Prevention Study (AMPS) in the United States and the School Health and Alcohol Harm Reduction Project (SHAHRP) in Australia (Leslie 54). Despite international evidence of successful harm-reduction programs for adults who misuse drugs (e.g., methadone maintenance programs, needle exchange programs), we could not find literature specific to harm-reduction strategies for adolescents who misuse drugs. Only one of the reviewed studies reported that parents tried to involve their adolescents in harm-reduction strategies, such as immunization (e.g., hepatitis B, hepatitis C) and safer sex (Usher et al. 427). Drug-Free Kids Canada (DFK), a registered charity, has a comprehensive website designed for parents to learn about drugs and adolescent drug misuse. The website provides helpful parenting tips because parents are the first line of defense in a drug prevention strategy and are essential for an adolescent's recovery from drug addiction (Chen et al. 1425). Healthcare providers need to include parents in strategies regarding adolescents' substance misuse in order to determine which strategies need to be implemented as prevention or as treatment.

For all the mothers in the studies reviewed, the ultimate step toward personal wellness was when they came to terms with their adolescents' substance misuse and recognized that it was not their addiction. This realization allowed the mothers to break the cycle of co-dependence and begin their own healing journey. This contributed to the mothers being resilient and seeking the help and support they needed to change their parenting practices and support their adolescent. Co-dependence within the family system can be adaptive or maladaptive. Adaptive co-dependence preserves the family from destructive forces and contributes to familial homeostasis (Scaturo 99). Maladaptive co-dependence rigidly prevents the family from adapting to normative changes as family members grow and family dynamics evolve (Knudson and Terrell 250; Scaturo 99). Co-dependence is a "dysfunctional pattern of relating to others with an extreme focus outside of oneself, lack of expression of feelings, and a personal meaning derived from relationships with others" (Fischer and Spann 87; Knudson and Terrell 245). Recovery from maladaptive co-dependence requires therapeutic intervention, which can occur through professional counselling or self-help groups (Scaturo 99). Co-Dependents Anonymous (CoDA) is a self-help group that provides supports and education for co-dependent persons that may be a useful resource for mothers of adolescents who misuse substances.

During this qualitative synthesis, literature emerged that described interventions to help parents cope with the stress associated with having an adolescent who misuses substances. Two therapies appear to be particularly relevant for improving parental coping: behavioural exchange systems training (BEST) and sand tray group therapy (Bamberg et al. 188; James and Martin 390). BEST is a intervention program designed to teach parents strategies to assertively manage family problems (Bamberg et al. 189). Sand tray group therapy is a treatment approach for parents to cope with their adolescents' substances misuse through reflection on their own life challenges. The therapy incorporates the use of miniature figures, creative elements, and artistic abilities to facilitate the creative expression of thoughts and emotions related to the challenges faced by the parent (James and Martin 392). Further research into the efficacy of these interventions with a variety of different parents and geographic contexts is warranted.

LIMITATIONS OF THE STUDY

There are three limitations to consider when interpreting the findings of this study. First, as with all metasynthesis studies, there is a possibility we have misrepresented the original experiences and interpretations. This can occur any time one synthesizes aggregated qualitative data from multiple sources (Sandelowski et al. 367-69; Walsh and Downe 207). To minimize this potential bias, we followed a rigorous systematic review methodology (Joanna Briggs), which involved double screening and verification of the data extracted. The research team also had expertise in review methods, substance use and addiction treatment, and mothering, which further enhances the validity of our results. Second, it is possible that the search strategy failed to identify all pertinent literature; however, a library scientist with expertise in systematic reviews created the searches using both MeSH headings and keywords. Finally, the database search was limited to studies written in English and published after 1995. It is possible that we omitted pertinent studies published prior to 1995 or that our aggregated understanding is biased toward English-speaking cultures.

CONCLUSION

This study synthesized the qualitative literature on the experiences of mothers of adolescents who misuse substances. The familial complexities and social processes influencing mothers' experiences with their adolescents' substance misuse were highlighted. The five categories emerging from this review could inform the development of new interventions to help mothers navigate the challenges of parenting an adolescent who misuses substances. Assessing mothers' experiences is essential to appropriately targeting these new interventions. For example, mothers who experience feelings of guilt, sorrow, blame, and humiliation may reach out to healthcare and social service providers to help them cope with their adolescents' substance misuse. This review also supports the need for healthcare and social services providers to become more sensitive to the differing needs of mothers and communities where adolescents who misuse substances live. Healthcare providers should recognize that being judgmental, stigmatizing, and discriminatory against adolescents who misuse substances is detrimental to entire communities. Adolescents are our future, and our future depends on effectively addressing the needs of adolescents who misuse substances so they can become productive members of society. Although some interventions exist to enhance mothers' coping skills so they can help their adolescents through the challenges of substance misuse, more work is needed to examine intervention use and effectiveness.

WORKS CITED

Bamberg, John, et al. "Change for the BEST: Family Changes for Parents Coping with Youth Substance Abuse." *Australian and New Zealand Journal of Family Therapy*, vol. 22, no. 4, 2001, pp. 189-98.

Barnard, Marina. *Drugs in the Family: The Impacts on Parents and Siblings.* Joseph Rowntree Foundation, 2005.

Barrett, Anne E., and R. Jay Turner. "Family Structure and Substance Use Problems in Adolescence and Early Adulthood: Examining Explanations for the Relationship." *Addiction*, vol. 101, no.1, 2006, pp. 109-20.

Borawski, Elaine A., et al. "Parental Monitoring, Negotiated Unsupervised Time, and Parental Trust: The role of Perceived Parenting Practices in Adolescent Health Risk Behaviors." *Journal of Adolescent Health*, vol. 33, no. 2, 2003, pp. 60-70.

Brody, Gene H., et al. "Family-Centered Program Deters Substance Use, Conduct Problems, and Depressive Symptoms in Black Adolescents." *Pediatrics*, vol. 129, no. 1, 2012, pp. 108-15.

Butler, Rachael, and Linda Bauld. "The parents' experience: coping with drug use in the family." *Drugs: education, prevention and policy,* vol. 12, no. 1, 2005, pp. 35-45.

Buitelaar, Jan K. "Adolescence as a Turning Point: For Better and Worse." *European Child & Adolescent Psychiatry,* vol. 21, no. 7, 2012, pp. 357-59.

Chen, Gila, et al. "Parents' Perceptions of Their Adolescent Sons' Recovery in a Therapeutic Community for Addicted Clients." *International Journal of Offender Therapy and Comparative Criminology,* vol. 57, no. 11, 2012, pp. 1417-436.

Chick, Norma, and Afaf Ibrahim Meleis. *Transitions: A Nursing Concern.* Aspen Publication, 1986.

Choate, Peter W. "Adolescent Addiction: What Parents Need?" *Procedia-Social and Behavioral Sciences,* vol. 30, 2011, pp. 1359-364.

Cohen-Filipic, Katherine, and Kia J. Bentley. "From Every Direction: Guilt, Shame, and Blame Among Parents of Adolescents with Co-occurring Challenges." *Child and Adolescent Social Work Journal,* vol. 32, no.5, 2015, pp. 443-54.

CoDA. *Co-Dependents Anonymous International,* 2018, coda.org. Accessed 1 May 2018.

Daire, Andrew P., et al. "Parental Bonding and Its Effect on Adolescent Substance Use and Sexual Debut." *Adultspan Journal,* vol. 12, no. 1, 2013, pp. 54-64.

Demant, Jakob, and Signe Ravn. "Communicating Trust between Parents and Their Children: A Case Study of Adolescents' Alcohol Use in Denmark." *Journal of Adolescent Research,* vol. 28, no. 3, pp. 325-47.

Dion, Kimberly. "'That's What I Mean by a Hundred Little, a Thousand Little Deaths ...': A Case Study of the Grief Experienced by the Mother of a Substance Abusing Child." *MedSurg Nursing,* vol. 23, no. 6, 2014, pp. 397-403.

Drug-Free Kids Canada. *DFK Canada,* 2018, www.drugfreekidscanada.org/. Accessed 1 May 2018.

Fauber, Robert, et al. "A Mediational Model of the Impact of Marital Conflict on Adolescent Adjustment in Intact and Divorced Families: The Role of Disrupted Parenting." *Child Development,* vol. 61, no. 4, 1990, pp. 1112-123.

Fischer, Judith L., and Linda Spann. "Measuring Codependency."

Alcoholism Treatment Quarterly, vol. 8, no. 1, 1991, pp. 87-100.

Geier, Charles F. "Adolescent Cognitive Control and Reward Processing: Implications for Risk Taking and Substance Use." *Hormones and Behavior,* vol. 64, 2013, pp. 333-42.

Gillies, Val. *Marginalized Mothers: Exploring Working Class Experiences of Parenting.* Routledge, 2007.

Gilligan, Conor, and Kypros Kypri. "Parent Attitudes, Family Dynamics and Adolescent Drinking: Qualitative Study of the Australian Parenting Guidelines for Adolescent Alcohol Use." *BMC Public Health,* vol. 12, no. 1, 2012, pp 1-11.

Grant, Maria J., and Andrew Booth. "A Typology of Reviews: An Analysis of 14 Review Types and Associated Methodologies." *Health Information & Libraries Journal,* vol. 26, no. 2, 2009, pp. 91-108.

Hawkins, J. David, et al. "Risk and Protective Factors for Alcohol and Other Drug Problems in Adolescence and Early Adulthood: Implications for Substance Abuse Prevention." *Psychological Bulletin,* vol. 112, no. 1, 1992, pp. 64-105.

Irons, Daniel E., et al. "Tests of the Effects of Adolescent Early Alcohol Exposures on Adult Outcomes." *Addiction,* vol. 110, no. 2, 2015, pp. 269-78.

Jackson, Debra, and Judie Mannix. "Then Suddenly He Went Right Off the Rails: Mothers' Stories of Adolescent Cannabis Use." *Contemporary Nurse,* vol. 14, no. 2, 2003, pp. 169-79.

Jackson, Debra, et al. "Fractured Families: Parental Perspectives of the Effects of Adolescent Drug Abuse on Family Life." *Contemporary Nurse,* vol. 23, no. 2, 2007, pp. 321-30.

James, Linda, and Don Martin. "Sand Tray and Group Therapy: Helping Parents Cope." *Journal for Specialists in Group Work,* vol. 27, no. 4, 2002, pp. 390-405.

Jander, Astrid, et al. "Determinants of Binge Drinking in a Permissive Environment: Focus Group Interviews with Dutch Adolescents and Parents." *BMC Public Health,* vol. 13, no. 1, 2013, pp. 1-13.

Kaynak, Övgü, et al. "Providing Alcohol for Underage Youth: What Messages Should We Be Sending Parents?" *Journal of Studies on Alcohol and Drugs,* vol. 75, no. 4, 2014, pp. 590-605.

Knudson, Theresa M. and Heather K. Terrell. "Codependency, Perceived Intraparental Conflict, and Substance Abuse in the

Family of Origin." *American Journal of Family Therapy*, vol. 40, no. 3, 2012, pp. 245-57.

Leyton, Marco, and Sherry Stewart. *Substance Abuse in Canada: Childhood and Adolescent Pathways to Substance Use Disorders.* Canadian Centre on Substance Abuse, 2014.

Leslie, Karen Mary. "Harm reduction: An Approach to Reducing Risky Health Behaviors in Adolescents." *Paediatric Child Health*, vol. 13, no.1, 2008, pp. 53-56.

Luk, Jeremy W., et al. "Parent-Child Communication and Substance Use among Adolescents: Do Father and Mother Communication Play a Different role for Sons and Daughters?" *Addictive Behaviors*, vol. 35, no. 5, 2010, pp. 426-31.

Lincoln, Yvonna S., and Egon G. Guba. *Naturalistic Inquiry.* Sage Publications, 1985.

Lifeline Australia. *What is Substance Misuse and Addiction*, 2010, www.lifeline.org.au/static/uploads/files/what-is-substance-misuse-and-addiction-wfyzigyyljub.pdf. Accessed 1 May 2018.

May, Vanessa. "On Being a 'Good' Mother: The Moral Presentation of Self in Written Life Stories." *Sociology,* vol. 42, no. 3, 2008, pp. 470-86.

Martins, Silvia S., et al. "Adolescent Ecstasy and Other Drug Use in the National Survey of Parents and Youth: The Role of Sensation-Seeking, Parental Monitoring and Peer's Drug Use." *Addictive Behaviors,* vol. 33, no. 7, 2008, pp. 919-33.

Moher, David, et al. "Preferred Reporting Items for Systematic Reviews and Meta-Analyses: The PRISMA Statement." *Annals of Internal Medicine*, vol. 151, no. 4, 2009, pp. 264-69.

Parker, Jennifer S., and Mark J. Benson. "Parent-Adolescent Relations and Adolescent Functioning: Self-Esteem, Substance Abuse, and Delinquency." *Adolescence,* vol. 39, no. 155, 2004, pp. 519-30.

Ribeiro Gomes, da Mata Betânia, et al. "The Context of Alcohol Consumption among Adolescents and Their Families." *International Journal of AdolescentMedicine and Health,* vol. 26, no. 3, 2014, pp. 393-402.

Sandelowski, Margarete, et al. "Focus on Qualitative Methods. Qualitative Meta Synthesis: Issues and Techniques." *Research in Nursing and Health,* vol. 20, no. 4, 1997, pp. 365-72.

Scaturo, Douglas J. *Clinical dilemmas in psychotherapy: A Trans-theoretical Approach to Psychotherapy Integration.* American Psychological Association, 2005.

The Joanna Briggs Institute. *Joanna Briggs Institute Reviewers' Manual:* The Joanna Briggs Institute, 2014.

Usher, Kim, et al. "Shattered Dreams: Parental Experiences of Adolescent Substance Abuse." *International Journal of Mental Health Nursing,* vol. 16, no. 6, 2007, pp. 422-30.

Van Hout, et al. "Mothers' Experiences of their Children's Detoxification in the Home: Results from a Pilot Study." *Community Practitioner,* vol. 85, no. 7, 2012, pp. 30-33.

Walsh, Denis, and Soo Downe. "Meta-Synthesis Method for Qualitative Research: A Literature Review." *Journal of Advanced Nursing,* vol. 50, no. 2, 2005, pp. 204-11.

Winters, K., et al. "Advances in Adolescent Substance Abuse Treatment." *Current Psychiatry Report,* vol. 13, 2011, pp. 416-21.

World Health Organization. *Adolescence: A Unique Time Requiring a Tailored Response.* WHO, 2013.

III.
Prevention and Treatment Approaches for Mothers Living with Addiction

8.
Confronting the Addictive Nature of Eating Disorder Behaviours

How Mothers Can Provide Support to Daughters with Eating Disorders through a Meaning-Centred Framework

CAITLIN SIGG AND LAURA LYNNE ARMSTRONG

"LIZ" KNELT OVER THE TOILET gazing intently, and thought to herself, this has to be the last time ... just one more time. *Given the large amount of food she had frantically consumed at dinner in front of her mother, she became increasingly determined to rid herself of the calories. She pushed her face deeper into the toilet and forced her finger toward the rear of her mouth. Within moments, Liz convulsed and regurgitated a mouthful of partially digested food into the toilet. She proceeded to repeat these steps several times, and felt a surprising sense of relief from the clandestine nature of her behaviours. Liz had been engaging in binging and purging more frequently throughout the past few months, as she strongly believed it would give her a more covert sense of control in her life. However, these recurrent episodes soon provoked a terrifying sense of loss of control and self-disparagement in her. She felt alone, ashamed, empty, and unsure of how to tell her mother about her compulsion to binge and purge.*

This clinical vignette accentuates a young woman's attempt to fill a void—an insatiable hunger—with disordered eating behaviours. In many ways, the case example is not solely limited to the experience of one young woman; rather, it is a painful expression of psychological, emotional, existential, and physical distress that resembles the experience of many women suffering from disordered eating syndromes and other addictions. Eating disorders, such as bulimia nervosa and anorexia nervosa, often serve as an illusory mechanism for coping with deep chasms, including, but not limited to: loneliness, emptiness, and despair (Knapp 17; Levine 243). From an existential-humanistic perspective, such behaviour can be conceptualized as an addiction to fill a sense of meaninglessness (Frankl 107; Thompson 457). Like other addictions, behaviours appearing grossly disordered—compulsively gorging and vomiting, as in the case of bulimia—seemingly oppose the human experience of connection, fulfillment, and hope. An attempt to fill the void ends up incarcerating the sufferer in isolation through attempts to hide the behaviour from others.

Given that many individuals with eating disorders tend to be reluctant to receive treatment and support from both parents and professionals (Fassino and Abbate-Daga 282; Jarman and Walsh 774; Kaye et al. 110), they are often perceived as complex disorders to treat. The chronic nature of these syndromes—especially the potential medical risks and complications—often leads to many challenges for caregivers, particularly for mothers of daughters with eating disorder syndromes (Tuval-Mashiach et al. 620). Mothers of these young women are often forced to reexamine and rethink their own mothering roles, especially since such eating disorders have "unfolded right beneath their roofs and around the kitchen table" (Hoskins and Lam 157).

Eating disorders are demanding not only on the individual but also on the caregiver and family unit. Secrecy, guilt, and shame remain central themes for both mothers and daughters in the presence of these illnesses (Hoskins and Lam 158). Unfortunately, this secrecy—and the silence that accompanies it—often leaves both sufferers of eating disorders and their mothers feeling lost and adrift while both attempt to cope with the devastating effects of the syndrome (Hoskins and Lam 157). To complicate matters further, mothers are often held more accountable than fathers for their child's health and wellbeing, including their psychological difficulties and eating disorders (Caplan 38; Lee 28). This sense of culpability often leaves mothers blaming themselves for their daughter's illness and desperately attempting to make sense of the syndrome (Hoskins and Lam 163). For this reason, this chapter focuses on how mothers can provide meaningful support to daughters with eating disorders, especially given how theoretical attention has historically focused on precarious aspects of the mother-daughter relationship in accounting for the daughter's eating disorder (Bruch 77; Masterson 260; Tuval-Mashiach et al. 614). Furthermore, although some young males also experience eating disorders, little is known about the mother-son dyad in this experience, so the focus of the current chapter is on the mother-daughter one. In addition, this chapter reviews both the clinical features and addictive behaviours of eating disorders; it demonstrates how the compulsive nature of these syndromes often leaves young women feeling imprisoned in their own minds and bodies. Given the complexity of these syndromes, and the accompanying stigmatization that mothers with daughters who have eating disorders often experience, this chapter also discusses strategies from a meaning-centred framework for mothers to use in supporting daughters afflicted by eating disorders.

CLINICAL FEATURES OF ANOREXIA NERVOSA AND BULIMIA NERVOSA

Eating disorders are defined by abnormal eating practices that may involve either excessive or insufficient food intake, which affects daily functioning (*Diagnostic and Statistical Manual of Mental Disorders* [DSM-5] 329). Moreover, eating disorders are characterized by maladaptive attitudes and behaviours around eating, weight, and body image (*DSM-5* 329; Steiger and Bruce 431). Although these syndromes are generally considered to occur far less frequently in men than in women, there is evidence that eating disorder prevalence is increasing in males (Cottrell and Williams 50). Approximately one-third of those diagnosed with anorexia remain ill for five years following their preliminary diagnosis, and less than half of those suffering from an eating disorder (both anorexia and bulimia) ever fully recover (Fairburn et al. 663). Recovery is considered the cessation of binging and purging symptoms, attaining a sufficient body weight in accordance to an appropriate body mass index, and experiencing the resumption of menstruation (Jarman and Walsh 775). Many so-called recovered women, however, continue to experience existential issues such as finding meaning and purpose outside of the syndrome (Elran-Barak et al. 207; Knapp 2). Accordingly, eating disorders tend to be chronic and pervasive syndromes, with periods of remission and relapse that may last a lifetime (Steinhausen 1288; Steinhausen and Weber 1331).

The major clinical features of eating disorders are described below, with emphasis on symptoms presented in the fifth edition of the *Diagnostic and Statistical Manual of Mental Disorders*. Although the *DSM-5* remains a categorical classification system, it provides a common language in communicating the fundamental characteristics of these syndromes, including their course and development.

Anorexia Nervosa

Anorexia is characterized by "a relentless pursuit of thinness and a phobia of the consequences of eating" (Steiger and Bruce 431). The intense fear of eating and gaining weight results in a deliberate restriction of food intake, excessive exercise, or purging that can lead the affected person to become significantly underweight or dangerously emaciated (*DSM-5* 340). In anorexia, the fear of gaining weight is so intense that actual (or perceived) weight gain, in an already thin or emaciated person, can provoke profound anxiety, irritability, and/or feelings of loss of control (*DSM-5* 340). People with anorexia often eat a restricted range of foods; they may avoid social situations involving food, or they may consume their food in a prescribed order or in painstakingly calculated, hypocaloric amounts (*DSM-5* 341; Steiger and Bruce 431). The major distinguishing feature between anorexia and other eating disorders is a body weight less than 85 percent of what is expected for one's age and height (Uher and Rutter 86; Walsh and Sysko 760).

Course and Development

Anorexia typically manifests in females during mid to late adolescence during a period of dramatic psychological and physical development (*DSM-5* 341; Walsh 480). The onset of anorexia is generally associated with dieting or exercising behaviours that may evoke little, if any, concern, especially given the presence of reinforcing compliments (Walsh 479). With time, however, the commitment to dieting, excessive exercising, or purging increases, coupled by several secondary features, such as physically adverse effects, social withdrawal, rigidity, and perfectionism (*DSM-5*

341). Recovery outcomes from anorexia vary—some affected by this disorder recover fully, whereas others continue to suffer from patterns of great fluctuation between weight gain and significant weight loss cycles. Sadly, some individuals experience a progressive decline of health, which can last several years (Steinhausen 1288). Mortality rates in anorexia are among the highest in psychiatric disorders; thus, early detection and appropriate treatment are crucial (Arcelus et al. 728).

Bulimia Nervosa

Bulimia is characterized by frequent episodes of binge eating followed by frantic efforts to avoid gaining weight, which include fasting, self-induced vomiting, or purging (*DSM-5* 345). An episode of binge eating is characterized by food consumption over a brief period of time that would be considered excessive in comparison to that which most individuals would consume in the same time period(*DSM-5* 345). Many women with bulimia often use one or several different methods and behaviours to compensate for binge eating (Steiger and Bruce 432). Compensatory behaviours to eliminate the calories consumed (or to reduce the impact of the calories consumed) during the binge typically include self-induced vomiting, the use of diuretics or laxatives, fasting, and/or excessive exercise (*DSM-5* 346). However, self-induced vomiting is among the most common technique and is frequently reported by women with this syndrome (Grave et al. 680).

Course and Development

Bulimia commonly manifests itself among females during adolescence or young adulthood (*DSM-5* 347). However, many women often present with the disorder in their twenties and thirties after having secretly lived with it for a significant period of time (Steiger and Bruce 433). Bulimia is associated with a more favourable course and outcome compared to anorexia (Steinhausen and Weber 1337). For example, in a direct comparison of standardized mortality rates between anorexia and bulimia, Pamela Keel and his colleagues argue that bulimia is less likely to result in premature death compared to anorexia (64). Nonetheless, the course of bulimia can be unremitting, especially if untreated, and can result in several medical complications, including death (Mehler and Rylander 95; Mitchell and Crow 438; Westmoreland et al. 30).

ADDICTION AND EATING DISORDERS

A commonly held view of eating disorders is that they are analogous with addictions (Davis and Claridge 464; Wilson 27). There are now several addiction models of eating disorders informing various treatment and support groups—Anorexics and Bulimics Anonymous and Overeaters Anonymous are prominent examples (Bemis 410). Patterns that appear common in both eating disorders and addictive disorders include a sense of loss of control, preoccupation with the substance in question, use of the substance to regulate emotion and cope with stress, secrecy about behaviour, and maintenance of the behaviour despite negative repercussions (Hatsukami 435; Wilson 28). Given these common features and shared behaviours, some people view eating disorders as definitive of addiction (Davis and Claridge 472).

It should be noted, however, that suggesting eating disorders are analogous with addictive disorders, such as substance use disorders—due to shared characteristics or commonalities—risks adhering to "selective reduction," in which certain similarities are accentuated and differences overlooked (Vandereycken 96). Therefore, the following section provides a brief overview of Aviel Goodman's (1990) addictive disorder criteria to provide readers with greater contextual understanding of how eating disorders can invoke behaviours and processes seemingly addictive in nature.

GOODMAN ON ADDICTIVE DISORDERS

To provide theoretical coherence to the concept of addiction, Goodman proposed the term "addictive disorder." At the time, Goodman noted how addiction was poorly understood and accompanied by ambiguous or imprecise definitions: "some being so all-inclusive, [so] as to leave the term devoid of pragmatic value" (1403). According to Goodman, addiction is defined as a process whereby a behaviour—that can serve to produce both pleasure and to provide escape from inner discomfort—is used in a pattern marked by (1) repeated failure to control the behaviour (powerlessness) and (2) maintaining the behaviour despite significant negative consequences (unmanageability) (1404). In addition, Goodman proposed two sets of factors shaping the development of an addictive disorder: (1) those that involve an underlying addictive process and (2) those that relate to the selection of a specific substance (or behaviour) as the one that is favoured for addictive use (1404).

After reviewing Goodman's definition of addiction, it becomes apparent that addictive disorders as a group is not a collection of distinct disorders, but rather an underlying process that can be expressed in one or more of various behavioural manifestations (Speranza et al. 183). To operationalize this process, Goodman also proposed a set of diagnostic criteria in a format corresponding to the *Diagnostic and Statistical Manual of Mental Disorders* making it applicable to both psychoactive substances and behavioural addictions (Speranza et al. 183). Goodman also maintained that only the simultaneous presence of all the major criteria signified an addictive disorder (1404). Furthermore, in over 50 percent of individuals with an eating disorder, there is also a co-occurring substance abuse disorder, which makes these highly overlapping conditions (Denis and Helfman).

DISTINCTIONS BETWEEN EATING DISORDERS AND ADDICTIONS

Beyond Goodman's proposal, researchers have associated several behavioural patterns observed in eating disorders to those commonly seen in addictive disorders (Davis and Claridge 472; von Ramson and Cassin 16; Wilson 28). More specifically, some support the addition of eating disorders to the addictive spectrums. Specifically, the two main features, powerlessness and unmanageability of behaviours, are defining features of both eating disorders and addictions (Davis and Claridge 470; Speranza et al. 186).

Feelings of Powerlessness in Eating Disorders

Although many young women with eating disorders are aware of the deceptive and addictive nature of the syndrome, they often feel powerless in their attempts to overcome it (Redenbach and Lawler 153). The experience of having an eating disorder is frequently described as a lonely one, especially since it alienates those affected by the syndrome from their loved ones (D'Abundo and Chally 1099; Levine 248). The voice of the eating disorder tells these young women that "all you need to feel good is more food, less food, or no food" (Goodman and Villapiano 165). The eating disorder may initially provide protection from painful internal states of fear, hurt, and anger, but it quickly imprisons them—suppressing any sense of personal agency and self-determination (Hall and Cohn 54). Accordingly, it inevitably renders them feeling powerless and helpless.

Preoccupations with body shape may also serve as way for women to convert an internal concern to an external sphere. For instance, if the concern "am I good enough?" translates into "am I thin enough?" the young woman with an eating disorder creates an external and measurable standard for her self-worth, which seemingly offers a less painful and more tangible way to cope with her fears. Although women may experience a sense of control and mastery during the initial phases of their eating disorder, the syndrome inevitably creates chaos into the mind, body, and soul (Broussard 43; Hall and Cohn 26). They swiftly become consumed by the compulsion to binge and purge or to restrict caloric intake, with little potential to grow in other areas in their lives (Elran-Barak et al. 207).

Shifting from Unmanageable to Manageable Coping Strategies

An eating disorder becomes unmanageable for many reasons. There are not only psychological and emotional ramifications, but also serious physiological consequences of disordered eating that occur overtime (Hall and Cohn 51). However, eating disorders are not merely about binging and purging or eating and gaining weight. Rather, they can serve as an illusory mechanism for coping with the tensions of human existence that elude many women (Hall and Cohn 138; Knapp 17). In this sense, the addictive behaviours accompanying these syndromes seemingly attempt to assuage and curtail long-standing feelings of loneliness and disconnection (Levine 253; Richards et al. "Theistic Spiritual Treatment" 174; Knapp 8). Furthermore, young women with these syndromes tend to rely more exclusively on their disordered eating as their interpersonal relationships deteriorate (Richards et al., "Theistic Spiritual Treatment" 183). The binging and purging become a mechanism for coping with pain and loneliness (Levine 243; Richards et al., *Spiritual Approaches* 46). Though used as coping in the short term, addictive behaviours do not resolve loneliness but rather breed loneliness over the long term.

Psychological and Physiological Effects of Dieting and Starvation

An important distinction in viewing eating disorders as addictions is related to some of the psychological and physiological ramifications of dieting and starvation (Jaspers). For instance, it is common for a dieting or famished individual to become preoccupied with food, to experience strong urges to consume large amounts of food (binging), to display irritability and negative emotionality, and to be more likely to overeat in response to stress (Jaspers; Polivy 591). Indeed, some of these behaviours may appear to be symptomatic of addiction, especially given the increasing fixation toward the substance women with eating disorders feel addicted to—that is, food (Jaspers). In some ways, she may feel like a prisoner to the eating disorder, as she wavers between succumbing to the urges or thwarting them with further restriction. Given the psychological and physiological effects of starvation, she may feel addicted to food (Jasper). However, one must cautiously view the situation in this manner because it may only serve to intensify her efforts to avoid food altogether.

Normalizing Food as Opposed to Avoiding

Another important distinction in viewing eating disorders as addictions resides in how avoiding alcohol may be influential in resolving addiction to alcohol, whereas avoiding food will only increase one's obsession with it (Jaspers). Similarly, avoiding smartphones when addicted also increases preoccupation with them (Bian and Leung 74). Thus, it seems that avoidance can potentially lead to different prognoses, depending on the addictive behaviour avoided. In fact, this may be the reason why some eating disorders have a much poorer prognosis than many substance abuse disorders. Furthermore, in many alcohol or drug addiction treatment programs, the person is often encouraged to view themselves as an addict, even if he or she has stopped using the substance in question. Moreover, they are encouraged to see themselves as an addict, and, thus, they can never think they can use the substance in a casual manner (Jaspers). Instead, an addict must completely abstain. Although this may serve as an effective treatment philosophy in the process of recovery for those with substance addiction or dependence, it is increasingly problematic to employ this framework with an individual who has an eating disorder (Jaspers). For women with eating disorders, an important step in the process of recovering from the addictive nature of these syndromes is to learn how to eat a balanced, healthy diet (Polivy 591). The more an individual with an eating disorder begins to include a variety of foods in her diet with appropriate portions, the less likely she is to become preoccupied with food or to binge (Hall and Cohn 198; Polivy 592). In the early stages of recovery, if certain foods are avoided (e.g., sweets, or other high-calorie foods), it may precipitate binging and increase fixation. For this reason, an important step in the process of recovery is not food avoidance but normalization of eating and restoration of natural weight (Jaspers). Although normative eating and weight are key components of recovery, the relational or existential aspects of recovery are often ignored. Given this, an approach addressing these components—particularly one implicated the mother-daughter dyad—may be an important supplement to current treatment protocols.

INTEGRATING A MEANING-CENTRED APPROACH: HOW MOTHERS CAN PROVIDE MEANINGFUL SUPPORT TO DAUGHTERS WITH EATING DISORDERS

Mothers often experience a myriad of questions once they discover their daughter is struggling with an eating disorder. Some of the questions mothers ask themselves may stem from societal messaging, whereas others simply may stem from the lived experience of having a daughter with an eating disorder. Some questions mothers ask themselves are more logical or physical (e.g., "Did my comments about her weight contribute to it? How do I get her the support she needs? Is she going to ruin her teeth from the purging?"), whereas others are more existential in nature (e.g., How did this happen? What does it mean for her to have an eating disorder? What is my role in all of this?"). Mothers naturally seek to understand why their daughters are struggling to fulfill the basic human need of eating or why they place such prominence on weight and physical appearance that they become more significant than anything else in life. In the process of attempting to locate a cause for their daughters' eating disorders, mothers inadvertently take on the blame themselves (Hoskins and Lam 164). In doing so, they risk further isolating themselves from their daughters, including their ability to provide meaningful support to them during the recovery process.

Paul Wong's meaning-centred approach (MCA)—which is grounded in his meaning therapy practice and theory—is one framework through which mothers may be able to use practical tools to support daughters with eating disorders. Furthermore, the MCA can be employed to complement traditional treatment approaches for eating disorders and to assist in addressing the existential needs of women with eating disorders. MCA, however, should not be used exclusively in the treatment and support of women with eating disorders. Rather, it should be integrated with standard medical and psychological modalities, especially given the potentially damaging physiological and psychological consequences of eating disorders. In many ways, the integration of a MCA can help women to discover a sense of meaning and purpose beyond or as a result of their eating disorder.

MEANING THERAPY THEORY AND PRACTICE

MCA is a second wave positive psychology (PP 2.0) approach (Wong, "Meaning Therapy" 88; "Positive Psychology" 72). In PP 2.0, both darker and lighter experiences of life are valued as a dialectic, as two sides of the same coin (Ivtzan et al. 131; Wong, "Meaning-Centered Approach" 6). The experience of positive emotions or situations depends on the experience of negative emotions or situations in order for one to experience meaning. More specifically, from the dark side of life, transformation, growth, and flourishing can emerge and be appreciated (Ivtzan et al. 55). Within the MCA, meaning therapy is an integrative and positive existential perspective, which focuses on the human capacity to discover and create meaning out of exceedingly difficult and, often painful, life experiences (Wong, "Meaning Therapy" 85). Meaning therapy emerges from logotherapy (Frankl 77; Wong "Logotherapy" 619), and employs personal meaning as its main organizing construct through an integration of various models such as cognitive behaviour therapy and positive psychology (Wong, "Meaning Therapy" 85).

Meaning therapy is shaped by both the meaning–management theory and the dual-system model (Wong "Meaning Therapy" 89). The former is concerned with meaning-related psychological processes, whereas the latter is concerned with the self-regulation processes involved in survival and attaining positive life goals (Wong "Meaning Therapy" 89). As a PP2.0 approach, meaning therapy acknowledges the paradoxical and dual nature of human existence—specifically, "the co-existence of good and evil, benefits and cost, happiness and suffering, hope and despair" (Wong "Meaning Yherapy" 90). Accordingly, this theory not only addresses people's difficulties, but also facilitates their quest for meaning. In many ways, it underscores the paradoxical nature of eating disorders. These syndromes initially function to protect women from the painful aspects of life, but it soon holds them hostage to their bodies and mind in the process. Such an experience holds potential long-term existential consequences, but paradoxically, it is from such an experience that meaning can also emerge.

Meaning is critical in our quest for understanding and developing a sense of coherence against uncertainty (Wong "Meaning Therapy" 89). Meaning-management theory is based on the central role of meaning in human survival (Wong "Meaning Management Theory" 70). Furthermore, meaning involves the human quest for meaning, purpose, and understanding as well as the human capacity to discover and generate meanings out of complexing life experiences (Wong "Meaning Therapy" 89). Arguably, meaning is also critically significant for women with eating disorders because the syndrome often leaves them feeling void of meaning and purpose. Therefore, mothers can accompany their daughters in their quest for finding a sense of meaning and purpose stemming from or beyond the syndrome. The meaning therapy approach has successfully been used to treat other types of addictive behaviours and disorders (Thompson 429); given this, it may be appropriate to use within the context of eating disorders.

PURE STRATEGY IN MEANING THERAPY

The PURE strategy provides an ideal framework to restore meaning in the life of women with eating disorders because it addresses significant components of meaningful living (Wong "Meaning Therapy" 90). Similarly, it can provide practical tools for mothers to employ with daughters struggling with eating disorders.

According to meaning-management theory (Wong "Meaning Therapy" 90), meaning consists of four interconnected parts: purpose, understanding, responsible action, and evaluation (PURE):

Purpose (motivational component): A life driven by purpose is one engaged and committed to pursuing an ideal future. In other words, it includes goals, values, ambitions, and objectives addressing the following questions. What does life require of me? What should I do with my life? What do I value in my life?

Understanding (cognitive component): A life with understanding includes consistency and integrity. Simply put, it involves developing a sense of coherence, making sense of situations, understanding one's own identity and relationship to others, and successfully communicating. It involves addressing the following questions. What has happened and what does it all mean? Who am I and how do I make sense of my surroundings?

Responsible action (moral and behavioural component): A responsible life is grounded in employing human freedom and personal agency. This involves encompassing appropriate reactions and actions, doing what is morally right, finding the right solutions, and making amends that involves addressing the following questions. What is my responsibility in this situation? What is the right thing to do? What options or alternatives do I have? What choices should I make? Is there a more helpful way I can think or act in this situation?

Evaluation (affective component): A meaningful life consists of using reflection and judgment. This involves assessing the level of satisfaction (or dissatisfaction) with circumstances or life on a whole, which involves addressing the following questions. Have I accomplished what I strove to do? Am I happy and content with how I have lived my life?

Practical Implications of the PURE Strategy and Eating Disorders

Each of these components contains various intervention skills (e.g., goal setting, decision making, reality checking, Socratic questioning, and challenging irrational or unrealistic thoughts, etc.), which is typically facilitated by a psychotherapist. However, mothers can tailor the questions from each domain of PURE to engage in both meaningful and fruitful conversations with their daughters. More specifically, these questions can be tailored to target meaningful interactions about what life could look like for their daughter outside of her eating disorder (e.g., What would you like to do with your life? What do you value in life outside of the eating disorder? What is your responsibility in addressing the eating disorder? What might my role be in assisting you? What options do you have in seeking support and finding meaning?). The intention for mothers is neither to assume responsibility for their daughter's eating disorder nor to assume the role of psychotherapist. Instead, the purpose of applying and investigating these domains serves to assist both mothers and daughters in finding meaning and strengthening their bond through the experiences of empathy and mutual collaboration.

Avoidance Systems and Eating Disorders

The four components of PURE function collectively to create an upward spiral feedback loop (Wong, "Logotherapy" 637). The successful completion of each component of PURE has been found to increase well-being (Wong, "Logotherapy" 637). However, when one experiences a serious hindrance or obstacle, one will shift to the avoidance system to attempt managing the negative circumstances (Wong, "Logotherapy" 637). In other words, one may return to their previous addictive habits to avoid experiencing pain or suffering. Avoidance inhibits the experience of meaning or growth.

In the case of an eating disorder, avoidance often leads to a return to eating disorder behaviours. As previously mentioned, women will often succumb to food, as it acquires an emotional quality and can be used to numb feelings of loneliness, worthlessness, and disconnection (Hall and Cohn 138; Knapp 17; Levine 253). Although this can be an exceedingly difficult, and perhaps vexing, experience for mothers, they should remain open and supportive during these setbacks. In fact, these setbacks or "slips" can provide both mothers and their daughters an opportunity to further investigate the implications of returning to disordered eating in the face of adversity. Reframed in this manner, setbacks become an occasion for both parties to develop additional insight and to discover meaning and positive growth away from disordered eating.

PURE AND MEANING MAKING IN ACTION

The following is a demonstration of how mothers could use the PURE strategy to facilitate discussions with daughters to create meaning from, or outside of, the eating disorder. Although this is only one of many potential dialogues that could be carried out, it shows how mothers could engage their daughters in these conversations.

Purpose (Motivational Component)

Mother: I'd really like it if we could talk about something that's been on my mind. Is now a good time to talk?
Liz: Okay...
Mother: I've been wondering... when you plan binges and purge, what's been helpful about that for you?
Liz: Maybe it made something feel in my control.
Mother: So, if I understand correctly, it sounds like you've been feeling like some things are out of your control and restricting gave you a sense of control.

Liz: Yes, except I now feel like things are so out of control with my eating.

Mother: So, initially, the eating disorder fulfilled the purpose of giving you a sense of control, and now, like other things in your life, it too seems uncontrollable.

Liz: Yes.

Mother: It sounds overwhelming. To get away from that, what you would like to see in your life outside of the eating disorder?

Liz: To be honest, I feel like my eating disorder is my life.

Mother: I understand that it's been tough lately, but you have made some big strides.

Liz: You think so?

Mother: Of course. I even heard you playing the piano again last night after dinner.

Liz: Yes, my counsellor mentioned that it could be a good distraction after my meals.

Mother: What was it like for you to play the piano again?

Liz: I forgot how much I loved playing the piano. I think I want to study music.

Mother: I noticed your face light up when you said that. What does music bring for you?

Liz: It's hard to explain, but it silences that voice.

Mother: It makes sense why you enjoy it so much because it gives you a sense of peace.

Liz: Yes, that's exactly it.

Mother: I'm wondering if the piano may give you a sense of control, as well joy....

Liz: I guess it does. It really does.

Understanding (Cognitive Component)

Mother: So, you're thinking about studying music after high school?

Liz: It's the only thing I think I would really enjoy studying. Do you think I could study something like music?

Mother: I think there are many possibilities that music can offer like teaching or performing.

Liz: Yes, I think I could teach or something. I just realized how rusty I am now though. I haven't been practising lately because I haven't had the energy. Well, I mean, the purging took a lot out of me.

Mother: Do you find that you have more energy lately? I know you mentioned that you haven't purged in about a week or so.

Liz: Yes, it's been about a week now, so I do have some more energy lately. I have more time now too. I guess I didn't realize how much time planning binges took.

Mother: What if you gave yourself some time each night to play and practise? And try to fill up that extra time like your counsellor suggested?

Liz: I think I could try it. It would give me time to brush up on my skills and focus on my music.

Responsible Action (Moral and Behavioural Component)

Mother: Is there something I could do to support you with your music?

Liz: Well, you could come listen to me play after dinner. I just feel so antsy after eating.

Mother: That's a good idea. Plus, I love hearing you play. What if I can't for some reason? I am just thinking out loud here. Would you still be able to practise?

Liz: Well, I could play the piano for least thirty minutes after dinner. I just need to make sure I keep my meal times structured.

Mother: That sounds like a good plan. So, you will commit to playing piano after dinner for at least thirty minutes?

Liz: Yes, but it might become longer once I get started.

Evaluation (Affective Component)

Mother: How about we try this plan for a few days and see how you feel?

Liz: That sounds good.

Mother: If something about the plan doesn't work, then we

can figure out what might work. If it does work, then we can see about having you set up an appointment with your guidance counsellor, if you would like. That way, you can get a sense of different music programs after high school.

Liz: That's not a bad idea. So, you would be okay with me studying music?

Mother: I would be okay with anything that you're passionate about.

Liz: Thanks, Mom.

The ABCDE Strategy in Meaning Therapy

Suffering is unavoidable in life and is often more pronounced in the face of illness. Given the inevitability of suffering, it is necessary to find effective strategies to overcome adversity. In MCA theory and practice, the ABCDE strategy is an important tool for confronting challenging life circumstances (Wong, "Meaning Therapy" 91). This strategy, however, is different from the sequence seen in the rational-emotive therapy process (Ellis 140). Rather, this strategy corresponds with acceptance and commitment therapy in its focus on action rather than thinking (Wong, "Logotherapy" 637).

The ABCDE stands for the following: acceptance; belief and affirmation; commitment to action and specific goals; discovering new meaning and understanding; and evaluation of the outcome and enjoying positive outcomes. In addition, the ABCDE strategy encompasses several psychological principles (Wong, "Logotherapy" 637-638; "Meaning Therapy" 91):

Accept and confront the reality (the reality principle): Acceptance does not suggest submitting or acquiescing to difficult life circumstances. Instead, it entails acknowledging the darker aspects of the human condition with honesty. In doing so, it allows one to feel empowered in confronting reality by evoking their longing for positive change.

Believe that life is worth pursuing and living (the faith principle): Believing life is worth living breeds hope, which is essential to persevere against adversity. Whether belief is religious or humanistic in nature, it creates hope and inspires one to continue moving forward.

Commit to goals and actions (the action principle): Committing to specific goals can lead to engaging in meaningful action. Tangible change is only possible when one begins to take actual steps toward a new direction.

Discover the meaning and significance (the AHA principle): Meaning is discovered more than it is created (Frankl 163). Discovering meaning involves an "Aha" or "Eureka" response, which allows one to feel inspired for living against darkness and despair.

Evaluate the first four principles (the self-regulation principle): Evaluation involves assessing levels of satisfaction (or dissatisfaction) with the situation. It is an important step in ensuring self-regulation because it allows one to make the necessary changes or improvements in their iotation to pursue positive life goals.

Practical Implication of the ABCDE Strategy for Eating Disorders

The ACBDE strategy can be helpful for women in confronting negativity they might experience during the process of recovery. For example, the process of weight restoration can be particularly challenging during the initial stages of recovery (Hall and Cohn 62). Research demonstrates that although mothers seek to actively support their daughters during recovery, they often display intense anger toward them (Tuval-Mashiach et al. 619). For some mothers, this rupture in the relationship can be incredibly painful (Tuval-Mashiach et al. 619), so it is important for them to work through their own painful and negative reactions. Although many women initially use eating disorder behaviours as an attempt to fit in and reconnect with family and peers, the disordered behaviours only intensify their feelings of disconnection from themselves and significant others (Patching and Lawler 17). Once women recognize and understand this level of disconnection, it can eventually compel them to pursue an enhanced lifestyle, which involves reengaging in life and reconnecting with themselves and others (Patching and Lawler 17). Therefore, the ABCDE intervention can be a tool for both mothers and their daughters with eating disorders in dealing with prolonged negative life experiences (Wong, "Meaning Therapy" 91).

ABCDE AND MEANING MAKING IN ACTION

The following are some different phrases—inspired by Wong's AB-CDE strategy—that could be used to help guide a mother-daughter conversation to set concrete goals and supports. There are several different ways mothers can approach daughters with eating disorders through the ABCDE principle.

However, it must be noted that these questions are intended as a starting place to demonstrate how mothers can facilitate dialogues seeking to empower their daughters in confronting the reality of the eating disorder while awakening their longings for positive change.

Step One: Accepting and Confronting the Reality (Reality Principle)

Cognitive Acceptance
- What was going on in your life that led to the start of the eating disorder?
- When it started, what did you end up doing?
- How was this helpful for you at the time? In other words, what purpose did it serve?
- What happened as it started to get worse? Could you tell me about that experience?

Emotional Acceptance
- How do you feel about having an eating disorder?
- What painful feelings do you experience from having the eating disorder?

Integrative Acceptance
- How does having an eating disorder affect other things in your life?

Existential Acceptance
- Beyond the eating disorder, what sorts of things do you look forward to in life?
- What brings you a sense of meaning or joy?

Transcendental Acceptance
- If a miracle were to happen and you were to wake up tomorrow without an eating disorder, what would be the first small thing you would notice different in your life?
- What would be the next thing you would notice to let you know this miracle would have happened?
- What other small or big things would be different in your day?

Transformative Acceptance
- By having experienced an eating disorder, is there any way this experience could be helpful for you? Could you use this experience to help others?

Step Two: Believing Life Is Worth Pursuing and Living (Faith Principle)

- Have there been moments when you've been lying to yourself about your eating behaviour? What have you noticed?
- Are there ways you can think about your eating disorder differently in order to be more honest with yourself?
- How have your attitudes toward your body and eating affected your life?
- How have your beliefs toward your body and eating affected your life?
- How are those attitudes and beliefs helping you? Are they getting in your way?
- What do these beliefs and attitudes tell you about yourself?
- What attitudes and beliefs do you think you may need to change about your body and eating?
- What beliefs and attitudes do you want to develop about your body and eating?
- Is there anything I can do to help make this easier for you?

Step Three: Committing to Goals and Actions (Action Principle)

- What can you do each day to keep your motivation high

to help you get over your eating disorder?
•Is there a way I could help keep you motivated?
•What obstacles do you see getting in your way?
•What can you do right now about those obstacles?
•Is there anything you or I could do to help you improve your situation of having an eating disorder?
•What action can you take to "own" having an eating disorder in order to begin moving forward?
•What can I or others do to help you in overcoming an eating disorder?

Step Four: Discovering the Meaning and Significance (AHA Principle)

•What is the meaning or purpose of having an eating disorder to you?
•What have you learned about yourself by having an eating disorder?

Step Five: Evaluating the Above (Self-Regulation Principle)

•Have you experienced a decrease in your eating disorder symptoms?
•Have you have experienced an improvement in the pursuit of your positive life goals?
•Do you think we need to review or change some of your goals to make them more doable?

CONCLUSION

The existential-humanistic approach, specifically the MCA, described in this chapter offers strategies for mothers to help daughters with eating disorders. Although further validation research is needed in this area, an existential-humanistic approach could assist in the treatment of eating disorders using the meaning therapy framework for addictions. Similarly, it could also provide mothers with practical tools to provide their daughters with meaningful support. Women afflicted with eating disorders are often reluctant to receive treatment, as they feel consumed by the addictive nature of the syndrome as well as misunderstood by those around them. Moreover, eating disorders are often considered perverse and conflicting syndromes; thus, they evoke negative reactions, such as bafflement, suspicion and apprehension in both mothers (Tuval-Mashiach et al. 619) and healthcare professionals (Jarman and Walsh 774). Accordingly, it is often perceived as an exceptionally difficult disorder to treat.

The treatment and recovery process for women afflicted by eating disorders is neither a fixed nor static pursuit; rather, it is an enduring quest including relapses and remissions (Elran-Barak et al. 208). However, this journey can offer women with many opportunities to discover meaning. Eating disorders are not merely about binging and purging or eating and gaining weight. To a certain extent, eating disturbances and their addictive nature also function as a mechanism for coping with the tensions of human existence, which either provoke or elude many women (Knapp 9).

The search for meaning and connection often leads women suffering from eating disturbances to the necessity of a meaning-centred approach. However, such an approach is not often presented within mainstream treatment protocols. Moreover, the concepts of meaning and ongoing existential suffering are also ignored in the definition of recovery. This gap in treatment and conceptualization of eating disorders is problematic because it is the existential concerns of disconnection, loneliness, or emptiness that often lead to relapse of the addictive eating disorders. If incorporated into the understanding of eating disorders, the ability to create meaning outside of the eating disorder can be a catalyst of transformation from "enslavement to liberation, from chaos to order," and from disconnection to connection (Elran-Barak et al. 205).

Therefore, the incorporation of a MCA framework with existing treatment and recovery processes could potentially ameliorate deep feelings of turmoil, loneliness, and sorrow that imprison the minds of women suffering from eating disorders (Levine 244; Richards et al., *Spiritual Approaches* 44) as well as alleviate the challenges that may develop in the mother-daughter dyad. Within the mother-daughter dyad, finding meaning from suffering may ultimately strengthen their relationship and bridge the loneliness to form deeper connections.

WORKS CITED

American Psychiatric Association. "Feeding and Eating Disorders." *Diagnostic and Statistical Manual of Mental Disorders: DSM-5.* 5th ed. American Psychiatric Association, 2013, pp. 329-54.

Arcelus, Jon, et al. "Mortality Rates in Patients with Anorexia Nervosa and Other Eating Disorders: A Meta-analysis of 36 Studies." *Archives of General Psychiatry*, vol. 68, no. 7, pp. 724-31.

Bemis, Kelly. "'Abstinence" and 'Nonabstinence' Models for the Treatment of Bulimia." *International Journal of Eating Disorders*, vol. 4, no. 4, 1985, pp. 407-37.

Bian, Mengwei, and Louis Leung. "Linking Loneliness, Shyness, Smartphone Addiction Symptoms and Patterns of Smartphone Use to Social Capital." *Social Science Computer Review*, vol. 33, no. 1, 2015, pp. 61-79.

Broussard, Brenda. "Women's Experiences of Bulimia Nervosa." *Journal of Advanced Nursing*, vol. 49, no. 1, 2005, pp. 43-50.

Bruch, Hilde. *Eating Disorders: Obesity, Anorexia Nervosa, and the Person Within.* Basic Books, 1973.

Caplan, Paula. "Don't Blame Mother: Then and Now." *Maternal Theory: Essential Readings,* edited by Andrea O'Reilly, Demeter Press, 2007, pp. 592-600.

Cottrell, Damon, and Jeffrey Williams. "Eating Disorders in Men." *The Nurse Practitioner*, vol. 41, no. 9, 2016, pp. 49-55.

D'Abundo, Michelle, and Pamela Chally. "Struggling with Recovery: Participant Perspectives on Battling an Eating Disorder." *Qualitative Health Research,* vol. 14, no. 8, 2004, pp. 1094-106.

Davis, Caroline, and Gordon Claridge. "The Eating Disorders as Addiction: A Psychobiological Perspective." *Addictive Behaviors*, vol. 23, no. 4, 2008, pp. 463-75.

Denis, Amy, and Bethany Helfman. "Substance Abuse and Eating Disorders: What Parents and Families Need to Know." *NEDA,* 10 June 2017, https://keltyeatingdisorders.ca/wp-content/uploads/2016/03/NEDA-Substance-Abuse-and-EatingDisorders. pdf. Accessed 2 May 2018.

Ellis, Albert. "The Revised ABC's of Rational Emotive Therapy (RET)." *Journal of Rational-Emotive and Cognitive Behavior Therapy*, vol. 9, no. 3, 1991, pp. 139-72.

Elran-Barak, Roni, et al. "The Road to Liberation: Metaphors and Narratives of Illness of Women Recovered from Bulimia Nervosa." *Treatment and Recovery of Eating Disorders*, edited by Daniel Stein and Yael Latzer, Nova Sciences Publishers, 2012, pp. 203-16.

Fairburn, Christopher, et al. "The Natural Course of Bulimia Nervosa and Binge Eating Disorder in Young Women." *Archives of General Psychiatry*, vol. 57, no. 7, pp. 659-65.

Fassino, Secondo, and Giovanni Abbate-Daga. "Resistance to Treatment in Eating Disorders: A Critical Challenge." Editorial. *BMC Psychiatry*, vol. 13, 2013, p. 282.

Frankl, Viktor. *The Doctor and the Soul*. 2nd. Random House, 1986.

Goodman, Aviel. "Addiction: Definitions and Implications" *British Journal of Addiction*, vol. 85, no. 11, 1990, pp. 1403-408.

Goodman, Laura, and Mona Villapiano. *Eating Disorders: The Journey to Recovery Workbook*. Brunner-Routledge, 2016.

Grave, Riccardo, et al. "Self-induced Vomiting in Eating Disorders: Associated Features and Treatment Outcome." *Behaviour Research and Therapy*, vol. 47, no. 8, 2009, pp. 680-84.

Hall, Lindsey, and Leigh Cohn. *Bulimia: A Guide to Recovery*. Gürze Books, 2011.

Hatsukami, Dorothy, et al. "Similarities and Differences on the MMPI between Women with Bulimia and Women with Alcohol or Drug Abuse Problems." *Addictive Behaviors*, vol. 7, no. 4, 1982, pp. 435-39.

Hoskins, Marie, and Eugenie Lam. "The Impact of Daughters' Eating Disorders in Mothers' Sense of Self: Contextualizing Mothering Experiences." *Canadian Journal of Counselling*, vol. 35, no. 2, 2001, pp. 157-75.

Ivtzan, Itai, et al. *Second Wave Positive Psychology: Embracing the Dark Side of Life*. Routledge, 2016.

Jarman, Maria, and Susan Walsh. "Evaluating Recovery from

Anorexia Nervosa and Bulimia Nervosa: Integrating Lessons Learned from Research and Clinical Practice." *Clinical Psychology Review,* vol. 19, no. 7, 1999, pp. 773-88.

Jaspers, Karin. "Are Eating Disorders Addictions?" *NEDIC, National Eating Disorder,* nedic.ca/sites/default/files/files/Are%20 Eating%20Disorders%20Addictions.pdf. Accessed 2 May 2018.

Kaye, Walter, et al. "'Nothing Tastes as Good as Skinny Feels': The Neurobiology of Anorexia Nervosa." *Trends in Neuroscience,* vol. 36, no. 2, 2013, pp. 110-20.

Keel, Pamela, et al. "Long-Term Outcome of Bulimia Nervosa." *Archives of General Psychiatry,* vol.56, no. 1, 1999, pp. 136-38.

Knapp, Caroline. *Appetites: Why Women Want.* Counterpoint, 2003.

Lee, Christina. "Health, Stress and Coping among Women Caregivers: A Review." *Journal of Health Psychology,* vol. 4, no. 1, 1999, pp. 27-40.

Levine, Martha Peaslee. "Loneliness and Eating Disorders." *Journal of Psychology,* vol. 146, no. 1-2, 2012, pp. 243-57.

Masterson, James. "Paradise Lost—Bulimia, a Closet Narcissistic Personality Disorder: A Developmental, Self, and Object Relations Approach." *Adolescent Psychiatry,* edited by Richard Marohn and Sherman Feinstein, Analytic Press, 1995, pp. 253-66.

Mehler, Philip, and Melanie Rylander. "Bulimia Nervosa: Medical Complications." *Journal of Eating Disorders,* vol. 3, no. 1, 2015, pp. 95-104.

Mitchell, James, and Scott Crow. "Medical Complications of Anorexia Nervosa and Bulimia Nervosa." *Current Opinion in Psychiatry,* vol. 19, no. 4, 2006, pp. 438-43.

Polivy, Janet. "Psychological Consequences of Food Restriction." *Journal of the American Dietetic Association,* vol. 96, no. 6, 1996, pp. 589-92.

Redenbach, Joanna, and Jocalyn Lawler. "Recovery from Disordered Eating: What Life Histories Reveal." *Contemporary Nurse,* vol. 15, no. 1-2, 2003, pp. 148-56.

Richards, Scott, et al. "A Theistic Spiritual Treatment for Women with Eating Disorders." *Journal of Clinical Psychology,* vol. 35, no. 2, 2009, pp. 172-84.

Richards, Scott, et al. *Spiritual Approaches in the Treatment of*

Women with Eating Disorders. American Psychological Association, 2007.

Speranza, Mario, et al. "An Investigation of Goodman's Addictive Disorders Criteria in Eating Disorders." *European Eating Disorders Review*, vol. 20, no. 3, 2012, pp. 182-89.

Steiger, Howard, and Kenneth Bruce. "Eating Disorders." *Oxford Textbook of Psychopathology.* 3rd ed. Edited by Paul Blaney, Robert Krueger and Theodore Millon, Oxford University.

Steinhausen, Hans-Christoph. "The Outcome of Anorexia Nervosa in the 20th Century." *American Journal of Psychiatry*, vol. 159, no. 8, 2002, pp. 1284-293.

Steinhausen, Hans-Christoph, and Sandy Weber. "The Outcome of Bulimia Nervosa: Findings from One-Quarter Century of Research." *American Journal of Psychiatry*, vol. 166, no. 12, 2009, pp.1331-341.

Thompson, Geoffrey. "Meaning Therapy for Addictions: A Case Study." *Journal of Humanistic Psychology*, vol. 56, no. 5, pp. 457-82.

Tuval-Mashiach, Rivka, et al. "Attacks on Linking: Stressors and Identity Challenges for Mothers of Daughters with Long Lasting Anorexia Nervosa." *Psychology and Health*, vol. 29, no. 6, 2014, pp. 613-31.

Uher, Rudolf, and Michael Rutter. "Classification of feeding and eating disorders: Review of Evidence Proposals for ICD-11." *World Psychiatry*, vol. 11, no. 2, 2012, pp. 80-92.

Vandereycken, Walter. "The Addiction Model in Eating Disorders: Some Critical Remarks and a Selected Bibliography." *International Journal of Eating Disorders*, vol. 9, no. 1, 1990, pp. 95-101.

Walsh, Timothy, and Robyn Sysko. "Broad Categories for the Diagnosis of Eating Disorders (BDC-ED): An Alternative System for Classification." *International Journal of Eating Disorders*, vol. 42, no. 8, pp. 754-64.

Walsh, Timothy. "The Enigmatic Persistence of Anorexia Nervosa." *American Journal of Psychiatry*, vol. 170, no. 5, 2013, pp. 477-84.

Westmoreland, Patricia, et al. "Medical Complications of Anorexia and Bulimia." *The American Journal of Medicine*, vol. 129, no. 1, 2016, pp. 30-37.

Wilson, Terence. "The Addiction Model of Eating Disorders: A

Critical Analysis." *Advances in Behaviour Research and Therapy*, vol. 13, no. 1, 1991, pp. 27-72.

Wong, Paul. "From Logotherapy to Meaning-Centered Counseling and Therapy." *The Human Quest for Meaning: Theories, Research, and Applications*. 2nd ed. Edited by Paul Wong, Routledge, 2012, pp. 619-47.

Wong Paul. "Meaning Management Theory and Death Acceptance." *Existential and Spiritual Issues in Death Attitudes*, edited by Adrian Tomer et al., Lawrence Erlbaum Associates, 2008, pp. 65-87.

Wong, Paul. "Meaning Therapy: An Integrative and Positive Existential Psychotherapy." *Journal of Contemporary Psychotherapy*, vol. 40, no. 2, 2010, pp. 85-93.

Wong, Paul. "Positive Psychology 2:0: Towards a Balanced Interactive Model of the Good Life." *Canadian Psychology*, vol. 52, no. 2, 2011, pp. 69-81.

During my first pregnancy, everyone was happy to provide advice and anecdotes about their own parenting or pregnancy experiences. What nobody mentioned was the loneliness that comes along with raising an infant. I came home from the hospital exhausted, full of awe and wonder, joy, and hormonal tears. I was prepared for these things and for the poop-shooting-across-the-room diapering experiences and feeding challenges. My friends had all shared similar experiences with me before my baby was born. What I wasn't prepared for was the feeling of disconnection from other adults. Prior to motherhood, I was used to continual adult contact as a social worker in a hospital as well as to relaxing evenings with my partner. After the initial whirlwind of visits by friends and family to the hospital and home, no one came. Days and nights were spent feeding, diapering, reading, and playing with a small human being who couldn't speak back to me. During the evenings, my partner took over baby duty so that I could shower or attend to other basic needs. By the time the baby was sleeping, I was too exhausted to have a meaningful conversation with my partner. I would pick up my smartphone and surf Facebook, Twitter, and Instagram to feel a connection to the adult world beyond. Eventually, short bursts of online time grew into far longer stretches. My phone would buzz in the middle of reading a book to my infant, and I would reach to check it. It would buzz while my partner was speaking, and I would try to discretely look at it. When my phone wasn't in the same room, I would search for it, feeling a bit lost without it. This was my lifeline to the adult world, and it seemed to quell my loneliness. My smartphone was becoming a problem. It was becoming an addiction taking me away from my partner and child.

—Stephanie, age twenty-six

9.
REAL Education to Prevent Smartphone Addiction

A Rational-Emotive, Attachment, Logotherapy Approach for Expectant Mothers

LAURA LYNNE ARMSTRONG

THE TRANSITION TO PARENTHOOD can be a particularly challenging time for the couple's relationship (Shapiro et al. 337). Even the most stable relationships are often strained by the arrival of a new baby (Gottman and Gottman). In fact, up to 67 percent of couples report decreased marital satisfaction and stress up to four years after the birth of a baby (Gottman and Gottman). During such times, mothers in particular often report loneliness (Cronin 265). Loneliness is not surprising, as heterosexual couples report significantly poorer conflict management, sudden declines in relationship quality (more so for mothers than fathers), and less paternal investment in the marital relationship (Doss et al. 13). Couples also report struggling with lack of sleep and financial concerns (Gottman and Gottman). Relationship changes resulting in a breach in meaningful partner attachment can cause problematic behaviours, such as addictive smartphone use (Flores 128; Tan et al. 606). As the transition to parenthood is associated with decreased marital satisfaction, new parents may be particularly at risk for smartphone addiction. Smartphone addiction, as with any form of addiction viewed with an attachment lens, is a surrogate for meaningful attachment—a way of regulating emotions that can turn into a prison (Johnson). Addiction in this sense can be conceptualized as a compulsion, as it compensates for attachment and provides temporary relief from difficult emotions, such as anxiety or depressive symptoms (Flores 128; Johnson). However, since meaningful attachment is a primary motivational force for humans, the pains, joys, and purpose derived from attachment cannot be replaced by a substitute over the long term (Flores 3). Beyond attachment, from an existential-humanistic perspective, addiction is a response to boredom, loneliness, and meaninglessness (Frankl 107; Thompson 56). Smartphone use can temporarily fill the meaning void or can be pleasurable entertainment, but addictive use can be harmful over time.

Smartphones are ubiquitous in society. They are a helpful tool and positive source of interpersonal connection, but they are also a risk factor for addictive use, interpersonal problems, and emotional concerns (Chen et al. 858). Women, in particular, turn to smartphones for social communication and relationship building; they exhibit higher levels of attachment and dependence on phones than men (Hakoama and Hakoyama 19; Roberts et al., "The Invisible" 254). Such a dependence is predictive of anxiety and depression, and can compound partner relationship difficulties that may develop during the transition to parenthood (Chen et al. 858). Furthermore, with over 11 percent and 6 percent of mothers experiencing postpartum anxiety or depression, respectively, the more symptoms of depression and anxiety experienced, the more people turn to smartphones (Reck et al. 463; Saeb et al. 175). Smartphone use both reduces and increases symptoms of anxiety and depression (Saeb et al. 175). These concerns, along with an attachment focus on the smartphone instead of on the child, if addicted, can affect the mother-child bond as well as later child health, mental health, and peer interactions (Shapiro et al. 337; Teti et al. 375).

In the general population, one recent study has found that 4 percent of young adults are smartphone addicts, whereas 58 percent are likely addicts (Chen et al. 862). This problem is so prevalent in society that many people are not even aware of their dependence or addiction to smartphones (Roberts et al., "I Need" 13). An average usage of sixty-eight minutes per day is considered problematic, addictive, and an indicator of depressive symptoms, whereas an average use of seventeen minutes per day is found in nondepressed individuals (Saeb et al. 175). Since addictions in general, including smartphone addictions, are more likely to arise when attachment is insecure or when loneliness arises (Flores, 128; Tan et al. 606), smartphone addiction is, therefore, likely a greater concern for postnatal mothers than for fathers or for the general population.

Intervention or prevention may, therefore, be meaningful for this population. However, as this is an emergent issue for new mothers in contemporary society, there are scarce existing interventions or prevention approaches to minimize the risk of relationship difficulties, enhance mental health, and reduce the chance of maternal smartphone addiction. With further validation research, the following REAL approach could be incorporated into prenatal education programs or provided online to expectant parents in order to promote resilience.

COMPONENTS AND RATIONALE OF REAL TOOLS

REAL therapy or education is grounded in rational-emotive, attachment, and logotherapy practice and theory. It is a second wave positive psychology approach emphasizing the importance of all emotions, both lighter and darker emotions, in the journey toward meaning and wellbeing.

Rational Emotive Theory and Practice

Rational emotive [behaviour] therapy (RET) is a cognitive-behavioural approach developed by Albert Ellis to tackle problematic thinking, behaviours, and feelings as well as to teach problem-solving skills. In RET, it is believed that what people think leads to how they feel, and those feelings will last as long as they continue to have the underlying thoughts. Irrational, or "stinky thoughts," can mask the basic experience of pain and pleasure, healthy frustration, sadness, fear, and joy, and can lead to problematic or persistent anger, sadness, and fear. Stinky thoughts underlying these feelings generally include 1) *Should* statements, 2) *Must* statements, and 3) Awfulizing (catastrophic/spiralling) thinking. RET teaches more helpful ways of interpreting situations. In RET theory, people are responsible for their own wellbeing. In addition to learning how to think in a more helpful manner, RET also teaches helpful behavioural coping strategies. These RET skills aid in self-regulation, which, in turn, enables one to get along with others (Baumeister et al. 118), including within the family system, and to help build or maintain couple and mother-child attachment bonds.

Attachment-Building Theory and Practice

Hallmarks of secure attachment include missing beloved persons when they are away and contentment when they return (Scheff). Key features of attachment building include mutual attunement, empathy, and responsiveness to needs (Furnivall; Lieberman and Van Horn 11). Paying attention to a smartphone may prevent one from being attuned, empathic, and responsive to the needs of a child, or to a spouse's needs.

Mutual attunement involves the feeling and experience of being heard, seen, and understood by another (Siegel 3). Attachment injuries can occur through surrogates for attachment in the form of addiction, which interrupts mutual attunement and damages secure relationships (Johnson). Empathy involves understanding another person as if in their shoes while understanding how those experiences may be different (Rogers 78). Through a nonjudgmental stance, empathy includes asking questions to gain a true understanding of another's perspective or problem; empathy gives words to recognized feelings. Addiction, however, often hijacks empathy (Sack).

Responsiveness to needs involves understanding and addressing a child's or partner's needs in a timely, affectionate manner (Deward; Stephens). More specifically, responsiveness entails noticing distress (e.g., fear, anger, sadness, and frustration) and taking steps to offer comfort; it involves responding to the needs of the partner or child, setting boundaries, and providing consistent and predicable responses (Deward; Stephens). Responsiveness is also a skill that enhances a child's self-regulation and increases a child's resilience for mental health concerns. However, when primary attachment figures are addicted, including to smartphones, they are less responsive to a child's or to a partner's needs (Solis 135). Together, responsive and empathic attunement nurtures secure attachment in the couple and parent-child relationships.

Logotherapy Theory and Practice

Logotherapy is a meaning-based theory developed by Viktor

Frankl, an Austrian psychiatrist. Within logotherapy theory, people have freedom to make choices under any circumstance and with that choice, comes responsibility (Frankl 77). An awareness of smartphone addiction allows the freedom to make choices about smartphone use. It allows the freedom to choose meaningful or connective activities to minimize the potential for addiction, which is similar to the freedom to make meaningful choices if suffering from compulsion as in obsessive-compulsive disorder.

Another key tenet of logotherapy is that life has meaning under all circumstances and that each person must discover the meaning potential of each situation (Frankl 103). Pathways to meaning include the following: 1) doing a deed for others or creating work (e.g., personally valued work, volunteering, or baking together for the family); 2) experiencing something (e.g., engaging in valued activities, experiencing nature, or participating in mother-child activities); 3) encountering someone (creating secure relationships or attachment with others); and 4) choosing attitudes (changing though patterns). The most powerful of these meaning pathways, as well as the most sustainable, is secure attachment with others. Losing meaningful connections with others is so risky that individuals whose partner passes away have a 66 percent greater likelihood of death in the three months following the loss (Moon et al. 36). Given the critical importance of meaning derived from attachment security, the REAL framework singles out this pathway to meaning by including attachment theory in addition to logotherapy. Through using logotherapy tools to uncover meaning potentials, mothers can gain a sense of control over smartphone addiction. They can gain enhanced self-esteem, awareness of new possible experiences, and hope for the future (Erikson 5; Markstrom and Kalmanir 179; Search Institute; VanderVen 3).

Overall, the combination of rational-emotive, attachment, and logotherapy educational tools is designed to help couple and family suffering. As an educational approach to prevent maternal smartphone addiction and weather postnatal attachment storms, the goals are the following: 1) to reduce the risk of disconnection by building or maintaining attachment in the couple and mother-child relationship; 2) to enhance meaningful experiences and connections; and 3) to address "stinky" thoughts and behaviour, leading to healthy ways of thinking and acting that do not cloud the experience of pain, pleasure, and meaning.

A GUIDE TO REAL EDUCATION TO PROMOTE RESILIENCE TO SMARTPHONE ADDICTION AND BUILD MEANINGFUL ATTACHMENT

The following is a free resource aimed at enhancing meaningful couple and parent-child attachment as well as mental health, and reducing the risk of maternal smartphone addiction in the postnatal period. The brief exercises and psychoeducation presented in this chapter could be incorporated into existing prenatal programs for couples or could be used as a standalone approach.

Stage One: Enhancing Awareness

An awareness of potential problems facilitates change and openness to resilience-based information (Armstrong and Young 87; Prochaska and Velicer 38). As the majority of couples may be unaware that the postnatal period is risky for the marital bond, such information could be necessary for couples to take preventative action. The following is information for the program facilitator to help him or her provide information or as a take-home handout for couples.

Attachment Psychoeducation Script and Handout

Did you know that the transition to parenthood can shake the foundations of even the most stable relationship? This educational resource is designed to help you navigate the parental journey while maintaining secure partner and mother-child bonds.

Children and partners turn to important others for support, comfort, nurturance, meaningful connection, and protection. This is called "attachment."

There are three pathways to building secure attachment couple and parent-child bonds:

1) *Mutual attunement:* Mutual attunement means feeling heard, understood, and close to another person.
2) *Empathy:* Empathy is an awareness of another's needs

or feelings and then expressing or demonstrating this awareness.

3) *Responsiveness:* Responsiveness means responding to your partner's or child's needs or providing comfort in a timely, affectionate, and consistent manner.

Barriers to meaningful, secure attachment are as follows:

1) *Addictions:* Addictions are surrogates for meaning or meaningful attachment that people turn to for comfort when they feel distressed, bored, or lonely, instead of turning to one's partner. Addictions are not just alcohol, drugs, or smoking. Addictions are anything that takes the place of turning to one's partner to feel better or less stressed. Addictions are hard to give up and are time consuming.

2) *Difficulties with self-regulation:* This includes feeling stressed, angry, worried, or sad, without knowing how to feel better or calm down. When people can self-regulate, it means they can do things or think in ways that help them balance their mood.

3) *Neglect and dismissing:* When a child or partner is not put as a first priority, attention can be focused elsewhere. Neglect means not taking the time to hear or observe, understand, and respond to another's needs in a timely, consistent, and affectionate manner. Dismissing ignores another's needs by shutting down possibilities for a helpful or comforting response.

When couples introduce a baby into their world, barriers to secure attachment can creep in. These barriers could lead to increased conflict and a sense of loneliness, particularly for mothers. This resource provides hands-on tools designed to maintain and build secure, meaningful attachment, and helps to prevent a common emerging problem—namely smartphone addiction. These tools can also be applied beyond addiction to address other factors, such as mental health and wellbeing. They should not, however, be used in lieu of speaking to a mental health professional if you are experiencing significant stress, depressive, or anxious symptoms.

Awareness of Addiction Problem Script and Handout.

Research suggests that over half of younger adults may be smartphone addicts. Smartphone addiction risk rises as relationships become less secure or as symptoms of sadness (or "baby blues"), stress, boredom, or loneliness. Since increases in maternal loneliness, boredom, and anxiety are more common postnatal, new mothers may be at particular risk for smartphone addiction.

Smartphone addiction is a compulsion. Instead of turning to one's partner for comfort or to feel better, smartphone addicts will often turn to their device instead. Even if a person recently checked their smartphone and there was nothing of interest, the person may feel compelled to check again. In the short-term, smartphones can make a person feel better, calmer, and connected to a social network, but with chronic and addictive use, worries and depressive symptoms can increase. Smartphone addiction may also have negative consequences for the couple and parent-child relationship.

When parents pay more attention to their smartphone than to their immediate surroundings, this prevents them from responding to their baby or child's needs. It shows children that they are not as compelling as the smartphone. When children or partners are frustrated, worried, stressed, sad, or even excited, they have to compete for the attention and responsiveness of a smartphone-addicted person. Research has shown that this can have a negative impact on parent-child attachment security and on later child mental health. In partner relationships, smartphone addiction may contribute further to relationship challenges postnatal, as addicted partners can become less attuned, less empathic, and less responsive to one another's feelings; they can become more dismissive and neglectful, and have fewer meaningful interactions.

A key step to avoiding chronic smartphone addiction is preventing a problem or recognizing it as it emerges. The following is a checklist of smartphone addiction indicators based on the most common symptoms noted in the literature (Chen et al., 856; Saeb et al., 175). If you answer "yes" to any of these questions, some of the strategies described below may be helpful to minimize the risk of smartphone addiction.

Checklist of Addiction Risk for Smartphones (CARS)

•Do you spend more than an hour per day on your smartphone for nonwork-related activities?
•Do you find yourself passing time on your smartphone even though there could be more meaningful or productive things for you to do?
•Has the amount of time you spend on your smartphone been increasing?
•Do you interrupt activities, family meals, or time spent with others to text, tweet, answer emails, surf the Internet, Internet shop, or view social media?
•Do your check your phone many times a day even when you know there is likely nothing new or important to see?
•Do you spend more time texting, emailing, or participating in social media than participating in face-to-face interactions?
•Do you feel an intense urge to check your smartphone if it beeps, vibrates, or buzzes no matter what you are doing?
•If you forget your smartphone at home or it is out of service, do you feel stressed or uncomfortable?

Awareness of Choice and Responsibility Script and Handout

Life calls us to find meaning in our daily life through helpful actions and thoughts. At every moment, we have a decision to make about who we want to be, and how we want to respond in this moment and the next. Even under the most challenging circumstances, we have the freedom to choose our attitude. With freedom of choice, however, comes responsibility—accountability to ourselves to be the best we can be in any given moment, to make meaningful choices, and to do no harm to others. One of the most important harm-reduction choices is to engage in actions that enhance meaningful, secure attachment with a partner and child. The choice to focus on mutual attunement, empathy, and responsiveness, and to minimize neglectful, and dismissive behaviour has tremendous benefits for emotional health and wellbeing. When potential or existing problems come to our attention, we then have the freedom and responsibility to make healthy choices.

Stage Two: Building Meaningful Attachment

Practising Attunement (and Gratitude) Exercise

Sit face to face with your partner, knees touching. Look into your partner's eyes. Notice the colours and details you see—all the different flecks of colour, the length of lashes, the whiteness of the sclera, and the lines around the eyes (one minute). Listen to the movements your partner makes as he or she sits in the chair; hear the breaths your partner takes. Slowly take in the details of your partner's face, and observe the ridges of the bone structure, the shape of his or her nose, the softness of the lips, and the smoothness of the forehead. Observe your partner's hair. Hear your partner's movements. Feel the firmness of your partner's knees upon your own. Take your partner's hands and notice the feel of your partner's hands, the softness or roughness of the palms and fingers. Observe the lines and all the details of his or her hands. Think about what you appreciate about your partner as you return attention to your partner's eyes (one minute). When you are done, gently return your attention to the room around you and think about what this experience was like for you. What were you thinking? What were you feeling? Did you notice anything different than you do in your everyday interactions with your partner?

Practising Attunement Script Handout

Set aside time each day to observe your partner or child with as many senses as possible. Notice small details of their face or body language with your eyes. Listen to the sound of their movements or voice, the rise and fall of the sounds they make. Touch them and feel the softness or roughness of their skin, hair, face, or clothing. Drink in the scent of them or the taste of a kiss. Think about what you are appreciating during this time of observation. Taking time to truly notice another person and to think or express gratitude are building blocks of meaningful connection.

Empathy: Emotional Alarm Bells Script Handout

To be attuned to another—a partner, a baby, or a child—involves noticing subtle emotional cues. By the time a baby cries, they have already shown subtle body language cues indicating their needs and have moved to the crying stage.

To gain an understanding of another's concern, one can think of emotions as important "alarm bells." If you are sad, angry, or scared, or you see that another family member is sad, angry, or scared, this means you or they have a need—the emotional alarm is calling for a response. A partner could use empathic questioning in response to the emotional alarm bells and say something like the following: "I've noticed that you've been angry lately, and you also seem sad. What's going on? ...Could you tell me more about that? ...That must be really hard. Meaning is enhanced by actively listening to another special person, by truly understanding their need in the moment, and then by acting to meet that person's need,

Empathy: Baby Activity Worksheet

Scenario One: Your baby is kicking their legs with a smile on their face. What do you think this means? How could you respond?

___
___
___
___

Scenario Two: Your baby looks away from you as you're showing her a cool new toy with lights and sounds. What do you think this means? How could you respond?

___
___
___
___

Scenario Three: Your baby touches their mouth with their hand. Their jaw moves up and down. What do you think this means? How could you respond?

___
___
___
___

Scenario Four: Your baby mashes their eyes with the back of their hands. What do you think this means? How could you respond?

_____

_____

_____

_____

Scenario Five: Your baby twirls their hair, sucks their thumb, and then tugs or rubs another body part. What do you think this means? How could you respond?

_____

_____

_____

_____

Answers

Scenario One: The baby is happy. Share in the joy. Smile, talk, or sing back. If you were away from when the leg kicking began, this may alternatively be a sign that your baby was trying to get your attention. Go over and smile, talk, or sing.

Scenario Two: Looking away may mean that your baby is overstimulated. Respect your baby's need for a break. Engage in a more soothing activity.

Scenario Three: The baby may be hungry and be making a food face. These subtle cues often precede hunger cries. You could respond by feeding your child in a timely manner to appropriately meet this need. You can't spoil a baby. When babies have a need, they will show you. Responding to the need builds secure, meaningful attachment and reduces baby stress and anxiety. It shows the baby they can count on you.

Scenario Four: Eye rubbing or mashing is often accompanied by yawning and signifies tiredness. Even if your baby sleeps in different places (e.g., crib, stroller, or lap), have some predictable cues (e.g., soother, a sleep toy, or routine) to indicate to your child that it is time to sleep.

Scenario Five: Sucking, rubbing, tugging, or twirling can be a baby's attempt to self-soothe. If it seems they are not calming down, go to your baby, talk gently, rub them gently, or sing softly. If they tug their ear, it could mean that they are experiencing pain, such as gas pain or teething. Rub the baby gently, burp them, or get a teether if it seems teething may be the likely culprit.

Meaning-Building Problem Solving Using Empathy, Emotion-Recognition, Responsiveness, and Gratitude Exercise and Handout.

Problems that get in the way of meaningful interaction or lead to conflict are often predictable. Tricky issues and more minor ones often emerge in a similar manner or pattern each time and can, therefore, be addressed. Meaning-building problem solving can be done with one's partner or with a child (preschool age and older). It is a way to build attachment and make another feel heard and understood while solving the problem in a helpful manner. This method is a way to express one's need in a way leading to a productive discussion. With practice, meaning-building problem solving can feel more natural for even quite difficult situations.

To begin, for practice, think of a minor issue that's been bugging you—one that has come up more than once in your relationship (e.g., forgetting to put the toilet seat down; needing help from your partner with a certain aspect of baby care; child repeatedly doesn't wash hands after using the toilet). Follow these steps.

1) *Approaching the issue:* Approach your partner or child when you are both calm ("green" mood). It is challenging to solve problems with longer-term solutions if people are in a "yellow" (caution) or "red" (completely frustrated, sad, or afraid) mood. In relation to this recurrent small issue that's been bugging you, try to understand the problem from the other person's perspective without using blaming language (use safe "I" language, not "you" language): "I've noticed that X has been happening lately. What's going on?" (Other phrases may include "Could you help me understand that?").

2) *Empathic reflection:* When the person replies, reflect back your understanding: "If I understand correctly …" or "What you're saying is … ." Try to stay as close as possible to the other person's words (e.g., "I forget about the

toilet seat when I'm busy answering emails on my phone."
Reflection: "So what you're saying is that it's easy to forget
the toilet seat when you're on your phone.").

3) *Further clarification:* If the problem is still unclear, con-
tinue to ask probing questions. "I do not quite understand?"
"Could you help me to understand what is tricky about
this for you?" "Some people find this hard because of X.
Is that what's hard for you?" "Let's play a guessing game.
Let me know if I'm hot or cold. Is this what's tricky?"
"Can I take a guess?"

4) *Recognizing feelings and validating them:* Ask questions
such as "What was that like for you?" "How did you feel
about that?" Or make feeling statements. "You seem really frustrated when this happens." And make validation
statements: "That would be really frustrating." Addressing
feelings touches the person in a meaningful way at the
emotional level, which can lead to greater connection and
longer-term impact. Going beyond "content" into feelings
also helps people feel more heard and understood.

5) *Define the problem and check your understanding:*
Once you have a clear understanding of the problem, show
your understanding to the other person: "If I understand
correctly, the problem is…" "It sounds like the problem
is…" (e.g., "So you're not washing your hands because
you don't like the feeling of the wet towel.").

6) *Express your worry or frustration using "I" language:*
"My worry is that…" "It bothers me because…" (e.g., "It
worries me when you don't wash your hands because I'm
concerned that you might get sick." "It bothers me when
the full toilet seat is left up because I'm used to just the lid
being up and, sometimes in the middle of the night, I've
sat down on the porcelain and have almost fallen in.").

7) *Brainstorm potential solutions to the problem:* For this
step, it is important to be accepting and nonjudgmental of
all expressed ideas. Invite the other person to generate a
possible solution first. "Can you think of something that
we could try …" "What could we do about this?" (e.g.,
Mom: "Could you think of something that we could try so

that it may be easier for you to wash your hands?" Child: "We could get a big giant fan for me to dry my hands instead of the wet towel." Mom: "That would certainly dry your hands. That's one idea. I wonder if there are some other ideas too. Let's think about some. Maybe we could get you your own towel?").

8) *Open the door for further discussion:* Agree on a possible solution to try out next time the issue arises. Invite continued discussion if the solution does not end up solving the problem. (E.g., "Let's try your idea to put a night light in the bathroom so that I'll notice if the seat is up. If that doesn't work, then we can talk about this again.")

9) End with appreciation and gratitude to highlight the value of the meaningful discussion: "Thank you for taking the time to talk to me about this." "I appreciated...." "This was helpful. Thank you."

With practice, meaning-building problem solving can be used with more challenging issues.

Meaning-Building Problem Solving in Action

Mom: I've noticed that you start off playing nicely with your brother, but then you often ask for me to take him away. What's going on?

Child: This happened today. He was playing nicely with the dominoes, and I asked him not to knock down my pattern. He accidently stepped on my dominoes and knocked a few down. I put them back up, but he thought knocking them down was funny, so he did it again on purpose and he wouldn't stop knocking them down.

Mom: So, the two of you were playing, and then your brother started disturbing your play.

Child: Yes.

Mom: What was that like for you when he knocked the dominoes down?

Child: He was mean.

Mom: You thought he was being mean, so you were frustrated when he was knocking things down. Is that right?

Child: Yes. It's really frustrating when he wrecks my setups.

Mom: That would be frustrating. So, it sounds like the problem is that it's upsetting for you when the game suddenly changes to a "little brother tornado" that wrecks your setups.

Child: I want him to go away when he wrecks things so that it will teach him not to do that.

Mom: It makes sense that you don't want him to wreck your setup and that you'd like him to learn not to do that. My worry is that he is only two and two year olds may not understand that you're trying to teach him something. To him, he may just think that you're getting mad at him and don't want to play with him. It may even make him want to disturb your setup even more, since it becomes off limits or a game to him, and he gets attention. Then, you're so busy trying to force him not to play with the toys that he was enjoying that neither of you is having any fun. Hmm ... I'm wondering if there is a way that we could solve this problem so that you'll both end up having fun.

Child: I don't know. Maybe you could give him a Popsicle so that he'd be busy and I could keep playing with the toys.

Mom: That is one possibility. It would certainly mean that your setup wouldn't get knocked over. I'm trying to think if there are also some other possible ways that we could come up with to solve the problem. Hmm ... I'm wondering if it would work if you or I could distract him when he starts knocking things down. We could show him a part of the toy that he might enjoy or something similar that he might find very interesting, especially if you're playing with it. That way, once he started playing with the similar thing, or a part of the toy that you show him, then you'd both have something to play with that wasn't disturbing each other. Does that sound like a good idea?

Child: It may work.

Mom: How about we try that, and if it doesn't work, then let's try coming up with a different way to solve the problem.

Child: Okay.

Mom: Thank you for taking the time to talk to me about this. I appreciate that you were helpful and are willing to try something different so that you and your brother might both be happy.

Affection before Correction and Connection Script and Handout

To address a concern when a child or partner is in a "yellow" or "red" mood, begin with emotion recognition and acknowledge the difficulty so that the person feels understood. This shows attunement and affection. Emotional language also helps build longer-term self-regulation skills. Even in frustrating situations, affectionately acknowledge the emotion before correcting the behaviour. Then, correct the behaviour by stating your concern. Follow this with an offer to help, which can help the person feel supported and enhance connection (e.g., Affection: "I see that you are exhausted and frustrated that the baby is waking up in the night. It's rough for you. Correction: "I see how tired you are, but it's not okay that you yell at X when he wakes up in the night. He's just a baby and that's what babies do when they have a need. Your yelling scares him." Connection: "What can I do to help? Perhaps I could take him downstairs when he wakes up at 5:00 a.m. so that you can sleep in?"). Affection before correction and connection can be carried out with a child or a partner.

Stage Three: Invitation to Play the Game

Game Script and Handout

When it comes to smartphone addiction, the addiction is like a game. Who is going to win? You or the addiction? The addiction is trying to set the rules of the game. Check it whenever it buzzes. Check it even if you know there's nothing interesting. Surf aimlessly. Turn to the "hive mind" instead of your spouse when feeling sad, angry or scared. Get bored while watching your baby and hang out with the phone instead. Check the phone at the dinner table. Pay attention to your phone before you pay attention to your family.

Framing it as a game with rules means you can go on the offensive and set the rules yourself. As smartphone addiction is so common, and the postnatal period may be a particularly risky time for such addiction, it may be helpful to set your own limits or rules of the game for phone behaviour, such as time limits or blackout times for smartphone use. You may choose to check it during one of the day's meals and at another time of the day. You may choose to leave it in a purse or pocket while at the park or in another room while at the dinner table. Figure out what could work for you. If you stick to the rules, then you win the game. At times, it may be difficult to stick to the rules, but this can be a good indication or "alarm bell" that you're feeling stressed, sad, frustrated, or worried. When this happens, some of the tools described below may help you better manage your mood.

Brief Meaningful Engagement Exercise

Fill a balloon, hold it, and stand face to face with your partner. Now, think about a day that was quite frustrating. Imagine this day and the feelings you had. Really picture this frustrating day in your head. As you're thinking about this day, on a scale of zero to ten—with zero being "not at all frustrated" and ten being "completely frustrated"—think of how frustrated you are feeling right now as you're thinking about this day. Once you have thought about this, take the balloon, and for one minute, try to keep the balloon in the air with your partner without using your hands. If you drop it, just pick it up and keep going. After the minute is over, rate your frustration from zero to ten again. What did you notice?

Generate a list of five to ten brief and relaxing activities. Write this list down and put it somewhere visible. For some people, these activities may include listening to music, playing a musical instrument, having a shower or a bath, going for a walk, exercising, stretching or doing yoga for a few minutes, playing a short board game, petting a pet, reading, calling a friend, or having a hot drink. There are many possibilities.

Activities such as these can help us calm down, make healthier choices, and think in helpful ways.

Longer-Term Meaningful Engagement and Self-Care Script and Handout

To decrease the risk of boredom and enhance wellbeing, creating a self-care plan may be helpful. For self-care, there are often many free, subsidized, or lower-cost parent and baby activities offered in major cities (e.g., strollercize, mom-baby aqua fitness, community centre drop-in activities, and mom and baby yoga). Having regular opportunities to connect with other new mothers (or parents) can reduce stress and isolation, and can be quite meaningful for many. Regular date nights may also be helpful.

To give yourself time for something to look forward to each week, think of something that you could do that gives to others, allows you to experience something enjoyable, or provides you with joyful connection to others. Generate a list and make a plan for you and your partner to each have time to engage in these activities regularly, either together or individually. These activities may include a hobby, volunteering, exercising, or socializing with friends or family.

Relaxation Activities and Script and Handout

Pink elephant activity: Sit down on a chair beside your partner. I'd like you to imagine a pink elephant in the room. Is it big or is it little? Are its ears up or down? Is its tail curly or is it long and straight? Can you see the pink elephant? Really think about it. Imagine it in the room. Focus on the pink elephant.

Now stop thinking about the pink elephant. Stop thinking about it. Just don't think about the pink elephant. I don't want you thinking about that pink elephant.

What are you thinking about? (Most people are still thinking about the pink elephant.)

Do you notice your chair? Is it too hard? Is it too soft? Does it feel just right? Look at the colour of the chair and the colours you see around the room. Think about the sounds you hear in the room around you or anything you can smell. Notice how the light hits the objects in the room.

What's going on for you right now? What are you thinking about? What happened to the pink elephant?

This exercise illustrates that when we try to force ourselves to stop thinking or feeling a certain way, we often cannot. Similarly, when we are awake in the night and trying to get back to sleep, we cannot force ourselves asleep. Sleep will further elude us. However, when we take the time to notice our surroundings with each of our senses, or truly notice all the details of an activity that we're doing (e.g., eating, a walk outside), thoughts that are bothering us can become background noise, and we can experience our surroundings in a new way. Other relaxation and distraction activities can also help difficult thoughts and feelings become background noise. The goal, however, is not to abandon scared, angry or sad thoughts, but to just calm down a little bit so that we can think in a more helpful way. In fact, great meaning can emerge from fear, frustration, and sadness, so it is important not to abandon these feelings. It is just difficult to think clearly or find meaning when challenging feelings are too strong, so distraction and relaxation activities can help us to understand a situation with a new lens.

Mindful breathing activity: Sit comfortably and put one hand on your chest and one hand on your stomach. Breathe in deeply. Your chest should have little or no movement, but you should feel the hand on your stomach move. When we are stressed, we chest breathe, but when we are calm, we belly breathe. Similarly, belly breathing can calm our body down.

Now, close your eyes and focus on your breathing. Breathe in slowly through your nose and out through your mouth. Try to keep a nice, even pace. If you start to have other thoughts, gently return your attention to your breathing. Imagine your other thoughts like clouds slowly moving by. Don't judge your thoughts, just accept them as they are, and use your breathing as an anchor to return your attention.

After a couple of minutes, slowly open your eyes. How many times do you think that you breathed each minute? Fifteen times? Twenty times?

Now, try this exercise again, and see if you can breathe in and out three or four times in a minute. When you have done this and have opened your eyes, notice what you were thinking about compared to the first time that you tried this exercise. When we are truly focused on our breathing, our minds are often quieter. This exercise does, however, take practice. Try breathing three to four times in a minute for a few minutes at a time over the course of a couple weeks at a time that you set aside each day (e.g., during a baby feeding or while lying in bed). With good practice, many people find this tool helpful to calm spiralling thoughts in order to feel less stressed, worried, or frustrated.

Imagine if you were given a basketball and you had never played before. Could you get the ball into the basket? Would you even know how to do so? What would happen over time with practice? Breathing tools take practice to affect our thoughts and feelings in a helpful manner.

Imagery. Think of a relaxing scene. For some people, this might be lying on a beach, walking through the woods, petting their dog, or even standing on the ice in an arena. Pick something that would be relaxing for you. Now imagine this scene—all the little details that you can see, hear, touch, smell, and (potentially) taste. Think of it in as many details as possible.

Take a paper and draw this scene as a reminder to yourself. Don't worry about drawing ability. The goal is just to be able to remember the details or as a reminder to practice the activity. Imagery—or thinking about your relaxing scene with as many senses as possible—is another activity that can be used to quiet a racing mind.

Stinky Thoughts Exercise and Script and Handout

Left foot. Imagine that someone is walking across the room to get his cup of coffee. As he's going across the room, he steps on your left foot. What do you feel? (Pain?) How long do you think that feeling would last? (A short time?)

Now, as the man is walking back across the room, he steps on that same foot again. What do you feel this time? How long do you think that feeling would last?

The man finishes his coffee and is walking to the garbage with his empty cup, and he steps on your left foot again. What do you feel this time? (Anger?) How long do you think this feeling would last? (A lot longer?)

Isn't it interesting that the situation was the same, but you re-acted differently each time. What do you think caused to you feel different? It's not the situation that's different. I would suspect that thoughts started flowing in your head. As long as you have those "stinky" thoughts—such as "he should have been more careful" or "he must have done it on purpose"—you're going to continue to be angry, frustrated, worried, scared, or sad. Those thoughts block the brief, short-lived, and natural emotions of pain or joy in different situations. Often the thoughts are "shoulds" (I should/ he should have done that) or "musts" (I must do well/she must), or they are "awefulizing" thoughts (if this happens, then this will happen, and then this will happen). Our challenging feelings of anger, sadness, or worry will last as long as we continue to have these thoughts. If we can change our thinking, then we can change the way we feel. At certain times, we want to feel emotions such as grief following loss or fear in dangerous situations, but other times, we want to be able to have more control over our difficult feelings. We can do that by changing our thinking or our behaviours.

How we perceive the same situation differently: Story. Imagine if two people, Bob and Joan, were at work, and their boss became frustrated one morning with a project that they had done that didn't meet expectations. At lunchtime, their colleagues invite each of them to join them at a restaurant. Bob turned down the offer because he wasn't in the mood, as he was still feeling bad about the conversation with his boss. Joan, also still feeling bad about the conversation with her boss, decided to go out anyways. At the end of the day, Bob went home feeling sad and worried, thinking that he was going to fail at his job and that he was going to get fired and be a failure of a human being. At the end of the day, Joan went home feeling amused by some of the lunch hour conversations. She also thought about where she had gone wrong at work and came up with a good strategy based on her boss's feedback about what she could do differently next time to lead to a better outcome. She went to bed feeling calm.

Two people experienced the same situation, but the way they thought about the situation and the choices that they made led to different outcomes. Therefore, under any situation, we have the ability to choose our actions and attitudes in order to feel differently.

Thought detective activity. Think about your emotional alarm bells. Is there a situation that typically leads you to feel stressed, frustrated, or worried? What sort of thoughts get you feeling stressed, frustrated, or worried? This is a "stinky" thought. Now, imagine you are a thought detective. What does a detective do? A detective gathers evidence. Take the thought and gather evidence from a number of perspectives—whichever ones are applicable to the thought. What is the likelihood that this would happen? What would you say to a friend who had this thought? Do you have evidence to the contrary for this thought? Can you think of similar situations where the outcome was positive or you thought and felt differently? What is the opposite of this thought or a more balanced, helpful perspective?

As a detective, you want to make sure you have a solid case that can send the thought to court. After you examine the evidence, with your partner, take the opposite of the original thought or the balanced, more helpful perspective and defend it. Out loud, defend the more balance, helpful perspective. Initial activities—such as relaxation, distraction, and meaningful engagement—can help us slow down or calm down to be able to think in a more helpful way as a thought detective.

Thought Detective Example

Stinky thought: I must check my phone. Feeling: Mild anxiety until I check it.

What would happen if I didn't check it? I could miss something important. What is the likelihood that this would happen? I checked it not long ago, so I probably won't miss anything important. My family is more important, so my phone can wait.

What would I say to a friend who had this thought? You don't have to check your phone because you're doing, or could be doing, other things that may be more important or more meaningful right now.

Do I have evidence to the contrary? I've never missed anything important when I haven't checked my phone for a while, so I guess I don't have to check it right this second.

Similar situations. I spent all day at a waterpark with my family on the weekend and I didn't bring my phone. I had a great time with them, and I wasn't worried about missing anything important or checking my phone.

Opposite or more balanced perspective. It would be nice to check my phone, but I can do it later when my husband is reading the newspaper and the children are sleeping. Nothing bad will happen if I don't check it now.

Summary Script and Handout

The tools presented in this resource are aimed at improving mood and thinking; maintaining and building couple and parent-child attachment; enhancing meaning and helpful coping; and reducing the potential for smartphone addiction, which can potentially disrupt mood and attachment. With regular prenatal practice of these skills, it may be easier to draw on these tools postnatal to prevent possible difficulties. Babies do not come with a manual, but a toolkit of resources can help you more smoothly navigate the parenting journey.

CONCLUSION

The REAL program described in this chapter provides a standardized protocol for longitudinal research with pre- and postnatal couples. All of the tools presented are grounded in existing evidence-based theories of counselling, but rational-emotive, attachment, and logo-therapy approaches are often considered differing and opposing schools of thought. The amalgamation of these approaches into a second wave positive psychology framework is unique. This framework recognizes the importance of darker emotions, such as sadness in leading to positive outcomes (Ivtzan et al.131). In a REAL approach, darker emotions are "alarm bells" to indicate an opportunity to make choices about thoughts and actions that may lead to meaningful directions. With further research, this program will hopefully become a gold standard in a much-needed area to enhance postnatal attachment, provide helpful tools to manage mood, and potentially prevent maternal smartphone addiction.

WORKS CITED

Armstrong, Laura Lynne, and Kaitlyn Young. "Mind the Gap: Person-centred Delivery of Mental Health Information to Post-Secondary Students." *Psychosocial Intervention*, vol. 24, no. 2, 2015, pp. 83-87.

Baumeister, Roy, et al. "Self-Regulation as a Key to Success in Life." *Improving Competence Across the Lifespan,* edited by Dolores Pushkar, et al., Plenum, 1998, pp. 117-32.

Chen, Li, et al. "Mobile Phone Addiction Levels and Negative Emotions among Chinese Young Adults: The Mediating Role of Interpersonal Problems." *Computers in Human Behavior*, vol. 55, 2016, pp. 856-66.

Cronin, Camille. "First-time Mothers-Identifying their Needs, Perceptions and Experiences." *Journal of Clinical Nursing*, vol. 12, no, 2, 2003, pp. 260-67.

Deward, Gwen. "The Science of Attachment Parenting." *Parenting Science*, 2014, www.parentingscience.com/attachment-parenting.html. Accessed 2 May 2018.

Doss, Brian, et al. "Marital Therapy, Retreats, and Books: The Who, What, When, and Why of Relationship Help-Seeking." *Journal of Marital and Family Therapy*, vol. 35, no.1, 2009, pp. 18-29.

Ellis, Albert. *Rational Emotive Behavior Therapy: It Works for Me, It Can Work for You*. Albert Ellis Institute, 2004.

Erikson, Erik. *Insight and Responsibility*. Norton, 1964.

Flores, Philip J. *Addiction as an Attachment Disorder*. Jason Aronson, Inc., 2011.

Frankl, Viktor. *Man's Search for Meaning*. Simon and Schuster, 1986.

Furnivall, Judy. *Attachment-informed Practice with Looked after Children and Young People*. IRISS Insight, 2011.

Gottman, John, and Julie Gottman. "3 Tips for Couples to Stay Connected After Baby." *The Gottman Institute*, 2016, www.gottman.com/blog/3-tips-for-couples-to-stay-connected-after-baby/. Accessed 2 May 2018.

Hakoama, Mikiyasu, and Shotaro Hakoyama. "The Impact of Cell Phone Use on Social Networking and Development among College Students." *The American Association of Behavioral and Social Sciences,* vol. 15, 2013, pp. 1-20.

Ivtzan, Itai, et al. *Second Wave Positive Psychology: Embracing the Dark Side of Life*. Routledge, 2016.

Johnson, Sue. *Emotionally Focused Couples Therapy: 6-Week Training*. Jack Hilrose and Associates, 2016.

Lieberman, Alicia, and Patricia Van Horn. *Psychotherapy with Infants and Young Children: Repairing the Effects of Stress and Trauma on Early Attachment*. Guilford Press, 2008.

Markstron, Carol, and Heather Kalmanir. "Linkages between

the Psychosocial Stages of Identity and Intimacy and the Ego Strengths of Fidelity and Love. *Identity: An International Journal of Theory and Research*, vol. 1, no. 2, 2001, pp. 179-96.

Moon, J. Robin, et al. "Short- and Long-Term Associations between Widowhood and Mortality in the United States: Longitudinal Analyses. *Journal of Public Health*, vol. 36, no. 3, 2014, pp. 382-89.

Prochaska, J.O, and W.F. Velicer. "The Transtheoretical Model of Health Behavior Change." *American Journal of Health Promotion*, vol. 12, no. 1, 1997, pp. 38-48.

Reck, C, et al. "Prevalence, Onset and Comorbidity of Postpartum Anxiety and Depressive Disorders." *Acta Psychiatrica Scandinavica,* vol. 118, no. 6, 2008, pp. 459-68.

Roberts, James, et al. "I Need My Smartphone: A Hierarchical Model of Personality and Cell-Phone Addiction." *Personality and Individual Differences*, vol. 79, 2015, pp. 13-19.

Roberts, James, et al. "The Invisible Addiction: Cell-Phone Activities and Addiction Among Male and Female College Students." *Journal of Behavioral Addictions*, vol. 3, no 4., 2014, pp. 254-65.

Rogers, Carl. *A Way of Being*. Houghton Mifflin, 1980.

Sack, David. "Is Empathy an Outdated Concept?" *Psych Central*, 2015, /blogs.psychcentral.com/addiction-recovery/2012/03/empathy/. Accessed 2 May 2018.

Saeb, Sohrab, et al. "Mobile Phone Sensor Correlates of Depressive Symptoms Severity in Daily-Life Behavior: An Exploratory Study." *Journal of Medical Internet Research*, vol. 17, no. 7, 2015, pp. 175.

Scheff, Thomas. "Genuine Romantic Love: Attraction, Attachment, and Attunement." *New English Review,* 2010, www.newenglish-review.org/Thomas_J._Scheff/Genuine_Romantic_Love:_Attraction,_Attachment,_and_Attunement/. Accessed 2 May 2018.

Search Institute. *40 Developmental Assets for Children Grades K-3*. Minneapolis, 2010.

Siegel, Dan. *The Mindful Brain: Reflection and Attunement in the Cultivation of Well-Being*. Norton & Company, 2007.

Shapiro, Alyson F, et al. "Bringing Baby Home Together: Examining the Impact of a Couple-Focused Intervention on the Dynamics Within Family Play." *American Journal of Orthopsychiatry,* vol.

81, no. 3, 2011, pp. 337-50.

Solis, Jessica M, et al. "Understanding the Diverse Needs of Children Whose Parents Abuse Substances." *Current Drug Abuse Reviews,* vol. 5, no. 2, 2012, pp. 135-47.

Stephens, Karen. "Responsive Parenting Nurtures Infants' Secure Attachments." *Eastern Florida,* 2007, www.easternflorida.edu/community-resources/child-development-centers/parent-resource-library/documents/responsive-parenting-and-infant-attachment.pdf. Accessed 2 May 2018.

Tan, Cetan, et al. "Loneliness and Mobile Phone." *Procedia-Social and Behavioral Science,* vol. 103, 2013, pp. 606-11.

Teti, Douglas, et al. "Maternal Depression and the Quality of Early Attachment: An Examination of Infants, Preschoolers, and their Mothers." *Developmental Psychology,* vol. 31, no. 3, 1995, pp. 364-76.

Thompson, Geoffrey. "Meaning Therapy for Addictions: A Case Study." *Journal of Humanistic Psychology,* vol. 56, no. 5, 2016, pp. 457-82.

VanderVen, Karen. *Promoting Positive Development in Early Childhood: Building Blocks for a Successful Start.* Springer, 2008.

IV.
Rethinking Practice and Policy

I didn't find out I was pregnant until the beginning of my second trimester. I had gone out west to escape a bad relationship and just stumbled into another one. I was drinking a lot as well as using whatever drugs showed up where I was staying. I lived with this guy because I had a roof over my head, and he provided me with booze and drugs. When I took the pregnancy test, and it was positive, I was scared to death. I knew I wanted to keep it, but I also knew I had to get away from the father for me and my baby to have a chance. So I came back home, but my parents were less than thrilled, and they did not want me living with them. So now I was pregnant, homeless, and trying to stop using drugs and alcohol, but it was basically impossible. I had very few options available to me. I ended up staying at a shelter for pregnant women, which was good because I had good food and a place to stay, but they wouldn't tolerate anything but abstinence from drugs and alcohol. If you got caught, you would get kicked out, and they would call child-protective services. Most of us wanted to quit and hated ourselves for continuing to use. We had to hide it and just not talk about it. Hiding it made it worse because of the guilt and because we weren't actually getting the help we needed. I saw some of the girls get kicked out for getting caught. They packed up their stuff in garbage bags and sent them out on the street. I get that women have to try to quit stuff—I loved my baby, and I wanted it to be healthy. I knew I was having a boy, and I tried so hard to do everything right. I was already stressed that I had drank so much before I found out I was pregnant and had cut back a lot since then, but when I slipped, I couldn't tell anyone or I'd be on the street. I don't think we should be punished for making a mistake. I don't think I've gotten the help I needed, and I'm not sure what I will do once he is here. If I mess up then, they'll just take him away from me, and I will have nothing.

—*Brigitte, age nineteen*

10.
Beyond Abstinence

Harm Reduction during Pregnancy and Early Parenting

LENORA MARCELLUS, NANCY POOLE, AND NATALIE HEMSING

D RUG AND ALCOHOL USE during pregnancy remains a significant public health and social concern in Canada. Women of
childbearing age from all social and economic groups continue
to use tobacco, alcohol, prescription and street drugs, with levels and types of use varying according to age, ethnicity, income,
ability, and occupational/mothering roles and other determinants
(Poole and Dell 1). Over the decades, there have been shifts in
substances used, around street drugs in particular—from heroin
to cocaine to crystal methamphetamine to prescription opioids (S.
Boyd 28). In recent years, public attention has been drawn both
nationally and internationally to the issue of prescription opioid
use, and pregnancy in particular, because of the specific clinical
issue of neonatal withdrawal (or neonatal abstinence syndrome,
NAS). Suzanne Turner et al. report that the incidence of NAS in
Ontario has increased fifteen-fold from 0.28 per 1000 live births
in 1992 to 4.29 per 1000 live births in 2011(E57). Due to stigma,
shame, and legal and child protection consequences, it is highly
likely that the data available on patterns of use during pregnancy
is a significant underrepresentation of actual use (Lange et al. 9).

Substance use during pregnancy is linked to varying degrees of
harm for women and fetuses and/or infants—depending on the
level and type of use, the impact of broader social determinants of
health, and the intersections across these dimensions. Historically,
pregnant women who use substances or have substance problems
or addictions have been subjected to judgmental abstinence-based
messages related to their substance use, and they experience a lack

of assistance on these intersecting health dimensions. Supporting reduction in, and cessation of, substance use requires a comprehensive understanding of issues such as the following: the patterns or epidemiology of substance use, influences on this use, pathways to and from use, readiness to change, intervention strategies, and community context.

Harm-reduction approaches have developed globally as an alternative approach to the dominant abstinence discourse. This pragmatic spectrum of approaches has been a part of prevention and management activities for many years in Canada. In this chapter, we explore the concept of harm reduction in the context of pregnancy and early parenting. We provide an overview of the development of the approach, briefly review harm reduction literature from a gendered perspective, and highlight current evidence underpinning the development and implementation of prevention and management strategies for women and their families. We address the ethical and political tensions arising within health and social communities when care is organized within popular philosophies of woman and family-centred care, and we explore how determinants of health such as the experience of trauma and violence affect women's health. Exemplars from integrated maternity care programs across Western Canada are incorporated to demonstrate key components of an approach that is harm-reduction oriented and trauma informed. A broader conception of the support needs of mothers who use substances or have addictions, as well as the support needs of their children, is also presented.

DEVELOPMENT OF THE CONCEPT OF HARM REDUCTION

What Is Harm Reduction?

The Canadian Harm Reduction Network (CHRN) currently defines harm reduction as the policies, programs, and practices that reduce the negative health, social, and economic consequences of the use of legal and illegal psychoactive drugs without necessarily reducing drug use (CHRN). The focus is on reducing harm rather than preventing substance use (Tammi and Hurme 84). A number of key principles have been identified nationally and internationally that inform the harm-reduction approach. These principles are described in Table 1.

Two key pillars underpin harm reduction. First is a pragmatic approach that takes a value-neutral stance to drug use itself. Within a pragmatic approach, it is acknowledged that substance use can be a historical and cultural practice and that some level of use is inevitable and to some degree typical in society (Tammi and Hurme 85). Second, a social justice and human rights perspective provides the opportunity to approach substance use as a health issue that is affected by inequities in access to healthcare and resources for daily living, such as poverty, inadequate and unsafe housing, and lack of social support (Stimson and O'Hare 93; Pauly 4-6). Social justice as an ethical framework involves examination of structural barriers that can themselves cause harm, such as institutionalized stigma and punitive social policies. Together, these two pillars create a theoretical, philosophical and ethical foundation for creating services that can enhance access to health and social resources and can improve outcomes for individuals, families, and communities.

How Did This Concept Develop?

At the turn of the century in North America, medical providers saw abstinence as the only appropriate approach to management of the disease of addiction, and program models such as Alcoholics Anonymous grew in popularity across the country (Canadian Nurses Association 15; Einstein 260). In the early 1970s, harm-reduction researchers who conducted epidemiological studies received highly critical responses. As a result, there was a stifling of attempts to offer services that were anything except abstinence oriented.

At the same time, the roots of harm reduction were emerging in the Netherlands in response to a backlash against excessive police force against student substance use. Public commissions were established to pragmatically determine how to balance interpretation of the law and the best interests of individuals within the context of minor drug experiences (Roe 244). Drug-related law enforcement itself began to be seen as problematic. A wide range of social classes were engaging in drug use rather than it being restricted to small and socially marginalized groups. A balance of harms approach

Table 1. Principles of Harm Reduction and Program Exemplars: International Harm Reduction Association (http://www.ihra.net/what-is-harm-reduction)

Principle	Description	Program Practice Exemplars
Targeted at risks and harms	Focusses on specific risks, harms, and individual factors so that interventions can be tailored.	Acknowledgement that harms and risks emerge from factors in addition to the substance use itself Range of practical services are provided that address determinants of health.
Evidence based and cost effective	Based practice and policy on the strongest available evidence and on approaches that are practical and feasible within existing contexts and resources.	Teams use evidence from multiple fields and disciplines. Cost benefit analysis is included in program evaluations. Planning occurs within the larger community continuum of maternal and family services.
Incremental	Services designed to meet the needs of individuals where they are at in their lives from a facilitative perspective where any small gain or step is seen as a benefit.	Team members practice from motivational interviewing, brief intervention, and appreciative inquiry approaches. Women are supported to identify their most pressing needs and those are worked on first. This may not be the substance use.
Dignity and compassion	Accepting people for who they are and avoiding stigma, judgment, and marginalization.	Trauma-informed and culturally safe care is practised Careful use of nonstigmatizing language.

Universality and inter-dependence of rights	All individuals have the right to health, social support, and freedom from deliberate harm.	Access to required health and social supports is facilitated, using low barrier considerations. Rights of mother and baby are considered together Practices are examined to ensure they are not biased based on substance use.
Challenging policies and practices that maximize harm	Policies, laws, and practices themselves can be harmful, intentionally or unintentionally.	Community collaboration occurs to examine routine practices that can be harmful, such as universal drug testing and automatic child removal practices. Sex and gender based analysis is conducted with policies and practices.
Transparency, accountability, and participation	Encouragement of open dialogue, consultation and debate with a wide range of stakeholders. In particular, people who use drugs should be meaningfully involved in decisions that affect them.	Development of women's advisory councils to support programs. Continuous evaluation with strong qualitative component to highlight women's voices and experiences.

was recommended, which prompted consideration of the impact of strict drug enforcement for minor drug-related offences on the individual, society, and legal system (Roe 244).

At the same time that harm reduction was developing as an alternative to abstinence for substance use, a similar consideration of a balance of harms approach was being introduced in response to the issue of HIV/AIDS among injection drug users. Needle exchange programs were started in 1984 in the Netherlands, and by 1986, needle exchange programs were available in several European cities and in Sydney, Australia. In 1987, Russel Newcombe published the first paper on drug-related harm reduction. The first needle exchange program in the USA started in New York City in 1989, and the first in Canada started in Vancouver in 1989; similar programs began shortly after in Toronto and Montreal (Marlatt et al. 16). Harm-reduction strategies gained in popularity as public health and policymakers looked for alternatives to legal enforcement of drug laws and for pragmatic solutions to prevent the spread of infectious diseases such as Hepatitis C and HIV (particularly from drug users and sex workers to the general population). Health authorities and community activists increasingly evaded or challenged drug laws to provide clean syringes and condoms to drug users—marking a shift from identifying these groups as criminal subcultures to seeing these groups as a population with specific health needs (Canadian Nurses Association 21; Roe 244; Einstein 258).

In British Columbia, particularly Vancouver, HIV/AIDS and drug activists, public health officials and policymakers engaged as a coalition and developed the City of Vancouver four pillar approach, which included strategies from harm-reduction, prevention, treatment, and enforcement perspectives (MacPherson 31). This approach was seen nationally and globally as an innovative strategy for engaging with communities and addressing the issue at multiple levels. In 2003, InSite, a safe injection site, opened (Hathaway and Tousaw 124; N. Boyd 234). Despite strong evidence about the positive impact of this harm-reduction approach and continued spread of harm-reduction policies and practices globally, there have been continued political and ideological challenges to the approach (N. Boyd 236).

Critiques of the Concept

Gordon Roe notes that within the harm-reduction movement, there has been a historic divide between medicalized and activist forms of harm reduction. Medicalized forms of harm reduction typically occur within the realm of public and preventive health and are employed by those who view harm reduction as a means of reducing harm to the individual. Activist forms of harm reduction are typically espoused by community based and/or activist groups who view it as a means of addressing broader social-structural inequities (Roe 245). Roe argues that without the focus on social change and critical analysis of the roots of risk, the concept and practice of harm reduction will only function as another institutionalized regulation of behaviour rather than paving long-term solutions to underlying societal and political causes (248). A related critique is harm-reduction principles have been applied with limited critical analysis of risk factors that take into consideration sex and gender, culture, and other social determinants of health (Hathaway and Tousaw 14; Seddon 102).

BRINGING IN SEX AND GENDER

Of the many determinants of health that have a bearing on substance use, sex and gender factors and influences have not been well accounted for in the design of Canadian substance use prevention, treatment, or harm-reduction strategies. In 2007, *Highs and Lows: Canadian Perspectives on Women and Substance Use*, edited by Nancy Poole and Lorraine Greaves, brought attention to sex and gender issues as a collection of articles, interviews, narratives, and guidelines reflecting the thought and action being applied in the decade between 1996 and 2006. The over ninety contributors to the *Highs and Lows* book came from many disciplines and professions, research and practice, and from women themselves with experience of substance use problems. The contributors identified the challenge of providing appropriate responses to substance use issues, old and new, legal or illegal. They talked about how providing an empowering women-centred and mother-centred response is not always easy in complex, traditional, or male-dominated systems.

In the larger literature, sex-based issues and differences have been identified and include the following: metabolic differences, body shape and size issues, brain response characteristics such as dopamine receptivity, nicotine dependence trajectories, and links with depression (Baker et al. 51). These biological features of substance use need to be part of the evidence underlying harm-reduction programing and policy design affecting girls and women. There are also important gendered influences on, and pathways to, substance use to be considered. For example, sexual and physical abuse are strongly related to problems with substance use. Circumstances of homelessness or poverty (which can be experienced differently by women, men, trans, and others within the gender identity continuum) can further complicate the paths to treatment, recovery, and wellness (Logan et al. 336; Varcoe 264). Mothering and policies—such as child welfare policies, which disproportionately affect substance-using mothers—are critical gendered influences on women's substance use and engagement in support services (Drabble and Poole 128; Greaves and Poole 215; Reid et al. 231). Compounding the risks and pressures to use substances is the societal stigma directed at women and particularly mothers who use substances, which creates often overwhelming barriers to accessing support and treatment (Poole and Isaac 14).

In Canada, there has been some advancement of critical feminist and intersectional views, notably in the publications of Susan Boyd, who sees drug use as shaped by "the social and cultural environment, as well as by drug laws and by social service, medical and non-government policy" (S. Boyd 12). She describes women's and men's use of substances as "mediated by race, class and gender in conjunction with history, culture, politics and the legal and sociological environment"(S. Boyd 13). Such a gender lens highlights how "women are socially controlled in ways that differ from men, and how the regulation of women centers on reproduction, mothering, double standards of morality, social and legal subordination" (S. Boyd 13).

However, with the exception of thinkers such as Susan Boyd and Lenora Marcellus, the substance use field overall remains gender blind (111). Nancy Campbell and Elizabeth Ettorre state the following in the opening of their book titled *Gendering Addiction*: "Knowledge making practices in the drug research and treatment arena make it resistant to acknowledging the gendered, classed and racialized power differentials that structure the lives of drug-using women. Without such knowledge, we argue that what we need to know about women's specific needs will continue not to be known" (1). Some authors argue that an intersectional analysis should be applied to harm-reduction approaches to reflect the interconnections between substance use, gender, class, race, homelessness, poverty, violence, and trauma that women experience. Victoria Smye et al. critique harm-reduction strategies for focussing too narrowly on the direct harms of substance use, and for failing to address the underlying determinant of substance use (7-9). Applying an intersectional lens to analyze the experiences of women receiving methadone maintenance therapy (MMT) in Vancouver, BC, they found that women frequently cited challenges linked to the "intersectionality of disadvantages": how stigma and discrimination affect accessing and using MMT, and how the policy context of MMT intersects with women's social locations to limit women's lives and opportunities (Smye et al. 6).

Attention to sex and gender influences on substance use and addiction, and tailoring of harm-reduction approaches in response has fallen, as we shall see in the next section, to community-based services reaching and engaging pregnant women, mothers, and children—groups that are willing to work with gender, culture, trauma, harm reduction, and other complex concepts and approaches.

DEVELOPMENT OF INTEGRATED PROGRAM MODELS

Substance use during pregnancy is a highly contested territory. It has often been treated as a criminal act to be punished rather than a public health issue to be addressed via health promotion and harm-reduction measures (Lange et al. 9; Paltrow and Flavin 332). The punitive approach has the counterproductive result of preventing women from seeking prenatal care and restricting their access to support for substance use problems or prenatal care. In Canada, community-based programs reaching pregnant women have called for reframing the issue to address the structural issues that shape women's drug use. In the view of providers working in these programs, a harm reduction approach includes the following: supporting women's self-determination of their needs and readiness to change; addressing gendered determinants of health and wellness such as housing and experience of violence; delinking maternal drug use from child abuse in legislation and practice; and providing pregnant women and mothers with opportunities for treatment (Pauly et al. 8; Poole et al., *Women-Centred* 2; Cusick 7; Khandor and Mason 50). There are multiple indicators of a harm-reduction framework for pregnant and parenting women.

Specifically, these services engage program participants who are actively using alcohol and other substances; changes in substance use, not only abstinence and participation in treatment, are used as indicators of progress. In this context, participants find it safe to discuss the pros and cons of substance use, and any changes they would like to make in their use. Participants also have a legitimate say in all aspects of their services and supports and choice as to the level and type of change in substance use and related health concerns is honoured. Importantly, support addresses the stigmatization, blame/shame, guilt, grief, loss, trauma and related harms associated with substance use. Finally, a range of practical supports are offered in highly accessible ways. In this view, when a service provider supports a pregnant woman who is having difficulty stopping drinking to reduce her alcohol use and to take maternal vitamins, they are practising harm reduction (Nathoo et al. 97).

In the face of the complex, interrelated issues that women who are pregnant and use substances experience, abstinence advice is often ineffective in supporting reduction or cessation of substance use (S. Boyd 172; NDARC 1). Harm-reduction programs do not require abstinence as a condition for accessing services; they recognize that behaviours occur along a continuum of risk (Flavin and Paltrow 232; Nathoo et al. 97). New and innovative models of community care have been emerging in Canada over the past twenty-five years, which address the presence of these complex issues and incorporate harm reduction principles. These integrated program models are "one-stop-shop" types of programs. They include services for women that address mental and physical health issues and that provide practical support, including parenting or child services (e.g., prenatal care and parenting classes) and substance use treatment (Marcellus et al. 501; Nathoo et al. 97; Niccols et al., "Integrated Programs" 2).

In the early 1990s, two pioneering integrated programs emerged in Canada: Breaking the Cycle (BTC) in Toronto and Sheway in Vancouver's Downtown Eastside. Planning for BTC began when agencies in Toronto collaborated to consult with the community and scan for innovative models. Partners at the time represented health, social service, mental health, and addiction sectors, including Mothercraft, the Jean Tweed Centre, the Children's Aid Society, the Hospital for Sick Children, and the City of Toronto Public Health Department (Motz 5; Racine et al. 281). A key principle in developing BTC was to design services around the needs of families rather than having vulnerable families trying to access multiple fragmented services. Harm reduction was identified as a core element of the BTC theoretical framework.

The Sheway Program in the Downtown Eastside in Vancouver was another early innovator in this field. A 1993 study conducted by Chris Loock and colleagues provided evidence of the significant impact of substance use on births in that neighbourhood (6). At that time, nearly all women who were showing up at the hospital emergency room to give birth had their children removed from their care, and received little help or support with their substance use issues. This work sparked the development of a coalition of health and social services providers to bring an integrated program to the community. Initial funders were the BC Children's Hospital, Vancouver Health Department, the Ministry of Social Services and the Vancouver Native Health Society (Marshall et al. 19; Poole 2). A harm-reduction approach was considered a key value and component of the service-delivery model.

Since the launch of BTC and Sheway, teams from other communities across Canada have continued to learn from and adapt this model to their own context. Collectively, evaluation data and research evidence have validated the effectiveness of this model. There are currently a number of programs in different stages of development across Canada. Organizations such as the Canada FASD Research Network Action Team on FASD Prevention from a Women's Health Determinants Perspective provide opportunities for national networking and mentorship on program development and evaluation. The Prevention Action Team has developed a consensus document on the fundamental components of FASD prevention, including harm reduction (Canada FASD Northwest Research Network 1-3).

KEY COMPONENTS OF HARM-REDUCTION PROGRAMS FOR PREGNANT WOMEN AND MOTHERS

All integrated programs at their core are woman centred and

child focussed; they support mother and child together within the context of their families and communities (Marcellus et al. 509). In this model, efforts are made to support both mother and child rather than focussing narrowly on the wellbeing of the fetus or child. The framing of substance use as problematic is rooted in an individualized understanding of health agency and in gendered roles and responsibilities that position women as "fetal incubators" and the main caregivers of children (Benoit et al. 260). In contrast, women-centred harm-reduction programs work collaboratively with and advocate for women, and seek to empower women by engaging them in their own health and social care (Canada FASD Northwest Research Network 2; Nathoo et al. 100).

These programs offer various forms of parenting support or education and training to enable women to maintain care for their child or to support them if they choose other forms of parenting (e.g., part time, elder support, open adoption) (Niccols et al., "Integrated Programs" 10). Studies are emerging that demonstrate these programs are effective in reducing substance use by women, in facilitating access to prenatal care, and in improving maternal, child, and parenting outcomes (Kramlich and Kronk 325; Milligan et al. 551; Niccols et al., "Integrated Programs" 10; Niccols et al., "Maternal Mental Health" 472; Ordean et al. e468-9). Table 2 summarizes some of the key impacts being noted in harm-reduction programs. Programs are flexible and tailored to meet the immediate needs as prioritized by women themselves.

Supporting women from a harm-reduction perspective also requires considerations of a trauma-informed approach. A history of violence and trauma has been found to be a commonly shared experience for women who use substances (Canada Women's Foundation and BC Society of Transition Houses 7). In a recent study with pregnant women and mothers with substance use issues who had accessed harm-reduction services in Vancouver, women describe continuing experiences of trauma, extending from childhood into adulthood (Torchalla et al. 4). Individual and environmental and structural conditions of disadvantage exacerbate one another, which creates barriers to substance use and trauma treatment.

From pragmatic and social justice perspectives, components of harm-reduction programs are often developed at four intersect-

Table 2. Impact of Participation in Harm-Reduction Focussed Programs

Outcome	Studies
Increase engagement and retention in prenatal services and addiction treatment.	Motz; Racine; Poole; Wodinski, Wanke and Khan
Increase referrals to other health and social services and increase engagement in services following birth.	Racine; Poole; Wodinski; Wanke and Khan
Reduce alcohol and drug use and improve nutrition.	Racine, Poole; Nota Bene and BCCEWH; Wodinski, Wanke and Khan
Reduce healthcare costs.	Racine; Wodinski; Wanke and Khan; Thanh
Improve health outcomes for women and their babies, including fewer preterm births and babies born with low birth weight.	Marshall et al.; Racine; Wodinski; Wanke and Khan
Increase the number of babies discharged home with their mothers following birth.	Racine; Poole; Nota Bene & BCCEWH
Encourage breastfeeding, early attachment, and improve childhood development outcomes.	Motz; Poole; Niccols et al., "Integrated Programs"; Niccols et al., "Maternal Mental Health"

ing levels: specific prenatal and postpartum health services for women; social supports that address access to services related to determinants of health (income assistance, housing); program features (trauma informed, part of a continuum of community maternity services); and policy (child-protection regulations). As harm-reduction programs continue to develop across Canada, they all in some form address these levels in ways adapted to their local community resources and circumstances. In this next section, brief descriptions of program elements from six Canadian programs are provided that demonstrate how programs may be diverse in structure and function but also collectively grounded in harm reduction principles. Key program elements related to the principles of harm reduction are provided in Table 1.

Breaking the Cycle (BTC) Program

BTC is a community-based and cross-systemic early identification and prevention program, in which families receive multiple services in one setting, including the following: addictions counselling, health and medical services, parenting support, early childhood interventions, child development assessments, childcare support, FASD diagnostics, and support for basic needs. BTC also provides home visitation and street outreach services. Evaluation of this program reveals that the empathy and respect demonstrated by the outreach workers facilitated positive relationships and that this was associated with improvements in mother-child relationships as well as women's relationships with other women, friends, and family (Motz 53). Further evaluation has shown that women who accessed services were more likely to follow through with treatment plans, and were more likely to maintain child custody and sustain recovery from substance use following discharge (Racine et al. 286).

Sheway Program

The Sheway program focusses on fostering women's empowerment, choice, and control. Women choose which services they feel are most needed or useful as well as the staff who will support their care. Staff can then respond to women's identification of an issue by offering support in linking women with the services they need. The key goals of Sheway are to support mothers capacity as parents/caregivers, to support access to prenatal care, to provide services and referrals to reduce risk behaviours, and to promote the health and nutrition of children, and of women accessing Sheway services (Marshall et al. 21; Poole 3). The agency is open daily, and drop in sessions are offered, along with a hot lunch program, which is assisted by staff members to integrate social support.

Additional services include prenatal and postnatal services in which women are offered food, nutritional support, and support in accessing housing, clothing, legal, and social supports. Program staff members come from a variety of agencies, and include addictions counsellors, dieticians, social workers and outreach workers, infant development specialists, community health workers, peer support staff, and physicians with methadone administration training. A service coordinator manages the linkages between various agencies to support program operation. A review of service files reveals an increase in concurrent health and social issues among women at intake yet with steady or improved indicators of infant health. The authors note that this reflects positively on women's motivation and understanding of their own needs and on the service delivery model of the agency (Marshall et al. 32).

Maxxine Wright Place Program

Located in Surrey, BC, the Maxxine Wright Place program provides support for women who are pregnant or with young children affected by substance use issues, and/or violence and abuse (Nathoo et al. 96). Services include a shelter and housing program, a daycare, a community health clinic offering women-centred health and social care services—including a lunch program, Aboriginal women's outreach, medical and nursing care, dental hygienist, substance use counselling, infant development consulting, income assistance support, housing outreach, and social work services. Because concerns over child apprehension can contribute to women feeling unsafe to access treatment, the Maxxine Wright Centre has adopted policies to prevent child removals onsite and support women's safety while accessing services (Drabble and Poole 125; Poole and Isaac 17).

Healthy, Empowered, Resilient (HER) Pregnancy Program

The HER program in Edmonton, Alberta, is a women-centred, peer-support, harm-reduction oriented model (Wodinski et al. 1). The women served tend to be experiencing mental health issues, addiction, violence and trauma, unemployment, and homelessness; the majority of the women are Aboriginal. Services are designed to meet women where they are at. They are designed to be flexible, low threshold, strengths based, and focussed on relationship building. The program is delivered by a multidisciplinary staff including a registered nurse, social workers, and pregnancy support workers with street experience and knowledge. The staff members collaborate and coordinate with multiple sectors to connect women with a range of services. There are weekly drop in sessions and in-person visits available at the program as well as community-based outreach activities, and online- and text-based communication between staff and women. Some of the HER pregnancy program services that the team facilitates connections with include addictions support, advocacy support, crisis intervention, children's services, health services and education, housing, and supplementary income. Resources are also provided, and include informational materials, hygiene products, coupons and transit tickets, harm-reduction supplies (e.g., alcohol swabs, syringes, spoons, and filters), condoms, vitamins, and baby supplies. Based on evaluation, the strongest program impacts were connecting women to a range of services and childcare outcomes (Wodinski et al. 33). Women were accessing health and social resources that were previously inaccessible (including medical, housing, and income supports), and keeping custody of their children. They also reported positive improvements in substance use, sexual health, safety, and empowerment.

HerWay Home (HWH) Program

HerWay Home (HWH) stands for "housing first, empowerment, respect, women, acceptance, your choice, health, opportunity, mother and equality." The program began in 2013 in Victoria, BC. Program design was based on earlier models of integrated care that offered cross-sector, community based and culturally safe services for women, infants/children and families who encounter barriers to health and social care due to social disadvantages (Marcellus et al. 500; Nathoo et al. 97). HWH services include basic needs support such as childcare and nutrition, primary health and perinatal care, substance use, trauma and mental health counselling, and support to access housing. The HWH program is rooted in a harm-reduction and social determinants of health approach, which recognizes the value of offering services to reduce harms from substance use along with housing, income, nutrition, employment, education, and social supports. To achieve this, HWH combines the skills and efforts of a wide range of health and social care professionals, outreach agencies, government agencies, charitable groups, and an advisory committee of women who are representative of the service group.

Marcellus et al. note that with the emergence of community-based, integrated, primary care maternity programs for pregnant women with a history of substance use issues, it is critical to consider how to evaluate the success of a program (503-8). Based on experiences with the HWH program, they argue that abstinence as the marker of success is problematic, and fails to capture the achievements of such programs; abstinence focusses narrowly on a single event based on the binaries of failure or success.

The Mothering Project

The Mothering Project (Manito Ikwe Kagiikwe) is offered through the Mount Carmel Clinic in Winnipeg's North End. The name of the program has Ojibway roots and means "spirit woman teachings." This name refers to the collaborative and relational nature of the program that emerges from these roots, where women are honoured for carrying all the teachings that they need within them. The role of the program team is to help women remember those teachings. Team members incorporate multiple ways of engagement for women, including providing opportunities for authentic input, choice, and feedback within the program. The program provides obstetrics support, nutrition and cooking classes, parenting and child development support groups, and addictions support for mothers (Nathoo et al. 100). Women choose the issues to work on that are most important to them (e.g., access housing, medical care, and methadone maintenance) (O'Brien 2). Services and supports are provided in ways that are holistic and reflect the Indigenous worldview and cultural safety approach of the program.

Emerging Programs

As evidence builds about the impact of integrated harm-reduction programs, a growing number of communities across Canada and in other countries are convening to examine the evidence and consider how to bring this approach to care to a wide range of contexts, including large urban settings, rural and northern communities, and Indigenous communities. With diversity in de-mographics, substance use patterns, and local resources, a critical step for communities is to bring together stakeholders, create new partnerships, and generate possibilities for practice improvements and program development. For example, public health nurses and hospital maternity providers in Campbell River, BC, a small community of over thirty thousand people on Vancouver Island, worked together to improve how they provided care to women with complex challenges in their small community, with limited resources. They approached providing harm-reduction focussed care as a philosophy rather than as something that only happens within the walls of a specialized program. They focussed on shifting staff and community attitudes, developing effective relationships with partners outside the health system, being proactive about planning supports, and taking a long-term family-centred view of providing these supports (Forsyth et al. 70).

Together, these established and emerging programs and practices represent a significant shift in how care for women with substance use issues is conceptualized and provided (Sword et al., "Integrat-ed Programs" 14; Sword et al., "Partnerships" 346). Focussing narrowly on substance use does not acknowledge the complex life circumstances experienced by women, nor does it respect what the urgent needs are for women to begin their paths of recovery and healing. There are often many other more pressing concerns, including being in violent relationships, not having safe housing, or not having enough food to feed their children. Harm-reduc-tion approaches are one way to create responsive, effective, and tailored systems of care and interventions that have the potential to improve health and social outcomes for families.

Much remains to be studied in relation to these harm-reduction oriented programs. A recent national survey of gaps and best practice (Poole et al., "Prevention" 9) has identified important remaining questions. How has the programming been adapted for context in different locations in Canada? What subcomponents are help-ful from women's perspectives? And what outcome measures are being employed and what is being achieved? These questions can be studied locally to capture context as well as nationally through research and practice collaborations.

CONCLUSION

Since the 1990s, services for pregnant women and mothers using harm-reduction approaches have emerged in many areas of Canada. Such a perspective provides the opportunity to acknowledge that reducing or stopping substance use at any time during pregnancy can have positive effects on women's health and the health of the fetus (Wong et al. 371).

Providing services from a harm reduction approach can reduce stigma and encourage engagement, as women can interface with multiple providers in environments designed to be safe and respectful (Wright and Walker 117). A wider conception of what harm reduction means can be informed from sex and gender perspectives as well as critical feminist and intersectional ones. Social justice and human rights approaches can provide pragmatic frameworks for program developments and practice improvements, which meet the unique needs of women coping with substance use and other challenges.

WORKS CITED

Baker, Travis, et al. "Of Mice and Wo/Men: Transdisciplinarity in the Laboratory." *Transforming Addiction: Gender, Trauma, Transdisciplinarity*, edited by Lorraine Greaves, Routledge, 2015, pp. 72-90.

Benoit, Cecilia, et al. "Providers' Constructions of Pregnant and Early Parenting Women Who Use Substances." *Sociology of Health & Illness*, vol. 36, no. 2, 2014, pp. 252-63.

Boyd, Neil. "Lessons from Insite, Vancouver's Supervised Injection Facility: 2003–2012." *Drugs: Rducation, Prevention and Policy*, vol. 20, no. 3, 2013, pp. 234-40.

Boyd, Susan. *From Witches to Crack Moms: Women, Drug Law, and Policy*. Carolina Academic Press, 2004.

Campbell, Nancy, and Elizabeth Ettorre. *Gendering Addiction: The Politics of Drug Treatment in a Neurochemical World*. Palgrave Macmillan, 2011.

Canada FASD Northwest Research Network. *10 Fundamental Components of FASD Prevention from a Woman's Health De-*

terminants Perspective. Canada FASD, 2010.

Canada Women's Foundation and BC Society of Transition Houses. *Report on Violence Against Women, Mental Health and Substance Use.* Vancouver, 2011.

Canadian Harm Reduction Network. "What Is Harm Reduction?" 10 Aug. 2016, www.canadianharmreduction.com. Accesseed 2 May 2018.

Canadian Nurses Association. "Harm Reduction and Currently Illegal Drugs: Implications for Nursing Policy, Practice, Education and Research: Discussion Paper." Canadian Nurses Association, 2017. www.cna-aiic.ca/en/on-the-issues/better-health/harm-reduction. Accessed 2 May 2018.

Cusick, Linda. "Widening the Harm Reduction Agenda: From Drug Use to Sex Work." *International Journal of Drug Policy,* vol. 17, no. 1, 2006, pp. 3-11.

Drabble, Laurie, and Nancy Poole. "Collaboration between Addiction Treatment and Child Welfare Fields: Opportunities in a Canadian Context." *Journal of Social Work Practice in the Addictions,* vol. 11, no. 2, 2011, pp. 124-49.

Einstein, Stanley. "Harm and Risk Reduction: History, Theories, Issues, and Implications." *Substance Use & Misuse,* vol. 42, no. 2-3, 2007, pp. 257-65.

Flavin, Jeanne, and Lynn M. Paltrow. "Punishing Pregnant Drug-Using Women: Defying Law, Medicine, and Common Sense." *Journal of Addictive Diseases,* vol. 29, no. 2, 2010, 231-44.

Forsyth, Alice, et al. "One Woman at a Time: Bringing the Fir Square Model of Practice to a Community Hospital." *With Child: Substance Use During Pregnancy: A Woman-Centered Approach,* edited by Susan Boyd and Lenora Marcellus, Fernwood Publishing, 2007, pp.70-75.

Greaves, Lorraine, and Nancy Poole. *Highs & Lows: Canadian Perspectives on Women and Substance Use.* Centre for Addiction and Mental Health/Centre de Toxicomanie et de Santé Mentale, 2007.

Hathaway, Andrew D., and Kirk I. Tousaw. "Harm Reduction Headway and Continuing Resistance: Insights from Safe Injection in the City of Vancouver." *International Journal of Drug Policy,* vol. 19, no. 1, 2008, pp. 11-16.

Khandor, Erika, and Kate Mason. *The Street Health Report 2007*. Street Health, 2007.

Kramlich, Debra, and Rebecca Kronk. "Relational Care for Perinatal Substance Use." *MCN: The American Journal of Maternal Child Nursing*, vol. 40, no. 5, 2015, pp. 320-326.

Lange, Shannon, et al. "A Comparison of the Prevalence of Prenatal Alcohol Exposure Obtained Via Maternal Self-Reports Versus Meconium Testing: A Systematic Literature Review and Meta-Analysis." *BMC Pregnancy and Childbirth*, vol. 14, no. 1, 2014, pp. 1-11.

Logan, T.K., et al. "Victimization and Substance Abuse among Women: Contributing Factors, Interventions, and Implications." *Review of General Psychology*, vol. 6, no. 4, 2002, pp. 325-97.

Loock, Christine, et al. *Targeting High-Risk Families: Prenatal Alcohol/Drug Abuse and Infant Outcomes*. University of British Columbia, 1993.

Marcellus, Lenora, et al. "Reenvisioning Success for Programs Supporting Pregnant Women with Problematic Substance Use." *Qualitative Health Research*, vol. 25, no. 4, 2014, pp. 500–12.

Marlatt, G. Alan, et al. *Harm Reduction: Pragmatic Strategies for Managing High-Risk Behaviors*. Guilford Press, 2011.

Marshall, Sheila K., et al. "Sheway's Services for Substance Using Pregnant and Parenting Women: Evaluating the Outcomes for Infants." *Canadian Journal of Community Mental Health*, vol. 24, no. 1, 2005, pp. 19-33.

Milligan, Karen, et al. "Birth Outcomes for Infants Born to Women Participating in Integrated Substance Abuse Treatment Programs: A Meta-Analytic Review." *Addiction Research & Theory*, vol. 19, no. 6, 2011, pp. 542-55.

Motz, Mary. *Breaking the Cycle: Measures of Progress 1995-2005*. Hospital For Sick Children, 2006.

Nathoo, Tasnim, et al. "Voices from the Community: Developing Effective Community Programs to Support Pregnant and Early Parenting Women Who Use Alcohol and Other Substances." *First Peoples Child & Family Review*, vol. 8, no. 1, 2013, pp. 93-106.

NDARC. *Supporting Pregnant Women Who Use Alcohol or Other Drugs: A Guide for Primary Health Care Professionals*. UNSW Australia: Substance Misuse in Pregnancy Resource Development

Project, 2014.

Newcombe, Russell. "High Time for Harm Reduction." *Druglink*, vol. 2, no. 1, 1987, pp. 10.

Niccols, Alison, et al. "Integrated Programs for Mothers with Substance Abuse Issues: A Systematic Review of Studies Reporting on Parenting Outcomes." *Harm Reduction Journal*, vol. 9, no. 1, 2012, pp. 14-24.

Niccols, Alison, et al. "Maternal Mental Health and Integrated Programs for Mothers with Substance Abuse Issues." *Psychology of Addictive Behaviors*, vol. 24, no. 3, 2010, pp. 466-74.

Nota Bene Consulting Group and BC Centre of Excellence for Women's Health. *Her Way Home Phase 2 Evaluation Report*. Nota Bene Consulting Group, 2017.

O'Brien, Carole. *Mothering Project: Effective Prevention with Vulnerable Families*. Canadian Centre for Policy Alternatives, 2015.

Ordean, Alice, et al. "Integrated Care for Pregnant Women on Methadone Maintenance Treatment: Canadian Primary Care Cohort Study." *Canadian Family Physician*, vol. 59, no. 10, 2013, pp. e462-e469.

Paltrow, Lynn M., and Jeanne Flavin. "Arrests of and Forced Interventions on Pregnant Women in the United States, 1973–2005: Implications for Women's Legal Status and Public Health." *Journal of Health Politics, Policy and Law*, vol. 38, no.2, 2013, pp. 299-343.

Pauly, Bernadette. "Harm Reduction through a Social Justice Lens." *International Journal of Drug Policy*, vol. 19, no. 1, 2008, pp. 4-10.

Pauly, Bernadette, et al. "The Ethical, Legal and Social Context of Harm Reduction." *Canadian Nurse*, vol. 103, no. 8, 2007 pp. 19-23.

Poole, Nancy. *Evaluation Report of the Sheway Project for High-Risk Pregnant and Parenting Women*. British Columbia Centre of Excellence for Women's Health Vancouver, 2000.

Poole, Nancy, and Barbara Isaac. *Apprehensions: Barriers to Treatment for Substance-Using Mothers*. British Columbia Centre of Excellence for Women's Health Vancouver, 2001.

Poole, Nancy, et al. *Women-Centred Harm Reduction, Gendering the National Framework Series*. Vol. 4. British Columbia Centre of Excellence for Women's Health, 2010.

Poole, N., et al. "Prevention of Fetal Alcohol Spectrum Disorder: Current Canadian Efforts and Analysis of Gaps." *Substance Abuse Research and Treatment*, vol. 10, no. S1, 2001, pp. 1-11.

Poole, N. and C. Dell. *Girls, Women and Substance Use*. British Columbia Centre of Excellence for Women's Health, 2005.

Racine, Nicole, et al. "Breaking the Cycle Pregnancy Outreach Program: Reaching out to Improve the Health and Well-Being for Pregnant Substance-Involved Mothers." *Journal of the Motherhood Initiative for Research and Community Involvement*, vol. 11, no. 1, 2009, pp. 279-90.

Reid, Colleen, et al. "Good, Bad, Thwarted or Addicted? Discourses of Substance-Using Mothers." *Critical Social Policy*, vol. 28, no. 2, 2008, pp. 211-34.

Riley, Diane, et al. "Harm Reduction: Concepts and Practice. A Policy Discussion Paper." *Substance Use & Misuse*, vol. 34, no. 1, 1999, pp. 9-24.

Roe, Gordon. "Harm Reduction as Paradigm: Is Better Than Bad Good Enough? The Origins of Harm Reduction." *Critical Public Health*, vol. 15, no. 3, 2005, pp. 243-50.

Seddon, Toby. "Women, Harm Reduction and History: Gender Perspectives on the Emergence of the 'British System' of Drug Control." *International Journal of Drug Policy*, vol. 19, no. 2, 2008, pp. 99-105.

Smye, V., et al. "Harm Reduction, Methadone Maintenance Treatment and the Root Causes of Health and Social Inequities: An Intersectional Lens in the Canadian Context." *Harm Reduction Journal*, vol. 8, no. 1, 2011, pp. 1-12.

Stimson, Gerry V., and Pat O'Hare. "Harm Reduction: Moving through the Third Decade." *International Journal of Drug Policy*, vol. 21, no. 2, 2010, pp. 91-3.

Sword, Wendy, et al. "Integrated Programs for Women with Substance Use Issues and Their Children: A Qualitative Meta-Synthesis of Processes and Outcomes." *Harm Reduction Journal*, vol. 6, no. 1, 2009, pp. 1-17.

Sword, Wendy, et al. "Partnerships among Canadian Agencies Serving Women with Substance Abuse Issues and Their Children." *International Journal of Mental Health and Addiction*, vol. 11, no. 3, 2013, pp. 344-57.

Tammi, Tuukka, and Toivo Hurme. "How the Harm Reduction Movement Contrasts Itself Against Punitive Prohibition." *International Journal of Drug Policy*, vol.18, no. 2, 2007, pp.84-87.

Torchalla, Iris, et al. "'Like a Lots Happened with My Whole Childhood': Violence, Trauma, and Addiction in Pregnant and Postpartum Women from Vancouver's Downtown Eastside." *Harm Reduction Journal*, vol. 12, no.1, 2015, pp. 1-10.

Turner, Suzanne D, et al. "Neonatal Opioid Withdrawal and Antenatal Opioid Prescribing." *CMAJ Open*, vol. 3, no. 1, 2015, pp. E55-E61.

Varcoe, Colleen. "Inequality, Violence and Women's Health." *Health, Illness and Health Care in Canada*, edited by B.S. Bolaria and D.H. Dickinson, Nelson, 2009, pp. 259-82.

Wodinski, Lindsay, et al. *Impact Evaluation of the Her Pregnancy Program–Final Summary Report*. Consulting for the Alberta Centre for Child, Family and Community Research, 2013.

Wong, Suzanne, et al. "SOGC Clinical Practice Guidelines: Substance Use in Pregnancy: No. 256, April 2011." *International Journal of Gynaecology and Obstetrics: The Official Organization of the International Federation of Gynaecology and Obstetrics*, vol. 114, no. 2, 2011, pp. 190-202.

Wright, Alison, and James Walker. "Management of Women Who Use Drugs During Pregnancy." *Seminars in Fetal and Neonatal Medicine*, vol. 12, no. 2, 2007, pp. 14-118.

I want to be a good mom so that she knows I'm always there for her. I didn't have that. I want her to have her own room and all the stuff that will help her develop right. I didn't have any of that with my mom. She did drugs and had lots of boyfriends come and go. Even when I told her that her boyfriend was touching me, she wouldn't believe me. A good mom wouldn't do that. They would always protect their kids. My kid isn't going to have a rich life, but they will know they are loved. Everyone judges us because we don't have perfect little lives, but we love our kids, and you can have all the money in the world and be a bad mom.

—Sarah, age seventeen

11.
Mothering and Illicit Substance Use

A Critical Analysis of the Implications for Healthcare and Social Policy Development from a Feminist Poststructuralist Perspective

MICHELLE FOULKES

WITHIN THE FEMINIST LITERATURE, discourse around mothering is the linchpin or pillar around which feminist theory has evolved since its epistemological beginnings. At times, motherhood has served as a unifying thread that has bound women together in the struggle to own their biological and reproductive selves, whereas, at other times, it has been largely divisive and highly contested among and between women. It has been all at once celebrated by some as the essence of womanhood in our unique capacity to generate life within us while others have seen motherhood as the primary source of oppression for women when defined by the power structures of a patriarchal society (Klee et al. 39).

At the same time that this widely disparate and varying embodiment of mothering within the feminist community has saturated its discourse, the predominant construction of motherhood within the Western world has generated a powerful binary representation of women as either good or bad mothers (Carabine 31; Weedon, *Feminist Practice* 2). The purpose of this chapter is to critically examine the socially constructed ideologies of mothering that have resulted in these dichotomous and paradoxical images to emerge, and to explore the implications these presuppositions may have for health policy development for women who use illicit substances while pregnant and beyond. It is hoped through this analysis using a feminist poststructuralist framework, largely informed by the work of Michel Foucault, that a contribution to our understanding of mothering under these conditions can be illuminated to inform health policy development.

LAYING THE THEORETICAL UNDERPINNINGS OF
FEMINIST POSTSTRUCTURALIST THEORY

Poststructuralism does not represent a single fixed theoretical entity but rather represents an overarching framework under which several philosophical positions are housed. Poststructuralist thought finds its origins in the work of the Swiss linguist Ferdinand de Saussure in his publication titled *Course in General Linguistics* (1916), which has resulted in a succession of modern-day philosophers, including Derrida, Lacan, Kristeva, Althusser and Foucault, adopting and expanding Saussure's original thesis (Belsey 4). Although variances around their theoretical positions exist, they share commonalities in their fundamental assumptions rooted in Saussure's original work around language, meaning and subjectivity (Weedon, *Feminist Practice* 13). Collectively, poststructural theorists believe that social organization and power structures can be understood by analyzing language. Chris Weedon explains that "language is the place where actual and possible forms of social organization and their likely social and political consequences are defined and contested" while providing a space for the knowledge and values that constitute a culture to be transmitted. Language is also the location where our sense of self, known as our subjectivity, is constructed through social interaction and its constituted meaning. This is to say that language does not reflect a given social reality; it constructs a social reality for us (McHoul and Grace 31).

Language and the meaning tied to words has no fixed intrinsic meaning; it is rather an abstract chain of signs or words with each sign consisting of both a signifier (sound or written image) and a signified (meaning) (Weedon, *Feminist Practice* 23). The relationship between the signifier or sound of the word and the signified or concept it represents is arbitrary and holds no natural connection to the other. They are bound together by meaning that is constructed within the social world creating it. Furthermore, signs derive their meaning in relation to other signs in the language chain, and do not stand alone. Language and meaning are understood because of the comparisons or differences between signifiers. Therefore, the meaning of a "woman" is not inherent in its signifier; it is through comparison with other signifiers that one knows "woman-ness."

It is through differences that meaning is derived. As an extension of this, the meaning of "woman" is not fixed but transient and subject to historically specific discourses in which competing ways of giving meaning to the world are prioritized and legitimized. It is in these competing discourses that the structure of social power presents itself and becomes the site of political struggle (Weedon, *Feminist Practice* 25). The meaning of "woman" is therefore fluid, and meaning is assigned based on the discursive relations in which it is located in time. It is open to constant reinterpretation (McHoul and Grace 36).

The concept of subjectivity then becomes critical in feminist poststructuralist theory and stands in stark contrast to humanist discourses that assert that subjectivity is fixed and coherent, and represents the essence of the subject. For humanists, the meaning of "woman" remains unchanged with the essential elements of "woman-ness" necessarily present for an object to be labelled as a woman. Understanding subjectivity to be precarious and in process as understood within a poststructuralist paradigm provides a space for its meaning to be redefined and reconstructed. This has political significance for feminism when it assumes one of the primary assertions of Foucault's work: it allows for woman's voices to resist the social discourses reflecting the dominating values, class, gender, and racial interests of patriarchal power to move toward a redefinition of the historically and culturally located meaning of "woman-ness" (Weedon, *Feminist Practice* 35). For in doing so, the dominant ideology of the oppressed, passive, and victimized female existing within a patriarchal reality can be challenged so that different conceptualizations of "woman" can be asserted through women-centred agency. It is within this philosophical archetype that feminists—regardless of fundamental differences in thought around how our existence in a patriarchal world may be altered—emerges an emboldened look to the future.

SEX AND GENDER AS DEPENDENT VARIABLES

Integral to our understanding of the social construction of the good and bad mother binary is in distinguishing the defining characteristics of sex and gender as dichotomous yet virtually inseparable entities that influence and inform the other's existence from a paternalistic stance. "Sex refers to the genetic, hormonal, and anatomical differences that characterize the bodies of human males and females" (DiQuinzio 19) and is assumed to be invariant. Gender difference, not unlike sexuality in Foucault's work, is not naturally given but results from relationships between knowledge and power, and manifests itself in both private and public spheres (Weedon, *Feminist Practice* 123). Gender therefore "refers to the psychological, social, political, and cultural meanings that these bodily differences come to have in specific social contexts" (DiQuinzio 19). Although the same holds true for sex characteristics in Western society, for gender in particular, it is in the differences between characteristics hierarchically situated that some are more valued than others as determined by those who hold power. A discourse assuming the white male to be the norm against which all others are measured allows for women to be relegated to domesticity and motherhood, given her natural attributes of weakness, passivity, and emotionality (DiQuinzio 63). This is best exemplified in the following passage taken from the book *What a Young Wife Ought to Know* written in 1901 by Emma Frances Angell Drake:

> In place of the logical, she possesses the intuitive mind, which makes her capable of reaching a conclusion while man is thinking about it. She has less strength, but greater endurance; less daring in achievement, but more patience: less forcefulness, but more quiet insistence; less practicality, but more of the aesthetic; less ambition to assume the great responsibilities of life, but more painstaking in the little and no less important things which go so far towards making the days sweet and peaceful. (qtd. in Weedon, *Feminism, Theory* 28)

This social construction of "woman" as patient and intuitive while at the same time illogical, and lacking strength, fortitude, and ambition is perpetuated across generations through a set of complex social processes supported throughout infant and child development in contextually defined childrearing practices (DiQuinzio 46). These practices inform the development of personal identity and results in the organization of various elements of culture, including the division of labour between males and females. It is within these social processes that both overt and covert patriarchal power structures reside and we develop our understanding of self or our subjectivity. For both women and men, the internalized understanding of femininity and masculinity permits only a prescribed menu of sanctioned behaviours to be considered normal. Indeed, these gendered ways of being are so pervasive and interwoven in the experience of interacting in the world that alternative enactments of gender are almost inconceivable. It shapes our subjectivity so intimately that the meaning of femaleness and maleness can appear to be virtually unchangeable, not unlike sex, because gender is causally related within a patriarchal power structure. Feminists argue that this determinism based on sex must be deconstructed to allow gender to be expressed in a multiplicity of ways in order for women to fully actualize their individual and self-determined potentials (DiQuinzio 64). The biological imperative for all women to bear children and embrace mothering within the circumscribed embodiment of the good mother as an amplification of the social construct of "woman" will now be explored.

THE SOCIAL CONSTRUCTION OF MOTHERING

The social construction of mothering is circumscribed with women expected to fulfill their biologically determined place in the world where gender and sex are unconditionally tied. Images of mothers and mothering permeate popular culture through multiple modes of transmission, including the mass media, parenting manuals, medical textbooks, and popular literature. These portrayals communicate influential ideals of how mothering should look and be exemplified by women in order to be labelled as good mothers. Good mother imagery is portrayed as the quintessential standard of femininity through which all women are measured. It is neatly packaged within the confines of the signifiers of race, class, sexual orientation, marital status, and method of conception. The good mother prototype is a white, middle-class, and heterosexual female who bears children within the confines of the traditional family structure. From within this perspective, women are tied to a prescribed role of reproduction of the species and that to be a woman requires fulfillment of this role. As an extension of this, not only are women expected to desire to become pregnant and give birth as a result of their instinctual destiny, but they are also "expected to love their children unconditionally, empathize completely with their children, meet their children's needs selflessly, and be completely fulfilled and satisfied by the experience of child rearing" (DiQuinzio 89). For women who are unwilling or unable to fulfill these gendered expectations of essential mothering, they are stigmatized to the highest order.

For women who actively choose not to become mothers or who are unable to become mothers, lesbians, single women, women with disabilities, women suffering from mental illness and/or addictions, women of differing race and class are all measured against the essential motherhood. The differences between the exemplar of the essential mother and its lesser representation of the above classes of women are then calculated to inform social position, rights, and privileges. Imperfections—seen as the differences between the good mother prototype and other representations of mother—are almost intolerable, especially when a woman belongs to multiple stigmatized groups. In the struggle to be the essential good mother, women are further silenced, shamed, blamed, and socially excluded.

SUBSTANCE USE AND PREGNANCY: THE MOTHER OF ALL EVILS

There is no other collective of women who are more stigmatized and thwarted than mothers who use substances during pregnancy (Flavin and Paltrow 232). This is because of the profound tension between the socially constructed image of the good mother and the actual mothering behaviour exemplified by this group of women through their substance use. To use substances while pregnant is to defy the cardinal premise of mothering: women are expected to abandon her personal needs, desires, or interests to meet the needs of her fetus. Indeed, the use of substances during pregnancy is often equated with child abuse: "mothers-to-be are transformed into pregnant addicts who are considered at best sick and at worst criminal" (Rutman et al. 6). Only morally depraved women would choose to place their fetus in harm's way. For these women, punitive sanctions are necessary to restore social justice and harmony, which feeds into the continuing rhetoric of the good-bad mother dichotomy.

How woman with addictions have been perceived and constructed has largely occurred as a result of marked advancements in medicine and technology in the mid-twentieth century (Daniels 19). Pregnancy has been forced out of the private domain of the woman's body and into the public sphere where a demarcation between mother and baby was imposed—pitting one against the other (Weir 15). The two pivotal concepts that have driven discourse around pregnancy and substance use, relating to both mother and fetus as separate entities, are risk and the legal rights of mother and fetus. The movement of pregnancy to the public domain as well as the concepts of risk and legal rights will be explored from a historical perspective, which will further illustrate the social construction of mothering.

THE DIVISION OF MOTHER AND BABY AS ONE THROUGH THE POLITICS OF RISK AND LEGAL RIGHTS

The term "threshold" is defined in the Merriam-Webster dictionary as "the place or point of entering or beginning; the level, point, or value above which something is true or will take place and below which it is or will not." In philosophical terms, thresholds mark the transition from "inside to outside, the imperceptible to the perceptible, the non-reactive to the reactive and therefore marks the between. Women in pregnancy bear the between, the entrance across which the unborn must pass in order to be distinguished from those who carry them" (Weir 1). Though not a single point in time or space, when and where the between "begins" and "ends," which is the time when the fetus is separate from mother is socially, historically, and culturally defined.

Until the first two decades of the twentieth century the "beginning" of the between was difficult to determine with high rates of both infant and maternal mortality. Although the beginning was sometimes marked by "quickening" or the sensation of internal movements of the baby by the mother, this was a highly ambiguous measurement of fetal health and wellbeing (Weir 37). What did have a clear delineation was the "end" of the between with the birth of a baby. After passing to a place separate from the mother, the infant was recognized as having human status as both a person and individual (Weir 143).

With concerted efforts to reduce infant mortality rates at the turn of the century, childbirth was removed from the private sphere—where the birthing experience was between woman and midwife—to the public sphere where childbirth was medicalized and ownership of obstetrical care was transferred to physicians (Annandale 79). Under the guise of reducing risk, medical intervention into the birthing experience was now a matter of public debate and discourse.

Although levels of infant mortality were dropping throughout this period, many deaths continued to occur either before, during, or immediately following birth (Weir 48). Under the assumption that deaths occurring before or after childbirth were of similar causation, it was postulated that the body of the fetus late in gestation and the infant after birth were fundamentally alike, with shifting the "end" of the between to a different location in time and space. The clear delineation that had previously existed with the end requiring a live birth, the consolidation of the period before, during and after birth to a single interval erased the demarcation. In doing so, the birth threshold became unfixed and the relationship between mother and fetus blurred, as social and legal categories of what defines a person continued to shift (Weir 33).

By the 1950s, significant changes in technology were occurring. The introduction of the ultrasound machine visualized the fetus in-utero and provided animation and personification to the unborn prior to individuating from the maternal subject (Klee et al. 34). Scientific discourse at this time further defined "risk" as "the product of the probability and consequences (magnitude and severity) of an adverse event" (Lupton 19)—not something of natural causation. Risk was now measurable and amenable to intervention to reduce its impact. Efforts to reduce prenatal risks to the fetus through the introduction of systematic regimes of prenatal care beginning at sixteen weeks were instituted. The meaning of "risk" was, thus, reconstituted to meet the social ideologies of the time.

Technological advancement coupled with efforts to reduce perinatal risk factors led to increased governmental control over women's bodies in the 1970s (Weir 24). Discourse around the "beginning" of the between was again shifting from a relatively time-limited interval immediately before, during, and after birth to being centred on a viability argument. Defined as the time when a fetus can theoretically exist separately from the mother, the legal categories of the unborn as an individual were well positioned for a highly politicized debate. The primary determinant of fetal survival is correlated with lung capacity, which develops around twenty-four weeks. Despite advances in prenatal care including prenatal surgical intervention, technology has been unable to pass the biological boundary defined by lung development. Viability then remains at twenty-four weeks gestational age today, when the fetus becomes legally and politically independent from the mother and falls under the jurisdiction of public property (Daniels 19).

The concept of mother and fetus as one was irrevocably ruptured and separated; placing the rights of the mother and the rights of the fetus now in direct conflict as distinct entities. With the "beginning" of the between unfixed and now somewhat fluid in nature, the "end" of the between found itself firmly situated with the fetus at twenty-four weeks gestational age. At this socially constructed line in the sand, fetal rights supersede maternal ones, and the state can now interject in decisions around a woman's body because of their legal and moral obligation to intervene if deemed necessary. As a result, "a woman's freedom to control her body is circumscribed by the obligation she incurs to the fetus" (Daniels 25).

Since the 1980s, there has been great support to punish women with legal sanctions and forced treatment for behaviours deemed to place the fetus at risk from the time of conception onward (Lester et al. 3). Women who are pregnant and using substances, particularly illicit drugs, have been placed at the forefront of this debate and vilified for their deviant behaviour (Daniels 25). With a woman's biological potential realized at conception, the desire is to protect the fetus from the bad mother who is unwilling to shield the developing fetus from environmental toxins and disease. Control of the woman's behaviours and body must be swift and all-encompassing so that any potential harm to the fetus can be eliminated (Weir 16). The risk of harm to the fetus, therefore, invalidates a woman's right to self-sovereignty. The "beginning" of the between is now being relocated to the point of conception where a fetus is now being afforded individual rights and status separate from the mother.

Fetal advocates contend that to prevent exposing the fetus to any risk including drugs while in utero, which may result in a lifetime of suffering and disability, is more important than limiting the rights and freedoms of the body in which it is housed (Lester et al. 12). To impose a time-limited control over the mother for the gestational period is now seen to be entirely reasonable; the idea has informed much of our current legal and social policy (Greaves and Poole 220). The point of contention, however, resides in the assumption that imposing restrictions to maternal freedoms by focusing on a single risk factor of prenatal drug exposure is linear, overly simplistic, and faulty. Developmental outcomes for children exposed to substances prenatally are widely variable and must be considered and understood within the context of the broader social environment. Health and social policy must move beyond prosecutorial strategies criminalizing a woman's behaviour to challenging the child-welfare system, which overwhelming supports the apprehension of children from women who use drugs (Poole and Isaac 14). Instead, as our understanding of addictions grows and expands and moves from a place that believes substance use by pregnant women is grounded in a selfish and reckless desire to harm a developing fetus (a moral failing) to one that situates substance use within the mental health domain, we can then look to the research on substance use to inform policy development. This will allow us to acknowledge the complex and multifaceted determinants that influence and coalesce to adjudicate the health of mothers and their children (Lester et al. 30).

SHIFTING HEALTH AND SOCIAL POLICY TO A RESTORATIVE JUSTICE FRAMEWORK

A punitive approach toward illicit drug use during pregnancy reduces the blame of the behaviour to the individual so that ownership of one's moral failing falls securely on the so-called bad mother alone (Weir 37). Such a reductionist stance denies the context and everyday reality of many drug-using pregnant women who tend to be poor and often victims of profound violence and trauma (Clayson et al. 236). It also ignores the social and distributive justice arrangements in our society, which result in a political economy where healthcare, food, work opportunities, and correctional measures are unequally distributed based on gender, sexual orientation, class, and race (Sullivan and Tiff 37). Social and health policy can have a healing and restorative agenda rather than a punitive one that aims to correct socially constructed deviant behaviours.

Indeed, substance use for women in general has been found to "arise from a complex interplay of biological, genetic, psychological, social, cultural, relational, environmental and spiritual factors" (Cormier et al. 1). Research has indicated that as many as two-thirds of women with substance use problems have a concurrent mental health disorder—such as, depression, posttraumatic stress disorder, panic disorder, or an eating disorder—that they are struggling to manage often through their addictions (Lester and Twomey 68). Furthermore, the research also shows that a large proportion of women with substance abuse problems are victims of domestic violence, were raised in chaotic and dysfunctional homes with at least one parent who had addiction issues, and were victims of incest or sexual assault, child abuse, or neglect (Logan et al. 342). With each additional layer of risk contributing to the potential for health and social consequences, a proportion of women enter their childbearing years already entrenched in a substance use problem. A previous history of addictions often supersedes a woman's journey into motherhood. Within this context, health and public policy directed at substance use during pregnancy must be developed out of a shared responsibility for society's failings, which acknowledges that power differentials result in increasing health disparities and social exclusion within both broader society and the healthcare arena.

A movement toward health and social policy situated within a restorative justice framework rather than a punitive one is entirely commensurate with poststructuralist feminism and women's health across the lifespan. This is because poststructural feminism allows for women's voices to resist the social discourses that reflect the interests of patriarchal power and provides a space for discourses that eliminate the language and meaning assigned to the good mother and bad mother (Klee et al. 34). A restorative justice framework is a form of insurgency because it competes with the state and other power-based arrangements, and it is also subversive in nature because it challenges social arrangements and processes that limit human potential while preventing human needs from being met. Such a framework acknowledges that we are all co-creators of our collective social world. To assume a stance of restorative justice it is to encapsulate immense human compassion and accountability in order to facilitate the "personal empowerment and growth of each and the collective well-being of all" (Sullivan and Tiff 5). It assumes a societal responsibility to promote and ensure healthy fetal development and maternal wellbeing rather than assign individual culpability to a woman to protect her unborn child in the context of often horrific disadvantage and trauma.

Attending to the philosophical constructs of restorative justice opens health policy and program development to a participatory process helping women understand the sociocultural influences that perpetuate the use of substances to cope with their social reality. Barriers precluding pregnant women from receiving help are revealed to better service their needs.

A thorough review of the literature indicates that successful outcomes for women and children both during and after pregnancy can best be achieved if health policy and the services offered are grounded in women's experiences and adhere to the following essential elements. Care must be shifted from a sole emphasis on the fetus and child to a woman-centred and dyadic emphasis, since the dissection of the two entities has had grievous consequences for both women and children (Greaves and Poole 221). Treatment and recovery must be available during pregnancy in a safe and specialized environment free of shame and stigmatization; treatment and recovery following birth must be available within a setting that provides care for mothers and her children together (Miller 43). A harm-reduction approach must drive the philosophy of care, as a philosophy of complete abstinence has shown to reduce women's participation in treatment (Centre for Addiction and Mental

Health). The services available must provide comprehensive pre- and postnatal medical and nursing care (Poole 8); comprehensive psychological, psychiatric and counselling services must be available and intimately woven within the care environment to support concurrent mental health issues and emotional healing (Clayson et al. 236). In the absence of fundamental human needs not being addressed (the absence of food and shelter), any efforts to reduce harm to mothers and children will be ineffective. Programs must be grounded in growth-promoting relationships, which are pivotal to women's experiences in healing (Leslie 241). Such programs can help develop parenting skills and understanding of child development (Poole 9), and provide advocacy around housing and legal issues or referrals to ongoing community supports as well as transportation. Care must be provided in a nonjudgmental and genuine manner, which is respectful and understanding of the social climate in which women's substance use arises (Poole et al. 192). Finally, programs must include culturally sensitive and competent care. The elements listed above can help promote restorative justice and are rooted in the principles of feminism and empowered mothering.

HEALTHCARE AND SOCIAL POLICY IS GROUNDED IN THE POLITICAL

The healthcare system has a long and turbulent relationship with feminism, which remains tenuous at best. From a poststructuralist feminist perspective, the patriarchal structures that remain within our healthcare spheres have largely defined the care we provide. Without a critical feminist perspective to drive healthcare and policy development, the care we provide remains two-dimensional in its theoretical progress and simplistic in its understanding of the interaction between the environment, health, and illness, and human beings. By embracing a critical lens, we can illuminate the power relationships embedded within our social and institutional environments that influence health, limit human potential, and restrict full and conscious participation of all in society while reinforcing stigma and social exclusion in healthcare.

The healthcare system is political. To ignore how patriarchy has influenced how we care and, indeed, what we should care about is to remain passive to the political forces that continue to shape the health and wellbeing of women, children, and other oppressed groups. Caring requires engaging in discourses that open the spaces between and challenge the present social reality through subversive means.

As healthcare providers, we must challenge ourselves and admit that caring can be difficult at times and can create great conflict and anxiety within us. We can provide only measured care for women who use substances during pregnancy unless we acknowledge our interactions when caring for others are situated within the dominant discourses that stigmatize and demonize these women in our society. It is in attending to our abjection when working with this population that is socially located as unclean and polluted that we are able to reduce the distance between us. There is a tension in caring for pregnant women who use substances. It provokes an uneasiness in us in ways that extend beyond our educational preparation. But providing care and informing social and health policy require us to look in the mirror and reflectively acknowledge the assumptions and biases we bring to our practice. We can then begin to reconstruct the meaning of mothering in ways that can transform the care we provide so that it is not from a distance. By fully engaging in critical feminist discourses while holding a stance grounded in restorative justice, we begin to loosen the oppressive forces that hold these women and their children in the outer circles of society.

WORKS CITED

Annandale, Ellen. *Women's Health and Social Change*. Routledge, 2009.

Belsey, C. *Poststructuralism: A Very Short Introduction*. Oxford University Press, 2002.

Carabine, J. "'Constructing women': women's sexuality and social policy." *Critical Social Policy*, vol. 12, no. 23, 1992, pp. 23-35.

Centre for Addiction and Mental Health. *CAMH and Harm Reduction: A Background Paper on Its Meaning and Applications for Substance Use Issues*. CAMH, 2002.

Clayson, Z., et al. "Themes and Variations among Seven Comprehensive Perinatal Drug and Alcohol Abuse Treatment Models." *Health & Social Work*, vol. 20, no. 3, 1995, pp. 234-39.

Cormier, R., et al. *Women and Substance Abuse Problems.* Vancouver: British Columbia Centre for Excellence for Women's Health, 2004.

Daniels, C. *At Women's Expense: State Power and the Politics of Fetal Rights.* Harvard University Press, 1993.

DiQuinzio, P. *The Impossibility of Motherhood.* Routledge, 1999.

Foucault, M. *The Birth of Biopolitics.* Pan Books Limited, 2004.

Greaves, L. and N. Poole. "Pregnancy, mothering and substance use: toward a balanced response." *Highs & lows: Canadian Perspectives on Women and Substance Use*, edited by N. Poole and L. Greaves, Centre for Addiction and Mental Health, 2007, 219-25.

Klee, H., et al. *Drug Misuse and Motherhood.* Routledge, 2002.

Leslie, M. "Engaging Pregnant Women and Mothers in Services." *Highs & Lows: Canadian Perspectives on Women and Substance Use*, edited by W. Poole and L. Greaves, Centre for Addictions and Mental Health, 2007, pp. 239-46.

Lester, B., and J..E. Twomey. "Treatment of Substance Abuse during Pregnancy." *Women's Health*, vol. 4, no. 1, 2008, pp. 67-77.

Lester, B.M., et al. "Substance Use during Pregnancy: Time for Policy to Catch Up with Research." April 2004, https://harmreductionjournal.biomedcentral.com/articles/10.1186/1477-7517-1-5. Accessed 3 May 2018.

Logan, T.K., et al. "Victimization and Substance Abuse among Women: Contributing Factors, Interventions, and Implications." *Review of General Psychology*, vol. 6, no. 4, 2002, pp. 325-97.

Lupton, D. *Risk.* Routledge, 1999.

"Threshold." *Merriam Webster*, www.merriam-webster.com/dictionary/threshold. Accessed 6 May 2018.

McHoul, A. and W. Grace. *A Foucault Primer: Discourse, Power and the Subject.* Melbourne University Press, 1993.

Miller, A.F. "A Critical Need: Substance Abuse Treatment for Women with Children." *Corrections Today*, vol. 63, no, 1, 2001, pp. 88-91.

Poole, N. and B. Isaac. *Apprehensions: Barriers to Treatment for*

Substance-Using Mothers. British Columbia Centre of Excellence for Women's Health. Women's Health Reports, 2001.

Poole, N. *Evaluation Report of the Sheway Project for High-Risk Pregnant and Parenting Women*. British Columbia Centre of Excellence for Women's Health, 2000.

Poole, N., et al. "Influencing Women's Substance Use: The Role of Transition Houses." *Highs & lows: Canadian Perspectives on Women and Substance Sse*, edited by W. Poole and L. Greaves, Centre for Addictions and Mental Health, 2007, pp. 191-99.

Rutman, D., et al. *Substance Use and Pregnancy: Conceiving Women in the Policy-Making Process*. Status of Canada's Policy Research Fund. The Government of Canada, 2000.

Sullivan, D. and L. Tiff. *Handbook of Restorative Justice*. Routledge, 2008.

Weedon, C. *Feminism, Theory and the Politics of Difference*. Blackwell Publishers Inc., 1999.

Weedon, C. *Feminist Practice and Poststructuralist Theory*. Blackwell Publishing, 1997.

Weir, L. *Pregnancy, Risk, and Biopolitics: On the Threshold of the Living Subject*. Routledge, 2006.

12.
Concluding Thoughts

WENDY E. PETERSON, LAURA LYNNE ARMSTRONG,
AND MICHELLE FOULKES

WITH THIS COLLECTION, we have focused on the intersection of mothering and addiction. It is at this intersection where we hear the voices of marginalized mothers. Marginalization occurs as a result of the patriarchal construct of motherhood where the definition of a good mother allows no space for women with addictions to exist. As Michelle Foulkes identifies in chapter eleven, addiction in those who are pregnant and mothering is "the mother of all evils." Mothers are held to a high standard of goodness within our health, social, and justice systems. They are blamed for their addiction while the complex web of variables that give rise to addictions is ignored. More importantly, mothers' experiences with these systems can be damaging and perpetuate the intergenerational nature of addictions. Examples of harmful practices and policies are numerous: the stigmatizing behaviours of some service providers, the lack of appropriate and accessible treatment, the separation of mothers from their children, and incarceration.

There is an important limitation to this collection that we acknowledge—the voices of Indigenous mothers are largely absent. Without a doubt, Indigenous mothers were included among the participants in the research and programs discussed; however, their unique experiences have not been explored in any detail. This is a critical shortcoming of the book given the enduring effects of colonial genocide on Indigenous peoples that can result in high rates of addiction. Understanding of the unique perspectives of Indigenous mothers living with addiction is crucial, and our approach to collecting chapters for inclusion in this collection failed in this respect. It is with regret that we acknowledge this weakness and propose that future work endeavours to include the voices of Indigenous women and mothers.

Although the meaning of mothers' experiences with addiction is varied and personal, we hope this collection contributes to readers' understanding of their lived experience—that is, the experience is greater than the addiction, and it includes hope, recovery, and resilience. Contributors have made clear the role of trauma in the development of addictions and their feelings of shame and guilt. Other themes include the harmful nature of judgmental health and social service providers, maternal concerns about the intergenerational nature of addiction, and the need to move from a punitive approach to treatment to one that is compassionate and embraces a public health approach. Positive themes emerging from this collection include the following: mothering as motivation to heal, the role of spirituality in providing personal meaning to addiction, the fundamental need for relational care, recovery as a lifetime journey, and the promise of harm-reduction and restorative justice policies. Meaning-centred treatment and prevention strategies were also presented. Such strategies may be a potential alternative or supplement to traditional approaches for mothers at risk for, or experiencing, addiction.

With this book, we have endeavoured to prioritize the voices of mothers living with addiction. Their voices are clearly present in the personal narratives (chapters one to four), and in the study findings emerging from collaborative partnerships with researchers (chapters five to seven). The needs of mothers living with addiction are reflected in the promising programs based on harm reduction principles which are individualized and comprehensive (chapters six, and eight to ten), and the call for policy that is healing and restorative instead of punitive (chapter eleven). This book uniquely addresses all aspects of the journey of mothering with addiction from prevention, to meaningful recovery, and to ongoing societal challenges.

About the Contributors

Hadley Ajana lives in San Diego, CA, with her son. She is licensed to practice law in California and New York, and holds a master's degree in history from San Diego State University. Hadley teaches online and works as a tax analyst. When not working or playing with her son, you can find her on the tennis courts.

Laura Lynne Armstrong, PhD, C.Psych, is an assistant professor, clinical psychologist, and researcher at Saint Paul University. She also holds a diplomate clinician certification in logotherapy from the Viktor Frankl Institute of Logotherapy. She is the founder of REAL therapy (rational-emotive attachment logotherapy) and a resilience-based mental health promotion program for school children called DREAM (developing resilience through emotions, attitudes, and meaning). In addition to public presentations to enhance community mental health, Dr. Armstrong works clinically with children, youth, and adults.

Dorothy Badry, PhD, RSW, is an associate professor in the Faculty of Social Work, University of Calgary. Her research focuses on fetal alcohol spectrum disorder (FASD), birth mothers and families of children with FASD, substance abuse social problems for women and families, homelessness, and disability advocacy.

Kristin Bonot manages the projects of the Alberta Parent-Child Assistance Program (PCAP) Council in her role as provincial coordinator. Her interests are studying the impact of prevention models, and streamlining Alberta PCAP practices to effectively support workers. Kristin graduated from the University of Alberta with a BA in psychology.

Patricia P. Brethour practiced litigation in the fields of labour and human rights law for over twenty years. Her journey to health from addiction and posttraumatic stress disorder has led her into the helping profession. She is currently taking her masters in counselling and spirituality and is hoping to be practicing in Ottawa in 2019.

Michelle Foulkes, NP-PHC, PhD, is a healthcare nurse practitioner and has worked in a variety of nursing contexts over the last twenty-nine years. Her research and clinical interests are women's mental health and addictions across the lifespan, social justice, health policy, and integration of the nurse practitioner role in Canadian healthcare. She completed her PhD in nursing in 2015; her thesis work focussed on prenatal attachment in women with addictions.

Natalie Hemsing is a research associate at the British Columbia Centre of Excellence for women's health. Her research interests include women and tobacco use, and gender and substance use.

Tobi Jacobi teaches writing and literacy courses in the English Department at Colorado State University. She directs the Community Literacy Center (CLC) and the SpeakOut Writing Workshop—a literacy program aimed at fostering and celebrating the creative voices and spirits of confined youth and adults in northern Colorado.

Joni Joplin has been an early childhood educator and mother of two girls for twenty-four years. She is a native of the great state of Nebraska.

Erika Kates conducts action-oriented research on low-income women and their families. She founded the Massachusetts Women's Justice Network in 2011. The network focusses on alternatives to incarceration, and their action platform priorities are reducing the number of women imprisoned pending trial and the justice involvement of women with substance abuse and mental health problems.

Masoumeh (Bita) Katouziyan is a registered nurse with fifteen years of experience. Her research interests include adolescent mental health, drug abuse, and mothering. Her qualitative research explores the lived experiences of mothers of adolescents who misuse drugs.

Lenora Marcellus is an associate professor in the School of Nursing at the University of Victoria. She is also the director of the UVIC Institute for Studies and Innovation in Community University Engagement.

Kate Miller double majored in English and business at Colorado State University and worked with incarcerated women and men through her Community Literacy Centre internship.

Rhonda Nelson worked as an administrative assistant with the Alberta PCAP Council from 2012 to 2016. Rhonda has worked in human services for almost twenty years and her passion for service and prevention continues on in her work as an addiction counsellor with Alberta Health Services.

Sam Pecchio is twenty-five years old, a Colorado native, and a mother to three beautiful children.

Wendy E. Peterson, RN, PhD, is an associate professor at the School of Nursing, Faculty of Health Sciences, University of Ottawa. Her program of research aims to improve the quality and experience of maternal-newborn health services for marginalized women by addressing disparities in access to health services, facilitating woman-centred humanistic birth, and critically examining the role of registered nurses in interprofessional maternal-newborn healthcare teams.

J. Craig Phillips, PhD, LLM, RN, ARNP, ACRN, FAAN, is an associate professor of nursing and vice-dean governance and secretary in the Faculty of Health Sciences, University of Ottawa, and co-director, International Nursing Network for HIV Research. Dr. Phillips's program of research, the "ecosocial context of health as a human right," has documented social, structural, and ecological factors influencing health outcomes among persons living with HIV or experiencing complex trauma, in Botswana, Canada, Nigeria, and the United States. His significant contributions have advanced the nursing profession globally.

Nancy Poole is the director of the BC Centre of Excellence for Women's Health. She leads research and knowledge exchange initiatives related to girls' and women's health and substance use. She is co-editor of four books; the most recent is titled *Transforming Addiction: Gender, Trauma and Transdisciplinarity*, published by Routledge in 2015.

Caitlin Sigg is a PhD candidate in Counselling and Spirituality at Saint Paul University, Ottawa, Ontario. Her research interests include eating disorders and the existential implications of these syndromes. In addition to her research and clinical work, she teaches part-time with the Faculty of Human Sciences at Saint Paul University.

Amanda Vandyk, RN, PhD, is an assistant professor at the School of Nursing, University of Ottawa. Prior to joining the faculty, she worked as a registered nurse in psychiatric emergency services. Her program of research is focussed on clinically relevant and evidence-informed mental healthcare. She conducts research studies using qualitative, quantitative, and synthesis methodologies.

Renée Violette, MA, CADC, started Violet Healing and Recovery in Portland, Maine, where she practices deep healing techniques that create new neuropathways, alter old unwanted behaviors and reduce reactivity and anxiety. As an emerging writer she uses her insight gained from over ten years of personal recovery work from addiction and trauma to shed light on family dynamics and social experiences. Renée holds a master's degree in Interdisciplinary Studies – Peace and Reconciliation, from the University of

Maine and has been studying interpersonal neurobiology healing techniques for the past two years.

Chandera von Weller grew up in Oregon, lived in Alaska for ten years, and now resides in Colorado with her son Hunter. She has a degree in photography and follows this passion as her means of income.

Larissa Willkomm majored in English literature at Colorado State University students and co-facilitated a writing workshop with incarcerated women through her Community Literacy Centre internship.